Eating Peru

Eating Peru

A Gastronomic Journey

Robert Bradley

UNIVERSITY OF OKLAHOMA PRESS : NORMAN

Publication of this book is made possible through the generosity of the Center for Latin American Art at the University of Texas Rio Grande Valley.

Library of Congress Cataloging-in-Publication Data

Names: Bradley, Robert, (Robert Charles), 1959– author.
Title: Eating Peru : a gastronomic journey / Robert Bradley.
Description: Norman : University of Oklahoma Press, [2023] | Includes bibliographical references and index. | Summary: "A culmination of decades of Robert Bradley's personal travels and discoveries about the food and the history of Peru. The book moves from coast to highlands and back selecting the most interesting aspects of Peruvian cuisine while also referencing pre-Hispanic sites, art, and culture"—Provided by publisher.
Identifiers: LCCN 2022061291 | ISBN 978-0-8061-9278-9 (paperback)
Subjects: LCSH: Gastronomy—Peru. | Food habits—Peru. | Peru—Description and travel. | Bradley, Robert, (Robert Charles), 1959—Travel—Peru.
Classification: LCC TX641 .B725 2023 | DDC 641.01/30985—dc23/eng/20230104
LC record available at https://lccn.loc.gov/2022061291

The paper in this book meets the guidelines for permanence and durability of the Committee on Production Guidelines for Book Longevity of the Council on Library Resources, Inc. ∞

To my wife, Serenella, and our three wonderful children,
Gabriella, Moche, and Donovan

Contents

Recipes

Acknowledgments

I wish to begin by thanking my editor, Alessandra Jacobi Tamulevich, for guiding me to and through this project. I also thank the many authors of the Universidad of San Martín de Porres Press. Without their writings on Peruvian gastronomy, completing this book would have been an impossibility. A special thanks to the University of Texas Rio Grande Valley (UTRGV) interlibrary loan staff Norma Romero and Joe Reyna for negotiating the pared-down library staff of US repositories during the pandemic and Rose Flores from circulation for helping me check out many books for an extended period.

Thanks go to UTRGV's former dean of the College of Fine Arts Steve Block, former School of Art director Joy Esquierdo, and the new CFA dean, Jeffrey Ward, and School of Art and Design director, Ed Pogue, for their continued assistance. And great thanks go to the Center for Latin American Arts director Katherine McAllen for her financial and moral support for this project. And a second thanks to Katherine for being a great colleague. I would like also to thank UTRGV's Honors College Dean Mark Andersen for his assistance and his food-blogging wife, Tamara, for her photograph of my Moche stirrup-spout bottle. I wish to thank graphic designers Erika Balogh and Carlos Limas for their expert advice and assistance. For linguistic support I thank my friends Ignacio López-Calvo, professor of Latin American literature and culture at University of California Merced, and Galen Brokaw, head of the Modern Languages and Literatures Department at Montana State University.

For advice on fish, great thanks go to Philipe Béarez from France's Muséum national d'histoire naturelle, whom I look forward to meeting in person one day. I wish to thank Peter Lerche and his late wife, Elizabeth, for putting me on the path to becoming an Andeanist. In the same vein, I thank my advisor at Columbia University, Esther Pasztory, for guiding me to Chachapoyas. For advice on Peruvian cuisine, I must thank my mother-in-law, Sonia Lozada Samame, my wife's aunt Cecilia Ríos de Salazar, and Ricardo Sulem Wong. I also want to thank my mother, Kathleen, and my sister Kerry for their support and advice. And finally, I want to thank my Huaracino friends Gladys Jiménez and Jim Sykes for their expert advice on all things concerning the Peruvian highlands.

Introduction

My wife and I come from dissimilar cultures. My early years in the northeastern industrial city of Trenton, New Jersey, could not have been more different from her childhood in Ferreñafe, a small town on Peru's North Coast. Yet from the first moment I met her, we shared a common denominator that secured our relationship: the love of food. Mine was hard-earned because I needed to move beyond the Irish American table of my childhood. Fortunately, I lived in the Italian section of the city, Chambersburg. Soon I discovered, and later mastered, many Italian dishes. This cuisine guided me to my first career as a wine merchant. I sold wine to some of the finest restaurants in New York City: Gramercy Tavern, Chanterelle, and Follonico. My interest in the job had been strong early on but had waned by the mid-1990s. The corporate business model was pushing the artistic and historical aspects out of the work, replacing these subtleties with the grim American model of product and marketplace. The days for my rhetorical style of salesmanship were disappearing.

These circumstances put me on the 1/9 local subway heading to an appointment with Professor Esther Pasztory, the Lisa and Bernard Selz Professor of Pre-Columbian Art History at Columbia University. Pasztory was a Mesoamericanist, a specialist of Mexican and Central American history and culture before the arrival of Columbus and the Spanish conquistadores. I became determined to seek her out during an intentionally non-wine-drinking vacation in Belize. The choice to alter my vocation occurred atop the Maya pyramid at Xunantunich while I was staring down at some sweating archaeologists in their khaki clothing. I was intrigued by these people because I imagined they were seeking ancient truths while it seemed the focus of my life was negotiating the next wine-by-the-glass selection. As the subway rattled on up to Harlem,

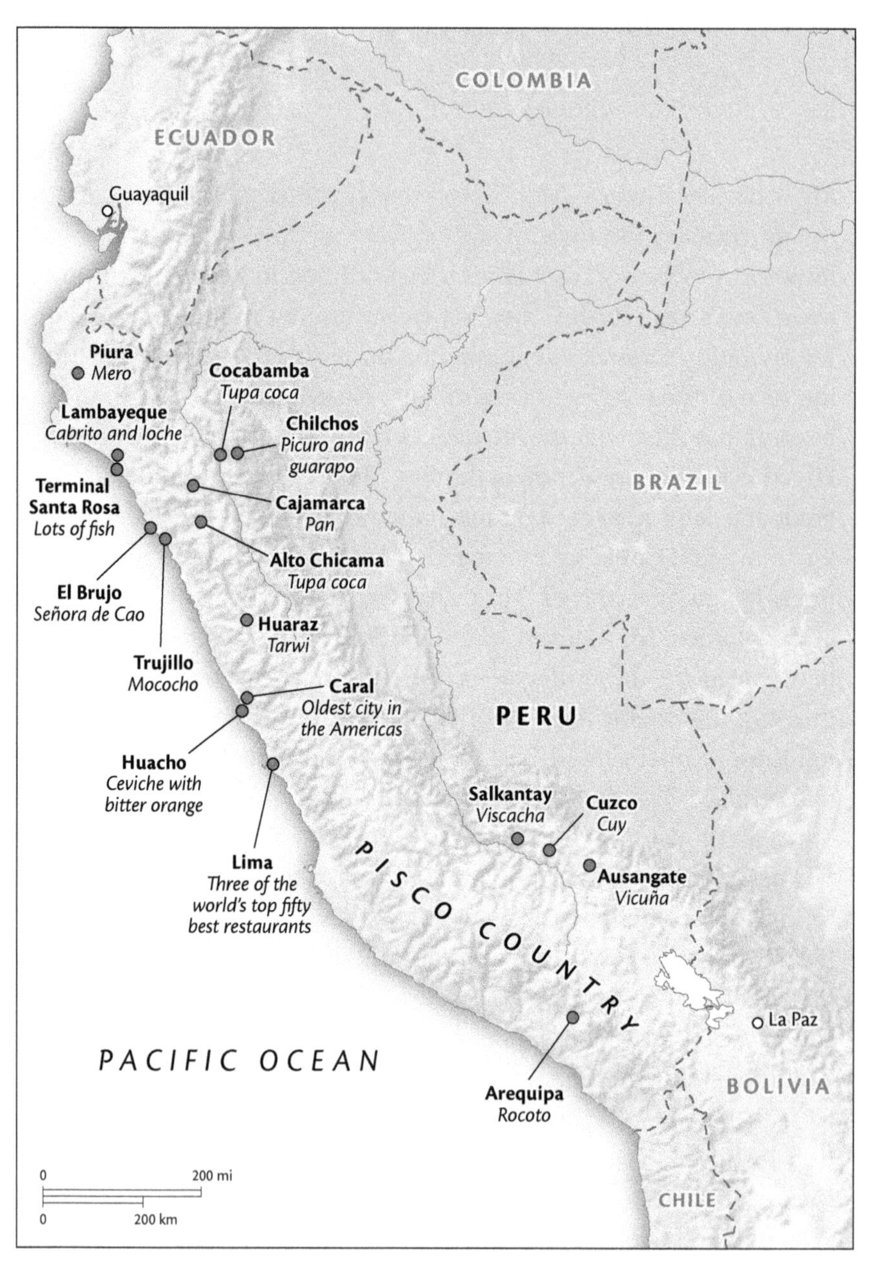

Peru with Food References. Map by Erin Greb.

I daydreamed about how Pasztory would understand my career crisis and about the different ways the celebrated professor would facilitate my new calling.

After briefly explaining my epiphany to Esther, I asked if she would recommend me for the part-time MA program in art history and archaeology. She said no. Instead, she suggested that I take the Maya Art course she was offering in fall 1995. I excelled in this class, and she then recommended me for the part-time MA. Three years later, about to leave the wine business, I asked if she would recommend me for the PhD program. Again, Esther said no. This time she raised the bar and advised me to go to my area of interest, the cloud forest of northeastern Peru. Esther had encouraged this Peruvian turn in my pre-Columbian focus toward the Chachapoya cloud forest people of ancient Peru. So there I was, flying aboard a Fokker turboprop bound for Cajamarca. I remember looking out of my window at the Andes Mountains below, concerned about my nonexistent Spanish and how I would find a driver willing to negotiate the twelve hours of dirt road switchbacks through the Marañón River canyon. Esther had set my journey in motion, and at that particular moment I had serious doubts about her judgment.

Of course, I survived, and even thrived, on the northeastern slopes of the Andes. But that story is for another time. This account is concerned with my idle time in Peru, after I came back from expeditions emaciated and hungry. I would return to Peru's North Coast in search of rest and relaxation. Each time I did, my foodie bona fides kicked in, directing me toward investigating the myriad markets and restaurants of Peru with even more enthusiasm than I had for scrutinizing Chachapoya architecture, the topic of my dissertation. But even in the Utcubamba Valley, the main artery for discovering Chachapoya culture, Peruvian cuisine was often my focus. For many years, I stayed at the farm of Peter and Elizabeth Lerche, and although Peter's gastronomic interest was zero (the locals would say Peter could be satisfied eating stones to fill his belly), Elizabeth was an endless source of information about highland offerings. She introduced me to my first cherimoya (*Annona cherimola*), which was the wild *Mamillata* type; *juanes,* a rice tamale variant; *chicha,* corn beer; and *cancha,* wholesome Peruvian popcorn. But to be fair to Peter, he was the first person to instruct me on the finer points of coca chewing, with a preliminary lesson one cold morning at the Chachapoya ruin Kuelap.

In Peru I rediscovered my love of food, always an integral part of my being. How could I not? By Western standards Peru is a poor country, but most Peruvians eat better than their richer and more entitled Western counterparts. Great food is omnipresent in their lives. The fiestas given by my wife's family introduced me to exquisitely fresh fish. Indeed, the fishmonger's offerings in any upscale city grocery pale in comparison to the seafood presented in the humble coastal markets of Peru. These places offer fresh fish as good or better than the Fulton Fish Market, and at a fraction of the price. On the North Coast, most celebrations begin with the raw fish salad ceviche, and move on to a *sudado de pescado* (fish stew). There, junk food snacks are unnecessary, because fresh bread is delivered to your door twice daily, a service provided to even people of modest income, and freshly made *cancha* (wholesome Peruvian popcorn) is always available.

These traditions began thousands of years ago on the desert coast. The elaborate architecture of the five-thousand-year-old trading center of Caral was contemporaneous with the pyramids of Old Kingdom Egypt, and in this place there is an ancient culinary tradition. For example, when the archaeologist Junius Bird excavated the remains of a woman at the four-thousand-year-old coastal site of Huaca Prieta, analysis of the undigested material found in her stomach showed her last meal to have been mussels, crabs, sea snails, and sea urchins with *ají* (hot pepper) along with three types of fruit abundant in her environment.[1] At this time, in any other corner of the world, not even powerful despots would have dined as well as this ancient Peruvian.

Three millennia later, compelling evidence of North Coast epicureanism is described in a post-Moche Sicán culture (also called

Lambayeque culture) legend of the cultivated ruler Naymlap. He migrated to the North Coast with a retinue that included Occhocalo, the royal cook, and Ñiñagintue, a male servant in charge of making the *chicha* (maize beer).[2] These servants are not only mentioned, the cook and the brewer are named and immortalized.

In this book I will define the Andean world as the mountains and the desert coast, although some references will be made to the eastern Andean cloud forest. I follow the model of the Andean world that has been used by scholars for decades. In this text I will intentionally move from the coast to the highlands and back, selecting the most interesting aspects of Peruvian culture and cuisine that I have encountered in more than twenty years of research in this marvelous country.

During my research for this text I noticed that articles and books examining Peru's recent gastronomic boom fell into two distinctly different groups. The first group was the South American/Peruvian school epitomized by scholars published by the University of San Martin de Porres (USMP) Press. Frankly, this book would have been an impossibility without these wonderful volumes, as I acknowledged in my opening remarks. These scholars take a very formal approach to Peru's culinary miracle. Their emphasis is on the history and categorization of plants and animals used in Peruvian cuisine. Their writings often show a sense of pride and a bit of nationalism, which is fair enough considering that the funding for these books comes from Peruvian governmental agencies such as PromPerú and Marca Perú. The second school of scholars examining Peru's gastronomic boom are the North American/European school. These scholars are mostly focused on theory and are highly critical of the boom, considering it a manifestation of the elite neoliberal order. They mostly see Peru's pricy restaurants and celebrity chefs as benefiting only the international haute bourgeoisie. In other words, according to the second school, there is no boom for your average Peruvian.[3]

I will say fair enough to this criticism. However, what I found most interesting while examining the writings of each school is that the focus is often solely on complementary texts in their specific genre. The USMP authors almost always write in Spanish and the lingua franca of the second is English, but I believe the divide is more than just language. This book is built on extensive research of the scholars published by USMP Press. Following the second school I also offer criticism of the elitist aspects of Peru's gastronomic boom. But as I finished writing this monograph I was delighted with the bibliography, because it contained a plethora of citations from both schools, and I believe that being attentive to the focus of both is a great strength of this book. Finally, in my conclusion I examine the interview between Raúl Matta, second school, and Mirko Lauer, first school. And I believe their compelling dialogue offers a way forward to Peru's gastronomic revolution 2.0.

Before detailing specific foodstuffs and historical culinary traditions, I highlight the markets and restaurants in Peru that I find unique and fascinating. These observations are far from comprehensive, but I hope to engage your interest by providing an overview of the myriad venues that even the smallest Peruvian town has to offer the visitor. For example, during the summer of 2015, our family stayed outside the North Coast city of Chiclayo. There we would frequently visit the market at Monsefú. *Chiclayanos* say that real descendants of the pre-Columbian Moche people live in Monsefú, and if these pre-Columbian coastal people even remotely share the outgoing and friendly manner of the people working in this market, then the first millennium of the Common Era must have been a glorious time on the North Coast. I will also discuss the markets and restaurants in Lima and Cuzco, the locales most likely to attract foreign visitors during their passage to Machu Picchu.

I will detail a North Coast Peruvian site that is unfortunately often bypassed by the Machu Picchu pilgrims, in the hope that the reader of my book will be intrigued by my description of Terminal Santa Rosa and the abundance of exquisitely fresh seafood that accumulates daily at this seafood depot. Of course, the Tsukiji Fish Market in Japan, now the Toyosu Market, moves more

Terminal Santa Rosa fishmonger with a medusa fish (*Seriolella violacea*).
Photo by Robert Bradley.

fish through its doors. But this less-well-known Peruvian facility, at the epicenter of the world's greatest piscary, is well worth a one-hour flight north from Lima. I will also provide an overview of outstanding Peruvian restaurants that are often omitted in the standard guidebooks, like the enigmatic and semi-private Chinese/Peruvian restaurant Mococho in Huanchaco, Picantería Campestre Los Delfines in Monsefú, El Cántaro Restaurant Turístico in Lambayeque and Punto Azul, Pueblo Viejo, El Cevichano and La Picantería in Lima.

The heart of Peruvian cuisine is fish, with an emphasis on ceviche. I will take time in this book to discuss the preferred fish for this famous Peruvian dish, *ojo de uva* (medusa fish), *lenguado* (flounder), *mero* (grouper), and *róbalo* (snook), with *lenguado* being the most expensive, a large fish can cost forty sols (fourteen dollars) a kilo, and the *ojo de uva* being the least expensive, around eighteen sols a kilo (six dollars). But any of these white-fleshed fish will serve as an excellent prime ingredient in a classic *ceviche de pescado*. *Tollo* will also be scrutinized. *Tollo* is the ever-present main ingredient of the myriad coastal *sudados* (fish stews). And although Elmo León defines *tollo* as smooth houndshark (*Mustelus* spp.), and spotted houndshark as *tollo manchado* (*Triakis maculata*), in my experience frequenting the fish markets of North Coast Peru, *tollo* or *toyo* is a generic term for any large predatory fish.[4]

I provide a brief history of the dish, imagining a pre-Columbian variant, and then move on to the colonial era and the arrival of limes, brought by the Spanish. I will outline the basic ceviche recipe in relation to the selection of fish and regional adaptations of the plate. Finally, the curious *life* catfish, an iconic image in Moche art, will be thoroughly analyzed. In the market of Monsefú you can buy the same *life* catfish for consumption that the Moche featured in their art. The fish range in size from four to six inches and are sold alive by the kilo. *Lifes'* thin bodies place them firmly in the Trichomycteridae family of pencil catfish. These catfish are named for the barbels (whiskers) emanating from the side of the mouth, and many examples of *lifes* in Moche artwork clearly depict this feature, like the catfish pattern mural from the Huaca Cao Viejo in the El Brujo complex. The Moche certainly consumed *lifes* because excavations at Huaca de la Luna revealed that 27.78 percent of the freshwater fish bones were *lifes*. This archaeological evidence clearly indicates that *lifes* were an integral part of the Moche diet, since they are rich in proteins, iron, and riboflavin.[5] Today they are found in dishes such as *panquitas de lifes* or *sudado de lifes* in and around the city of Chiclayo, particularly in the town of Monsefú. The ingredients to prepare these offerings affirm their pre-Hispanic origins. The recipe consists of *life* catfish, *chicha de jora, ají amarillo*, salt, and herbs. The main ingredient, *lifes*, are kept alive until they are ready to be eaten. They are killed when salt is poured directly onto the skin, a process that locks in the flavor of the dish.

The exotic fruits of South America are aptly famous but none more so than the paradoxical fruit we only enjoy in small amounts, hot pepper or *ají*. Curiously, the Quechua name for hot pepper (*uchu*) is confined to remote regions of the mountains and rainforests in Peru. The word *ají* is a Cariban name for *Capsicum* spp., and the term was introduced from the Caribbean by the Spanish during the conquest era.[6] I will spend time on the most important *ajíes* in Peru: *Capsicum baccatum* (common names are *ají amarillo, ají de causa, ají verde* [even though it is orange], and *ají escabeche*), *Capsicum chinense* (*ají limo*), and *Capsicum pubescens* (*rocoto*). Of the four, *Capsicum baccatum* is ubiquitous and exclusive to Peruvian cuisine. In its dried form, *ají amarillo* is called *ají mirasol*, but the most important dried pepper in Peru is *ají panca*, which is a mild coastal variety of *Capsicum chinense*.[7] The use of these *ajíes* in the most well-known Peruvian dishes will be scrutinized. I will also highlight a sweet fruit in the otherworldly offering of cherimoya (*Annona cherimola* Miller), which Mark Twain called the most perfect fruit in the world.[8]

Fermented and then distilled beverages have been a part of the Peruvian gastronomic tradition since the pre-Columbian era. In the mid-nineteenth century, the Limeño Manuel Fuentes recorded aguardiente, *chicha*, and *guarapo* as the most important national drinks in Peru.[9] Of course, the aguardiente (distilled liquor) to which Fuentes was referring was specifically an aguardiente of *uva* (grapes): pisco. I will detail the history of this celebrated beverage, which Rudyard Kipling called "the highest and noblest product of the age," from its early seventeenth-century invention to the historic impact of exported pisco on the Barbary Coast and San Francisco.[10] And no discussion of pisco could be presented without an elaboration of the invention and history of the pisco punch, the pisco sour, and the recent rise of the coca sour.

Fuentes's second national drink was Peruvian corn beer (*chicha*), which was the preferred beverage of the pre-Columbian Andean realm. The consistency of highland *chicha* is like the filtered liquid oatmeal that is enormously popular in Peru at breakfast. But the tradition of making *chicha* on the coast of Peru is also ancient, and although in the highlands the brewers are always female, the most celebrated coastal brewers were and still are male.[11] The seminal text defining this tradition is again the story of the seafaring king Naymlap recorded in the colonial chronicle of Father Miguel Cabello de Balboa. In this preconquest story, a haughty king sails to the North Coast town of Lambayeque with a great fleet of balsa rafts. The king travels with a retinue of forty retainers, who cater to his every whim, and the butler Ñiñagintue was the man in Naymlap's entourage "in whose care was the drink of that Lord."[12]

The style of fermenting coastal *chicha* is also markedly different from in the highlands. The most celebrated coastal *chicha* has a longer fermentation interval and is therefore drier (higher in alcohol) than highlands beers. Indeed, the best example of coastal *chicha*, the *chicha de jora*, is malted and often fermented for up to a year. This long fermentation gives the yeast enough time to consume all residual sugar. This beverage therefore is quite strong. The aging process and the lack of sugar give the *chicha* a flavor that could be, depending on the maker, favorably compared to an oloroso sherry.

Fuentes's reference to *guarapo* (sugarcane beer, but *chicha de azucar* is more specific) is interesting because this beverage doesn't have the prominence it once had in the nineteenth century. According to Fuentes, *guarapo* was the drink most favored by the Negroes. I will examine this interesting and somewhat racist statement in my discussion of African influences on Peruvian cuisine.

In the early colonial era, the Spanish replaced the hearty and sustaining indigenous crops and animals with more familiar European fare. But pre-Columbian agricultural traditions survived in many of the small hamlets and villages removed from the conquest and the destructive late-sixteenth-century policies of Viceroy Toledo. The first of the two crops that were never replaced—and indeed went on to conquer the world—was *Zea mays*, the genetic monster that mutated from *Balsas teosinte* thousands of years ago in southern Mexico.[13] I say "monster" because one unbiased look at an ear of corn reveals unnatural abnormalities. The vegetable has an overabundance of large grains, fruit really, that are aligned in straight lines facilitating access and consumption. Without human manipulation, and certainly modern genetic modification (GM) is only the latest manifestation of human manipulation, modern corn would cease to exist. In Mesoamerica maize was a dietary staple by the second millennium BCE, but in order to be effectively consumed by humans, maize required even more human alteration: alkali processing. But whereas in Mesoamerica maize was and is consumed as a grain (the region's daily bread, so to speak), in the Andean realm of South America it is used as a vegetable, or perhaps more succinctly as a fruit. The vegetable or fruit component of maize takes the form of *chicha* beer (think *chicha* wine) in South America, an ever-present refreshment, offering of tribute, and centerpiece of ritual feasting and exchange.[14] Maize (more properly, *choclo* from the Quechua) is also toasted to make *cancha,* boiled to accompany ceviche, and ground to make *humitias,* a non-nixtamal-processed South American tamale.

The second plant is the potato (*Solanum tuberosum*), the irreplaceable Andean tuber that went on to conquer the world. Although there are at least four hundred different varieties of potato in South America (and this is a very conservative estimate), few of these were introduced to Europe by the Spanish, so "only a fraction of the biodiversity that exists among the wild and cultivated potatoes of South America" was transferred to the Old World. And these tubers were propagated in a vegetative manner and not by the plant's seeds, so each plant is an exact copy of the previous—in other words, a clone.[15] Inevitably, this lack of biological diversity led to blight, famine, and death, and I will briefly note the potato's plight in the modern world.

Many unique Andean crops were studied by biologists in the early modern era, but unlike corn and potatoes, these super crops did not seize the Western imagination until the mid to late twentieth century, when Western commercial interests became interested in these nutritious Andean offerings. At least one of the superfoods—quinoa—suffered a similar boom-and-bust fate like the potato in the twenty-first century. Here the botany was sound, at least for the non-Andean world, but the economics of singling out one variety of quinoa and planting it worldwide was disastrous for the livelihood of Andean campesinos.[16]

The lupine *tarwi* has the potential to gain worldwide celebrity, or perhaps notoriety, like quinoa. In the highlands of Peru, nutritious dishes like *ceviche de chocho (tarwi),* which is *chocho* in key lime juice (*limones ácidos*) with tomato, onion, cilantro, and *rocoto* (*ají*), are common campesino lunchtime repasts. Inexpensive and extremely nutritious, *tarwi* was domesticated in pre-Inca times. It grows in marginal soils and adds nitrogen to the soil in which it is grown. The problem with *tarwi* is detoxifying the seeds. These nutritious bone-white seeds are what is consumed, in a manner like rice or quinoa, but first they must be rinsed for a week and boiled.[17] Another "superfood" is the amaranth grain *kiwicha,* which gained worldwide attention toward the end of the twentieth century. This attention soon waned, but recently there has been a resurgence of interest in the grain because of its health and nutritional benefits. Peru's edible freshwater blue-green algae *cushuro* and the fermented potato *tocosh* have now gone from a highland market curiosity on to celebrity chef Virgilio Martínez's four-star table. But as *cushuro* and *tocosh* ascend, the consumption of the original Andean superfood, the peanut, has unfortunately waned.

The domestication of plants in aboriginal America was prolific compared to the paucity of animal domestications, but because the highlands lack the maritime protein resources of the desert coast, camelids (llamas and alpacas) and the abundant kitchen-scrounging *cuy* (guinea pig) provided vital sources of protein. The Inca and their ancestors were pastoralists, and although camelids were a meat source, they were slaughtered most judiciously. Even the eating of the lowly *cuy* was reserved for auspicious occasions. Today *cuy* is a major source of protein in the Andes, and it is common to see them huddled in a highland kitchen waiting for table scraps.

I will also discuss the roadside stands of the Sacred Valley at Coya, Calca, and Lamay, where the women of these towns serve up *cuy al palo* (guinea pig on a stick) with *huacatay* (Peruvian black mint), and tasty *cuy* blood sausage, again flavored with *huacatay*, stuffed in rabbit intestine. I will discuss the history of the transfer of *cuy* from the Andean world to the West and its strange transition from a highland protein staple into an adorable pet.

But no discussion of a delicious mixture of fat and protein could end without mentioning the Peruvian North Coast specialty *cabrito norteño*. Although goats (in this case the reference is to kid goat) arrived with the Spanish, *cabrito norteño*'s main ingredient belie its pre-Columbian origins. *Chicha* beer, *ají amarillo*, and *loche* squash flavor this famous dish, and all these ingredients have strong pre-Columbian origins. I will spend time discussing *chicha de jora* and *ají amarillo*. But beautiful ceramic vessels depicting *loche (Cucurbita moschata)* date back to the Moche culture of North Coast Peru (100–800 CE), and Dillehay and Piperno have recorded *loche* cultivation at the site of Nanchoc, forty-five hundred years before the present era.[18] In fact, *loche* is grown only on the North Coast of Peru and is practically unknown elsewhere.[19] More specifically, the tradition of *loche* being an essential ingredient in *cabrito norteño* has an epicenter around the North Coast city of Chiclayo, and the archaeological site of Nanchoc is less than an hour's drive from this city. For several years my family and I vacationed in the beach town of Huanchaco, about four hours from Chiclayo. When my wife's mother would travel from Chiclayo to prepare cabrito for us, she would carry a *loche* with her, because she could not find this squash in the markets around the town. And she could not imagine preparing her cabrito without *loche*! Goats came to Peru with the Spanish, but pre-Columbian Moche ceramics have many representations of deer, so perhaps it was a pre-Hispanic Andean venison stew. The pre-Columbian hairless dog might have been another possible protein source.

In pre-Hispanic South America, coca was a food source, and this ancient tradition has resurfaced today. For example, at

Virgilio Martínez's high-altitude restaurant Mil in Maras, the celebrated chef serves a green-tinged coca bread with *saúco* (elderberry) butter. Indeed, the Peruvian historian María Rostworowski once confirmed that a coveted and aromatic variety of coca, which the Inca dubbed *tupa coca* (royal coca), was used as an ingredient in pre-Columbian food preparations.[20] This celebrated variety of coca, *Erythroxylum novogranatense* var. *truxillense,* is also the most desired variety of coca for both the ancient and the modern chewer. *E. novogranatense* var. *truxillense* is named after the Peruvian North Coast city of Trujillo—or more specifically, the parched region that typifies this ancient part of northern Peru.

Chewing coca is a lawful activity in the Andean nations of South America. Coca acts as a mild stimulant and helps ward off fatigue, hunger, and thirst; it is coveted in this rugged mountainous environment. Coca is a social lubricant, a ceremonial offering, and a stimulant that was shared by both emperors and peasants in western South America. The term *coca* comes from an Aymara word for "bush" or "tree," but in the pre-Columbian era, each variety of coca had its own unique indigenous appellation.[21] Wintergreen oil (methyl salicylate) is found in the leaves of *E. novogranatense* var. *truxillense.* This essence has made the leaf popular with the campesinos who chew the plant on a daily basis, and it is likely that the unique flavoring of this variety promoted the assignment of the appellation *tupa* for this plant in the pre-Columbian era. *Tupa coca* has always been cultivated for its taste. Indeed, the process of chewing coca mimics the ancient method of making corn tortillas, tamales, and hominy, which were and are the daily bread of the Mesoamerican world. Nixtamalization is a technique in which maize is soaked in a solution with quicklime (CaO). Likewise, coca is soaked in a solution of quicklime or wood ash with saliva in the chewer's mouth. Both wood ash and quicklime are alkalis that release vitamins and trace amounts of cocaine. The history of coca's introduction to the West is complex, to say the least, with curious concoctions such as the coca-infused red wine Vin Mariani and the coca special ingredient in the world's most popular soft drink, Coca-Cola.[22] Today the rise of the coca sour in Peruvian restaurants and bars and the ubiquitous Andean high-altitude placebo *mate de coca* (coca leaf tea) continue the tradition of coca being both clandestine and sought out at the same time.

Old World influences on Peruvian cuisine began with the arrival of the Spanish. Although the Europeans entered a land of plenty, soon after the conquest they imported the plants and livestock with which they were familiar. I will outline these environmental disruptions with an emphasis on Spanish imperial designs and then continue with an examination of the African and Asian culinary impact. José Carlos Mariátegui, the intellectual leader of Peru's early twentieth-century indigenous movement, lamented that neither the Chinese nor the African contributed cultural values or creative energies to the formation of Peru.[23] Obviously, the avowed Marxist never considered the bourgeois category of cuisine as creative. Because even though during Mariátegui's short lifetime, when the Chinese diaspora was in the initial stages of adding to the Peruvian culinary tradition, the descendants of African slaves had already had a profound impact on food preparations in Lima. Again, Fuentes's tome on mid-nineteenth-century Lima is insightful because he describes the celebrated Negro cooks of the time, called *Serapios*, who fetched a high price for their services.[24]

Certainly, the impact these former slaves had on Peruvian food was not recorded properly. Slavery was not abolished in Peru until 1854, and so it is likely that the history of these cooks would not have been properly reported. But the dishes that Fuentes specifically mentions—puchero (cabbage stew), *chupe* (chowder), *locro* (chicken stew), *carapulcra* (another pork and chicken stew), and *chicharrones* (pork rinds fried in lard)[25]—will be examined regarding other Afro-colonial and African cuisine, as will the modern dishes *cau cau* (tripe stew), *chanfainita* (stew with beef lungs) and *sangrecita* (cooked chicken blood with garlic and onion). And no study of African/Peruvian cuisine would be complete without a discussion of the ultimate Peruvian street food, *anticuchos* (grilled beef heart).

Chinese Peruvians (*Tusán*) began arriving in Peru in 1849 to work on sugar plantations and to extract guano from Peru's coastal islands. The majority left the hardships of Canton province only to embark on a hazardous sea voyage and then enter slavelike working conditions.[26] But after decades of immigration marked by racism, these industrious migrant workers started to establish businesses, the most important being the taverns of Capón Street, which fed Chinese and provided sustenance to poor Limeños. Years of progress led to the first celebrated Chinese restaurants, which were called *chifas*.[27] Kuong Tong was the first and most famous, and this restaurant served Cantonese food to the upper class, a segment of Lima's society who had never before ventured to Lima's Chinatown.[28]

Toward the end of the nineteenth century, Japanese workers arrived, first as miners and then as laborers assigned to the vast coastal sugar plantations. The Japanese never adapted to the harsh conditions of the plantations, but instead, several thrived in Peru's ancient cotton trade. During World War II many Japanese were deported from Peru, including Nikkei (ethnically Japanese Peruvians), but after this unfortunate era, another wave of Japanese immigration ensued.[29] In this migration, Chef Nobuyuki "Nobu" Matsuhisa arrived in Lima.[30] His experiments with the fusion of Peruvian and Japanese flavors helped to create Nikkei cuisine, and in the process he built a global network of restaurants and hotels. Although I believe the Nikkei chefs take too much credit for the prominence of fish and seafood in the Peruvian diet, an examination of the Japanese influence on Peruvian cuisine is essential for an understanding of the country's modern culinary tradition.[31]

As an art historian I am accustomed to looking at the past, but I will close this book with an attempt to look into the future. Twenty-five years ago, I made my first trip to Peru as a graduate student, and I recounted my awe and anxiety as I became immersed in this land of fantastic geography, ancient architecture, and exotic flavors. My first hike up from the Utcubamba River to the ruin of Kuelap, a three-thousand-foot ascent, seemed endless. Now there is a cable car connecting the river below to this Chachapoya city. When I started working in the area of the pre-Columbian Chachapoya, the site of Kuelap received about one foreign visitor a day. But recently, the *New York Times* listed Kuelap as No. 29 of the fifty-two places to travel to in the world. According to the article, the number of annual visitors to Kuelap has doubled in the past few years, from thirty thousand to sixty thousand. If you told me twenty years ago this ruin would have sixty thousand visitors a year, I would have laughed. In 2004 my wife and I hiked up to Kuelap as part of our honeymoon. At the site we had a difficult time finding accommodations for the night, the two "hotel rooms" were being used by archaeologists. We finally paid ten sols (three dollars) for a room in a nearby house but were chagrined to find out the owner had locked us in the room until morning, so he could secure payment. Had we known, we would have paid in advance. But the point here is that Kuelap, and indeed all of Peru, has changed so much—some for the worse, but a lot for the better. For me the cable car at Kuelap lessens the rigor of the visitor's experience, but I understand it is progress. However, the staggered entrance times (designed to maximize tourists) and the fixed walking direction now in place at Machu Picchu are nothing but onerous. Focus on Machu Picchu is important because a recent poll in Peru "found that 39 percent of Peruvians consider gastronomy to be the principal source of national pride—ahead of the ruins of Machu Picchu's 36 percent."[32]

The key here is to not let Peruvian cuisine be inundated by growing popularity, like Machu Picchu has been. We then must consider that we are in an exciting transformative era for Peruvian food. It has been a long journey from pre-Columbian to colonial to modern culture, with foreign cultural infusions leading to worldwide attention. COVID has stalled the Peruvian gastronomic boom somewhat, but my return to Peru in the summer of 2022 assured me that Peru's culinary landscape is alive and well. And perhaps the unfortunate pandemic interregnum will help the gastronomic tradition avoid Machu Picchu's plight of being "loved to death." My closing discussion focuses on the future of Peru's gastronomic boom, specifically referencing the previously mentioned interview between Raúl Matta and Mirko Lauer.

Chapter 1
Mercados and Restaurantes

Before the pandemic, Peru was named the No. 1 food destination in the world for eight consecutive years. Many travelers to this country can understand why, even if they are only doing the perfunctory trip to Machu Picchu and back. But to gain a profound understanding of the excellent culinary tradition embedded in Peru's DNA, a longer and more diverse itinerary is required. My goal is for this book to serve as a guide not only to places that should be visited but also to the reasons why these places are unique and special. The information I put forward here is by no means exhaustive, but it is a good start for initiating an awareness of the antiquity and complexity of Peru's gastronomic tradition.

Lima's Jorge Chávez International Airport perennially ranks as the best airport in Latin America. The functionality of the airport greatly benefits tourists but not so much the country, because at the turn of the last millennium a multinational consortium of companies was given a thirty-year concession to run Jorge Chávez.[1] And I must (reluctantly) add that the consortium has done an excellent job. Almost all tourists visiting Peru will pass through Jorge Chávez. Some, however, will enter through Cuzco's Alejandro Velasco Astete International Airport from neighboring South American countries. Going directly to Cuzco, to access Machu Picchu quickly, is a mistake, because Lima has so much gastronomy to offer. Even a short layover at Jorge Chávez is rewarded by a meal at Tanta, the best airport restaurant food I have ever had—and yes, I have been to New Orleans's Louis Armstrong International Airport, and no, I do not accept the Michelin Guide list of best airport food worldwide because they do not review South America.[2] Lima is a sprawling metropolis, unfortunately damp, overcast, and foggy most of the year, but around Christmas and New Year the shroud lifts and the sun scalds off the city's gray veil.

If you are staying in Lima, most likely you will lodge in the upscale district of Miraflores where there are numerous restaurants and shops, and the only bad thing that can happen to you is being overcharged. On the other hand, going to Lima's great markets like the Minka Fish Market or the Mercado Central is a daunting task made more difficult every year by Lima's increasing traffic congestion. Besides, without access to an extensive kitchen with pots and pans, plates, and utensils, you really cannot take advantage of these markets' offerings. But if you are renting in the city on a prolonged stay, then please enjoy. Miraflores does have the Wong and Vivanda supermarkets. These markets cater to upscale professionals, so their produce, meat, and fish selections are ridiculously overpriced, but they are good places to buy pisco, Peru's brandy, and especially hard-to-find pisco like Albilla.

Two Lima locations make it worth leaving the convenience of Miraflores, and these are the Museo Rafael Larco Herrera and Lima's famous Chinatown. The Larco Museum is the largest collection of Moche ceramics in the world. This was assembled by Rafael Larco Herrera's son, the autodidact archaeologist Rafael Larco Hoyle, whose contribution to the study of the pre-Columbian Moche was immense. Perhaps his most significant contribution was the museum in the Pueblo Libre district, which he named after his father. The beautiful architecture of the Larco Museum is complemented by exquisite landscaping and a pricy fusion restaurant. But after viewing the galleries, I suggest you have a glass of wine or a drink at the Cafe Museo Larco and then ask for directions to Antigua Taberna Queirolo. Taking a walk or a short cab ride to this tavern is an essential outing when visiting the museum, if only to have a glass of pisco at the old stand-up Western-style bar at the entrance of the tavern. The tavern was founded at the beginning of the twentieth century by an Italian businessman who then went on to become a pisco entrepreneur with his own Santiago Queirolo brand. The tavern's menu is a classic compilation of criollo food. And after imbibing at the Café Museo Larco, you will find the drinks both reasonably priced and just as expertly made. Lima's Chinatown is in the center of the congested city, so as in any large and overpopulated metropolis, I suggest you take a little caution when visiting. It would be best to take a cab to Fung Wen rotisserie, tea salon, and bakery. My *Tusán* (Chinese Peruvian) friend told me their pork is delicious and their moon cakes are the best in the world outside of China.[3]

For a more authentic market experience than upscale supermarkets in Miraflores, you can walk across an Avenida Paseo de la República overpass to Mercado No. 1 in Surquillo, about a twenty-minute walk from the centrally located Parque Kennedy. After browsing the market, try one of the excellent and affordable boutique fish restaurants in the area such as El Cevichano or La Picantería. And if you want to relax in cozy restaurant surroundings after walking around the market, Pueblo Viejo restaurant is located right above Avenida Paseo de la República. Full disclosure, the chef is my wife's aunt, and her specialty is the exceptional cuisine from the famous North Coast region of Peru. Try her ceviche with *tortita de choclo* (corn bread) in the style of the city of Chiclayo or her *cabrito norteño* (kid goat stew), one of the most famous dishes from this region.

Eating ceviche is a must in Lima, and my standard in the Miraflores district is Punto Azul. This restaurant is extremely popular with Miraflores office workers, so get there early for lunch (the main meal) in order to avoid a line. A restaurant that defies the rule that "only bad restaurants have beautiful views" is Punta Sal Cevichería, overlooking the Parque del Amor and the Pacific Ocean. Of course, the most famous *cevichería* is Gastón Acurio's La Mar, now one of seven in the chain. Acurio is the chef whose career ascended simultaneously with Peru's culinary boom; his flagship Astrid & Gastón is also worth a visit.

Currently, the new Peruvian culinary ambassadors are Virgilio Martínez Véliz and his wife, Pia Leon. Chefs Martínez and Leon are quite the power couple. They oversee a restaurant empire that includes his flagship Central, the fourth best restaurant in the world,

Chiclayo-style ceviche at Pueblo Viejo restaurant. Photo by Robert Bradley.

Cabrito norteño at Pueblo Viejo restaurant. Photo by Robert Bradley.

according to "The World's 50 Best Restaurants."[4] Central moved from Miraflores to the lovely adjacent neighborhood of Barranco in 2018, but it is still very accessible from Miraflores, if you can get a reservation. Leon's new venue is called Kjolle, and in 2021 she was named best female chef in the world. Pia Leon's growing global gravitas is on full display in a Netflix "Waffles+Mochi" episode produced by Michelle Obama, in which the master chef humbly makes potato stew in a rural highland setting.[5] Rounding out this family enterprise is Martínez's sister and her research center Mater Iniciativa. Malena Martínez oversees projects such as Virgilio Martínez's Mil restaurant located twelve thousand feet above sea level, at the top of the cold and windy Inca terracing at Moray.[6] The artistic district that is the setting for both Central and Kjolle is made up of flower-lined pathways and terraces that gradually descend to the Pacific. But if you make the pilgrimage to Central or Kjolle and have no luck getting a reservation, go eat at either Canta Rana or Canta Ranita in center of Barranco. Both places have great food and a good-looking and hip crowd that will make you forget why you came to Barranco in the first place.

Although Lima is one of the world's great food destinations, after a few days I look forward to leaving the crowds of the capital. Of late this always means a flight to Cuzco. I will talk about the capital of the Inca Empire in a bit. But first, a word everyone must know when frequenting a Peruvian market is the Quechua phrase *yapa.* The term is listed in González Holguín's early seventeenth-century Quechua dictionary as "an addition," or perhaps more precisely "a little extra."[7] *Yapa* is basically a baker's dozen, a little bit more, given as a favor to a good customer. It is universally spoken in all of Peru's markets, and the word will even work for gringos (in Peru the term *gringo* has no negative connotation and is synonymous with "foreigner," especially if you patronize a certain market daily). *Yapa* works like this. If you buy ten limes, the seller will throw in one or two more. Buy a bag of hot peppers, *ají,* and get an extra one or two for free. Interestingly, the term was exported two hundred years ago to a locale far from Peru. And the nineteenth-century wordsmith of repute Mark Twain noted and was delighted by the term:

> We picked up one excellent word—a word worth traveling to New Orleans to get; a nice limber, expressive, handy word—"*lagniappe.*" They pronounce it lanny-yap. It is Spanish—so they said. We discovered it at the head of a column of odds and ends in the *Picayune,* the first day; heard twenty people use it the second; inquired what it meant the third; adopted it and got facility in swinging it the fourth. It has a restricted meaning, but I think the people spread it out a little when they choose. It is the equivalent of the thirteenth roll in a "baker's dozen." It is something thrown in, gratis, for good measure. The custom originated in the Spanish quarter of the city. When a child or a servant buys something in

a shop—or even the mayor or the governor, for aught I know—he finishes the operation by saying—"Give me something for lagniappe." The shopman always responds; gives the child a bit of licorice-root, gives the servant a cheap cigar or a spool of thread, gives the governor—I don't know what he gives the governor; support, likely.

When you are invited to drink, and this does occur now and then in New Orleans—and you say, "What, again?—no, I've had enough"; the other party says, "But just this one time more—this is for lagniappe." When the beau perceives that he is stacking his compliments a trifle too high and sees by the young lady's countenance that the edifice would have been better with the top compliment left off, he puts his "I beg pardon—no harm intended," into the briefer form of "Oh, that's for lagniappe." If the waiter in the restaurant stumbles and spills a gill of coffee down the back of your neck, he says "For lagniappe, sah," and gets you another cup without extra charge.[8]

Webster has the word *lagniappe* derived from the Quechua *yapa*.[9] And Twain is correct that the word entered the French-influenced lexicon of antebellum New Orleans from Spanish merchants in the city during the Spanish interregnum (1763–1802), when Spain controlled the Louisiana territory before its sale to the United States. This global passage of words echoes the movement of foodstuffs, which I will return to often in this book. One last note about *yapa*. I noticed on my most recent trip to Cuzco that Yapa is the name for a money transfer service in Peru much like Zelle in the States, and an ancient name for a convenient digital service seems apropos.

No one will have to tell you the air is thin when you arrive at Cuzco's Alejandro Velasco Astete International Airport, because picking up and carrying your luggage, for me always my backpack, can leave you winded. Chewing coca can assuage altitude sickness, but do not buy coca from the women hawking small plastic bags of leaves in the airport parking lot—not because of legality, because chewing coca is legal in Andean nations, but because the sellers are grossly overcharging for the packets. Wait and check into a hotel or hostel and then walk (walking is great for acclimatization) to the San Pedro Market, which is about five blocks above Cuzco's Plaza de Armas. The San Pedro Market has myriad stalls serving everything from fresh smoothies to full-course meals at affordable prices. Go through the market, and at the southwest corner you will find stores selling coca leaves. Again, this is all perfectly legitimate. A one-pound bag of coca leaves should cost you around fifteen sols (four or five dollars), but you must buy the coca with *llypta,* quicklime and ash activator that releases the trace amounts of cocaine in the leaves. I will detail the specifics of coca chewing later, but here you should use your magic word *yapa* to have the vendor give you this activator agent as a bonus for the sale.

About an hour's drive outside of Cuzco the stalls and small restaurants in the Sacred Valley towns of Coya, Calca, and Lamay have excellent *cuy al palo* (grilled guinea pig on a stick). But please take some caution first.[10] As you read this book you will come to understand how food in Peru, or for that matter all of Latin America, is much fresher than what we have in the United States. However, outside of the supermarkets, most common markets lack refrigeration. And even though most of my study abroad Peru students are Mexican American and Mexican who are used to, as I am, of crossing the border for a taco lunch, I warn them to eat defensively and to pay more for their meals for the first few days in Peru. Unlike in Lima, I avoid raw fish in the highlands except for *ceviche de trucha* (trout), because this non-endemic species thrives in fresh Andean water.

However (back in Cuzco), Limo is an excellent, but expensive, sushi restaurant, and Barrio Ceviche, now just called Ceviche, on the plaza sometimes makes me think I never left the coast. Ceviche is always consumed at lunch in Peru, the earlier the better. After all, who wants to eat raw fish that has been sitting around all day? For dinner in Cuzco, I often eat pizza. But I typically take my evening repast at Museo del Pisco, which consists of a *butiffara* sandwich chased down by a few coca sours. Unfortunately, the *butiffara* sandwich was removed from Museo del Pisco's pared-down post-pandemic menu, but I hope when Peru's tourism industry recovers from COVID restraints the sandwich will reappear as an offering.

The upscale restaurants in Cuzco are first-class with excellent food to nourish you and help you acclimatize. In Peru I always think of the one-third rule. Peru has expensive restaurants, but relatively speaking they will cost one-third the price of an equally posh restaurant in New York City or Los Angles. Gastón Acurio has left his mark in Cuzco with his burger joint called Papacho's and a very fine restaurant called Chicha. Chicha is named after the famous pre-Hispanic corn beer. Try an alpaca steak at the upscale Uchu, named after the Quechua word for hot pepper. Sample Chinese Peruvian food at the restaurant Kion, with its wonderful ambience and beautiful bar. And then there is pizza.

I grew up a few blocks away from De Lorenzo's Tomato Pies, a pizzeria that is always in the running for the best pizza in the United States. So I know good pizza, and Cuzco has some of the best. The plethora of adobe ovens throughout Peru likely facilitates the great pizza here. And well-heeled tourists from around the world on their pilgrimage to Machu Picchu certainly fuel a healthy pizzeria market. La Bodega 138, a few blocks above the Plaza de Armas, is immensely popular. Expect to wait in line, but their red hot chili peppers offering is worth the wait. Be careful, because the pizza is covered with two very hot Peruvian peppers, *ají limo* and *rocoto*. Carpe Diem Cucina Italiana in Cuzco and the lavish Incontri del Pueblo Viejo in Aguas Calientes, the town below Machu Picchu and a few hours from Cuzco by car and rail, have the same owners and the same exceptional pizza. My study abroad group and I had wonderful pizza at Antica Osteria Pisac–Trattoria Pizzeria in Pisac, a Sacred Valley of the Inca town about an hour below Cuzco. This is just a pizzeria sampling, because there almost seems to be a pizzeria on every other corner in Cuzco. Go pizza hopping if you visit. You will not be disappointed.

One final note on the Cuzco region: Aguas Calientes is a major hub because of its access to Machu Picchu. But this jungle town is often very hectic, and lodging tends to be expensive for what are typically small rooms. The exception is Inkaterra Machu Picchu Pueblo Hotel. The hotel's beautiful gardens and bird watching possibly make the price tag of four hundred dollars a night well worth the cost. But obviously, this rate is out of reach for my study abroad group, so what we do is stay two miles outside of Aguas Calientes at the Mandor Lodge. The lodge is located by the Mandor Gardens, which have an amazing biodiversity of plants and animals. And the restaurant at the lodge offers an exceptional daily menu. If you want to try the numerous restaurants in Aguas Calientes, a trail runs along the railroad tracks, which you can take back and forth to the town. And don't worry about the train, it moves slowly and only passes a few times a day.

Cuzco and Machu Picchu are the major hubs on the "gringo trail," so there is no lack of restaurants catering to tourists in the areas. But if you are on a gastronomic tour of Peru, then go north. You will encounter the oldest pre-Columbian ruins in the Americas and the remnants of the Moche culture. Moche specialists Walter Alva and Christopher Donnan have found their artwork—weaving, ceramics, metallurgy, and so on—nothing short of astounding, and they use the oeuvre of the ancients Greeks as a valid comparison.[11] Moche art and architecture were created centuries before the Inca state came to fruition. Keep in mind that the Inca were the last major polity at the end of thousands of years of pre-Hispanic civilizations.

After a three-hour car ride going north from Lima, you will arrive at the ruins of Caral, the oldest city in the Americas dating back almost five thousand years.[12] If you are going to visit, leave Lima very early because the archaeological site is a complex with many structures, and you will need time to explore. For lunch go to the town of Huacho and look for ceviche made with bitter orange, or perhaps try the town's famous *chifas*. After a Caral visit, either drive back to Lima and fly to Trujillo (most internal Peruvian flights take about one hour) or drive another seven hours north to the city. The city of Trujillo has two famous pre-Columbian sites, Huaca de la Luna and Chan Chan. Both are almost part of the city's landscape with Chan Chan to the northwest and Huaca de la Luna to the southeast. Huaca del la Luna was built by the Moche people who thrived in this area fifteen hundred years ago. The city of Chan Chan was constructed by the Chimú people, a successor culture to the Moche, who were ultimately conquered by the Inca in the fifteenth century.

Both sites have museums, but the new Moche facility is not to be missed. Later, I will set up an itinerary for visiting this area and suggest a stay in the tranquil fishing village of Huanchaco about ten minutes to the north of Trujillo depending on the traffic. Huanchaco has many good *cevicherías*: the oddly named Big Ben is the most expensive, La Barca is our family favorite, and El Caribe is immensely popular with the locals. But the finest restaurant in Huanchaco is Mococho, named after the edible seaweed. If you want to dine in this unique Chinese Peruvian venue (*chifa*), go to the front entrance, knock on the door, and ask for the owner, Ricardo Sulem Wong. If Wen himself is not out for a run, he will discuss the specifics of your group and tell you when the dining room is available, likely the next day at lunch. A meal at Mococho typically consists of a ceviche for the first course and a second course of whole cooked fish with rice. The fish will probably be *chita*, Peruvian grunt (*Anisotremus scapularis*) pulled out of the ocean just a few hours before you arrive.

If you are having an extended stay in Huanchaco, a few blocks from the ocean the local market is friendly and accessible. While nowhere near as big as Trujillo's central market, Huanchaco's market has everything you need to cook Peruvian style. Several stalls have fresh fish, some of it supplied by the *caballitos de totora* fishermen whose reed boats line the village's *malecón* (pier). Here you can buy *chicha* (the pre-Columbian corn beer), *mochero* (hot peppers), and many of the fruits and vegetables I mention in this book.

The El Brujo Archaeological Complex (a must-see) is forty minutes to the north of Huanchaco on the right bank of the Chicama

Museo Cao. Photo by Robert Bradley.

River. This area of beach was of great importance to myriad pre-Columbian peoples for more than five thousand years. I reference the earliest site, Huaca Prieta, many times in this book because of the extensive floral and faunal remains uncovered there. Huaca El Brujo and Huaca Cortada are both Moche adobe pyramids. Huaca El Brujo was excavated twenty years ago, and you can see Moche era murals of catfish and rays. The pristine Huaca Cortada pyramid sits to the north of Huaca El Brujo and has not been excavated. Although small, Museo Cao is one of the finest museums I have ever visited. Most of the artifacts were dedicated to the Señora de Cao, an elite Moche woman who died in her twenties from complications of childbirth. The Señora is interred at the museum, and her mummified tattooed body is indirectly, and discreetly, visible through a reflective mirror. Just one glance at the Señora's gold and silver nose ornaments is worth the price of admission to the museum.[13]

One final note about this special place: the surf right off the El Brujo Archaeological Complex is designated Punta Prieta by Magic Seaweed, the oldest and most popular long-range surf forecast website. Indeed, Peru's North Coast is one of the best surfing destinations on the planet, with the iconic Chicama point, the longest left break in the world, being less than twenty miles to the north of the El Brujo Archaeological Complex. Nowhere in the world do you have such ancient archaeology and such natural wonders packed so close together into one place. It is like having the Great Pyramid of Giza sitting on the beach at Waimea Bay. Additionally, the history and distinction of the cuisine in the region demand visitors. Yet a tiny number of tourists go here compared to the multitude each year seeking out Machu Picchu.

The next important stop is Chiclayo, a coastal city three hours to the north of Trujillo. Chiclayo is Peru's gastronomic epicenter, with the towns and villages outside of the city being the most traditional and unique. Although Chiclayo is considered a coastal city, this urban center does not sit on the coast. Instead, the coastal town where *Chiclayanos* flock to the beach is the town of Pimentel, which is a sleepy fishing village with high-end condos and houses lining the *malecón* to the north of the pier. The pier is the longest in Peru, reaching two thousand feet out into the ocean. The tracks on the pier recall the nineteenth century when ships were loaded with huge bags of sugar from the coastal plantations.[14] On days when the surf is big, the pier facilitates brave surfers who walk halfway out and jump forty feet into the waves. The surfers then ride a wave in. Paddling back out in big surf is impossible, so they return to the pier to do it again (I only did it once). The guard at the pier gate usually waives the thirty-cent fee because they have already paid once, and he likely feels sorry for crazy people.

Pimentel has lots of restaurants specializing in seafood. The more expensive ones are north of the pier, and the more touristy budget restaurants line the beach to the south of the pier. My family and I have stayed in Pimentel several times over the past decade, and one of our favorite restaurants is Tienda el Pato, just north of the pier. For lunch, Tienda el Pato offers superb seafood dishes, typical of the region. At night the menu changes, with burgers being promoted (my children's favorite) and *anticuchos* (grilled beef heart). But most of the time during these stays, we eat in the house, because I have access to a kitchen and, therefore, I became well acquainted with the markets in the area. Pimentel's central market was only two blocks from our rentals. It reminded me very much of the market at Huachaco, and I would go there to buy key lime, *ají*, red onion, cilantro, and so on. But my most important purchase was fish, typically *lenguado* (flounder) and *mero* (grouper). Pimentel has numerous pre-Columbian-style reed boats or *caballitos de totora*. While there are some active caballitos in Huanchaco, most boats are now tourist attractions. In Pimentel the caballitos are an active fishing fleet, and when I observed the fishermen return with their catch I would often run to the boats with my mother-in-law and purchase fish. This fish was even fresher than the fish at the Pimentel market, but waiting for the boats was also a time-consuming process.

All my fish purchases changed with my first visit to Terminal Santa Rosa. If you are intent on sourcing the freshest big fish, you will be drawn to this large open building a mile south along the coast from Pimentel. Terminal Santa Rosa is a blue-and-white walled-in enclosure that really is just a parking lot for the trucks loading the catches from the trawler fleet operating from this busy port. But before the fish are taken away to other Peruvian destinations, local restaurant owners, fishmongers, and you all have a chance to purchase retail.

The cosmetics of the terminal leave much to be desired. However, smell the fish here and note the total lack of the aroma of decay. Instead, they smell like the ocean. Ask the fishmongers to show you the bright red color of the fish's gills (a sign of its health and freshness) when they lift their catch from the plastic bins. Anything you purchase here will be several days fresher than even the finest offerings at an upscale restaurant in the United States. If you visit,

Fish bins at Terminal Santa Rosa. Photo by Robert Bradley.

take your time and ask questions, because a purchase will be very expensive by Peruvian standards and even a gringo will be treated with great respect once the fishmongers know you are prepared to put down thirty to a hundred dollars for fish. If you want to prepare ceviche, try the exquisite *ojo de uva* (medusa fish), *lenguado* (flounder), *mero* (grouper), or *róbalo* (snook). The *lenguado* will be one of the most expensive, a large fish can cost forty sols (fourteen dollars) a kilo, and the *ojo de uva* the least expensive, around eighteen sols (six dollars) a kilo, but any of these white-fleshed fish will serve as an excellent prime ingredient for your ceviche.

The stalls for cleaning shellfish are in the back of the terminal, as is the filleting station. Purchases in the shellfish section are typically a kilo or more, which is quite a bit, so perhaps plan a meal of *arroz con mariscos* (a typical plate here) or a wonderful pairing of shellfish with pasta. *Conchas de abanico* (Peruvian scallops, *Argopecten purpuratus*) are one of the most delectable and exotic offerings.[15] These scallops can be prepared with Parmesan cheese, *a la chalaca*, with *ají* and *rocoto*, or served as a garnish for your ceviche. *Rocoto* is a pepper that resembles a small red or green bell pepper, but the veins are loaded with capsaicin, which gives the fruit its fiery flavor. Since many of the fish offerings here are in excess of three kilos (about seven pounds), leave the cleaning and filleting to the professionals at the fillet station in the back of the terminal. For six sols (less than two dollars) they will do all the squishy business promptly and deliver thick and meaty bone-free fillets. They will also give you the heads and bones. My mother-in-law uses these as the base for *chilcano*, a nutritious fish soup. If you have invited friends for a visit to Peru or befriended some residents, buy one of the larger fish and save one fillet for ceviche and the other to grill or pan sear. The social lubricant here is the pisco sour made from an aguardiente of *uva* (grapes), or grape brandy (I will share my musings on pisco and its history along with a detailed recipe for this cocktail later).

The village of Monsefú is only a few miles from Pimentel, making this pre-Columbian gastronomic center well worth the short trip. Again, many people in Chiclayo say the descendants of the Moche live in Monsefú. Have a taxi drop you off in the Plaza de Armas in the late morning so that you can experience the central market. There you can buy your *chicha* (homemade pre-Columbian corn beer), which in the ancient coastal tradition is fermented longer and has more alcohol than its milky highland counterpart. Buy your delicious cherimoyas for dessert here.

Before you concentrate on the fruit stalls, however, go to the first aisle of fishmongers and look for plastic bins with small snakelike creatures swimming in water. These highly prized freshwater catfish are called *lifes*. Imagery featuring these fluvial creatures has been uncovered on the walls of the Moche sites of Huaca de la Luna and Cao Viejo. *Life* bones have been excavated from Moche archaeological sites. Textiles and jewelry, uncovered from the spectacular 1987 Moche Sipán tombs, are replete with *life* icons. *Lifes* fetch a dear price at the Monsefú market, going for twenty-five sols (seven dollars) a kilo for the larger four-inch fish. To bring out the flavor of the catfish, *lifes* need to be killed in the old style, by adding salt and a bit of water to a bowl of the catfish until they stop moving. Then rinse and clean the fish. Because they have tough and unctuous skin, *lifes* are hard to clean so make sure your fillet knife is razor sharp. They also sell *lifes* at the Terminal Santa Rosa (for twenty-eight sols a kilo). The fillet station should be able to clean these river fish, but this task will almost certainly cost more than the price for cleaning the large ocean fish. I have cleaned *lifes* to make *sudado de lifes* (catfish stew) for my wife's grandmother, and I would highly recommend paying a bit more to have a professional complete this task. Add some *chicha,* cilantro, and spring onion to the *life* mix along with several tablespoons of *ají amarillo,* which can be purchased in any market stall selling fresh homemade sauces. Then cook the dish over low heat for about twenty minutes and serve with yuca. At the restaurant Los Delfines in Monsefú they serve the traditional *panquitas de lifes,* which are prepared exactly as in the preceding recipe except the *lifes* are cooked in a cornhusk. (I will return to *lifes* later.)

A twenty-minute taxi ride from Pimentel in the opposite direction will put you in front of the Museo Tumbas Reales de Sipán. This is the depository of some of the finest Moche artifacts in the world. The building is an interesting imitation of a Moche *huaca* (temple/pyramid), which dominates the pre-Columbian town of Lambayeque. The place name Lambayeque is associated with the pre-Columbian king who, more than one thousand years ago, entered the region from the ocean on a fleet of rafts and then proceeded to establish a dynasty. King Naymlap was no common ruler, because his entourage included attendants to make his food, make his beer, and spread rare shells at his feet as he walked. And although no one will litter the pavement with shells as you walk through the town, the tradition of great food in Lambayeque continues to this day.

The museum houses the artifacts salvaged from the 1987 Sipán archaeological find. Before this discovery, the sumptuous gold, silver, and semi-precious-stone regalia of the Moche lords—often depicted on fine-line-painted ceramics—was believed to be legendary. But the Sipán artifacts shifted these objects from legend into reality. After touring the museum and noting the superb Moche gold and turquoise duck ear spools, I suggest you settle down to a regional meal of *arroz con pato* made from the oddly named Muscovy duck. Later I will discuss this endemic fowl's introduction to the West and detail the famous North Coast recipes for *arroz con pato* and *cabrito norteño* (kid goat stew). For traditional dishes like these, the place to go in Lambayeque is El Cántaro Restaurant Turístico. Do not let the term tourist bother you. I know, in the West, tourist restaurants are to be avoided. But in Peru the moniker *turístico* is a badge of honor because, when Peruvians apply the word *turístico* to a restaurant, it is an accolade indicative of good service and a more elaborate menu. El Cántaro is very popular, so it is a good idea to get there either early for lunch (before noon) or later (after two). Before the duck or goat dishes, I would recommend an appetizer of ceviche, especially if they have *ceviche de róbalo* (snook), and/or *tortilla de raya* (a stingray omelet with hot pepper and spring onions).

An excellent, albeit very expensive, restaurant in the city of Chiclayo is Fiesta Restaurant Gourmet Chiclayo. Here you can order the same regional specialties as are served in El Cántaro. They will be more expensive but meticulously prepared and served in very elegant surrounds. It is worthwhile mentioning that Fiesta's Chiclayo locale will be much less expensive than their restaurant in Lima, even though the Chiclayo venue is in the epicenter where the ingredients for the regional specialties featured in both restaurants are sourced. Another very good and more reasonably priced restaurant in the center of Chiclayo is La Romana–Balta 512. Again, order the regional specialties *cabrito norteño, arroz con pato, tortilla de raya,* and so on. The last time I was there with my family, I had a wonderful *chinguirito.* This is a ceviche appetizer made from reconstituted stingray meat. In contrast to my citrusy and spicy fish dish, my wife's trips to Balta 512 are for the desserts.

Another recommended stay while visiting the Peruvian Departamento (state) of Lambayeque is Los Horcones de Túcume. This lodge is located next to one of the pyramids of the pre-Columbian center of Túcume, less than an hour's drive from Chiclayo. The lodge's architects used ancient materials from the area, like carob wood, to construct the buildings. They are also the architects for the beautiful Chachapoya museum in Leymebamba. The Túcume archaeological site covers more than five hundred acres and includes twenty-six pyramids and many smaller structures. The famous adventurer and ethnographer Thor Heyerdahl spent his last years here documenting the site. Following the twilight of the Moche culture in the region, the Lambayeque (Sicán) people were responsible for these massive constructions.[16] You can walk to the entrance of the Túcume museum and the Túcume Archaeological Project from the lodge—in fact, one of the pyramids looms over the lodge. The museum deserves at least a few hours especially if you walk the trails around the site. Look for the feisty burrowing owls who defend their nests until the very last minute. These creatures are celebrated in pre-Columbian art.

Los Horcones de Túcume has a very good restaurant with a friendly staff. Even though we were not guests, they were very accommodating when my study abroad group dropped in for lunch several years ago. If you stay here, I recommend that you buy fish at Terminal Santa Rosa, have it filleted there, and then pack the cleaned fish in a Styrofoam cooler with ice. Plan the night before with the cooks, and I am sure they will make some spectacular ceviche for you or prepare your catch any way you like.

Chapter 2
Fish

Before the end of the Pleistocene Epoch, the Ice Age, human beings migrated into unoccupied parts of the Americas. Peru was "probably first populated by way of a coastal route along the Pacific shoreline or from the crest of the nearby Andean high-lands sometime before 13000 BP [before the present]."[1] Andean archaeologist Tom Dillehay has summed up the survival strategies of these hunter-gatherers with one word, *diversity*.[2] These ancient Peruvians utilized and consumed every edible part of the living environment so as to thrive. This would include lizards, snakes, small rodents, shellfish, and small fish, and of course they foraged wild plants.

At some point in time survival strategies changed when these ancient Peruvians arrived at the most prolific fishing grounds in the world. Even though Peru is situated well within the temperate Tropic of Capricorn, a frigid current flows north from the sub-Antarctic and inundates the southern and central Peruvian coastline until it turns west toward the Galapagos Islands. Along most of Peru's beaches, bathers encounter cold Antarctic water. A few hundred miles from the coast of Peru the ocean becomes more temperate when warm ocean currents from the north push the cold current out into the Pacific. This icy coastal current is called the Humboldt Current, after the great German polymath Alexander von Humboldt, and this mass of Antarctic water is responsible for conditions advantageous for the plethora of sea life in Peru's coastal ocean. Clear, warm, and pleasant tropical waters are great for bathing, but they are mostly sterile. In contrast, the forbidding cold dark ocean of coastal Peru teems with life. Changes in Peru's unique coastal ecosystem occur once every ten years or so, when the Antarctic Humboldt Current gets pushed away from Peruvian coastal waters by a warm northern flow. For a time, El Niño ushers in the exile and destruction of the cold-water creatures that typically thrive in Peru's coastal waters.[3]

Early fishing in Peru is associated with a particular type of lithic spearpoint called Paiján. The Pampa de Paiján is a twenty-mile-wide stretch of barren North Coast desert, which has numerous ancient archaeological sites. These settlements were occupied from seventeen thousand to seven thousand years ago. Paiján spearpoints are long and thin and were mounted on hollow shafts.[4] This light and deadly stone-age spear was wielded by skilled fisherfolk for millennia. But even before the end of the Paiján Tradition, the fishing techniques used by these ancient Peruvians started to evolve. In the Las Pircas phase (5800 BCE) of the Peruvian North Coast archaeological site of Nanchoc, cotton (or more precisely, *Gossypium barbadense*) was first cultivated. This inedible plant continued to be grown in the later Tierra Blanca phase at the site, and one of the reasons to produce this crop was to fabricate fishing line and fishing nets.[5]

But *G. barbadense* is not ordinary cotton. It was and is the finest cotton in the world. After the arrival of the Spanish, *G. barbadense* was exported and (most famously) cultivated in the American South and Egypt. Today we are most familiar with the different brand names for *G. barbadense*: Pima Cotton, Sea Island Cotton, and Egyptian Cotton. *G. barbadense* is also called extra-long-staple cotton or ELS cotton because it has extra-long cotton fibers. And as the Nanchoc archaeology has suggested, ELS cotton is endemic to the dry coastal valleys of Ecuador and Peru west of the Andes.[6] The fisherfolk of pre-Columbian Peru were fortunate to have the best cotton to make their lines and nets. Any industrial production of this crop likely took millennia to develop, but by 2500 BCE this transition was complete. Andeanists refer to the time period from 3000 BCE to 1800 BCE as the Cotton Preceramic Period. And here a digression is necessary to explain this rather oddly named era.

About five thousand years ago, six geographical locations worldwide saw the rise of urban centers, cities: China, Egypt, India/Pakistan, Mesopotamia, Mexico, and Peru. These complex and stratified societies were necessarily supported by irrigation agriculture because hunting and foraging cannot feed the mouths of thousands in a city.[7] Four of these locations—India/Pakistan, China, Egypt, and Mesopotamia—had vast river networks in support of agriculture. Ancient Mexico, specifically Mexico City, had numerous shallow lakes and a system of using the rich mud from these waterways to enrich the soil.[8] All five of these places had ceramics early on. Ceramics are important because of the need to cook crops such as rice, wheat, barley, and so on, so that we can actually digest these foods. Evolution did not give human beings the four stomachs of a cow.

The final center, Peru, is an anomaly. Peru's coastal desert was where large urban centers first developed along small rivers with headwaters in the Andes. However, these were not the vast water networks of the Tigris and the Euphrates or the delta of the Lower Nile. More important, Peru had no ceramic tradition until after 1800 BCE, even though there are several complex sites in the Norte Chico (the central and northern Peruvian coastal region), which developed in the first few centuries of the third millennium BCE.[9]

The absence of an early ceramic tradition was an enigma for Andean archaeology. Toward the end of the twentieth century, Michael Moseley offered the Maritime Hypothesis. Simply put, the principal crop grown on Peru's coast from 3000 to 1800 BCE was cotton, specifically *G. barbadense*. This cotton was the essential material for the nets and fishing line that provided the maritime bounty to feed the early coastal populations.[10] Since its introduction, the Maritime Hypothesis has been intensely debated. Certainly, the third millennium rise of Norte Chico coastal centers was more complex and defies being categorized by one all-encompassing theory. But Moseley's observation that Peru's coastal biomass is the richest in the Western Hemisphere is not easily dismissed. I have often wondered: did Moseley come up with his theory while driving through one of Peru's coastal cities during the morning rush, when everyone from laborers to office workers can be seen eating small plates of ceviche, fish marinated in key lime juice with salt and hot pepper, dispensed from roadside stalls?

Recently, industrial cotton production (again *G. barbadense*) has been suggested as the industrial resource behind the urban center of Caral, a five-thousand-year-old settlement that has been designated the oldest city in the Americas. Peruvian archaeologist Ruth Shady has imagined the site as an agricultural center specializing in cotton production. The inhabitants of Caral, twelve and a half miles from the ocean, would trade cotton with coastal sites such as Aspero in exchange for great quantities of fish and mollusks.[11] Later, the evidence of vast pre-Columbian fishing activity on Peru's coast is overwhelming. Tom Dillehay's archaeological work at the four-thousand-year-old coastal midden of Huaca Prieta has revealed nearly two hundred faunal species of marine animals.[12] In the Common Era, the Moche culture (from the first to the eighth century) left reminders of their fishing tradition in the imagery on their ceramics as well as their ceremonial architecture. The fishing scenes first appear on ceramics in the middle of the Moche timeline and become frequently portrayed in later phases.[13]

Line fishing from shore and throwing nets from the beach and rocks have their limitations, so a floating platform on the sea, boats, greatly enhance maritime harvesting. The reed boat is a ubiquitous image in Moche art.[14] And these craft are still in use today among a few fishermen in Huanchaco, a fishing village near Trujillo. Farther north at Pimentel, a beach town near Chiclayo, an active fleet of boats works the coastline in all but the biggest surf. The only difference between these boats and their pre-Columbian antecedents is that the cotton that binds the vessels has been replaced with nylon fishing line, and empty plastic soda bottles now line the interior of these crafts to delay the vessels' becoming waterlogged. In the colonial era, Father Bernabe Cobo described the great lengths the reed-boat fishermen would go to in order to keep their boats from getting waterlogged, and the modern innovations are not surprising. Cobo also stated that these small fishing craft could venture out four or six leagues in the open ocean.[15]

It is difficult to determine the exact length of a Spanish league in the sixteenth century, but we can approximate the distance mentioned by Cobo to be about ten or twelve miles.[16] I have spent years surfing breaks and fighting currents on Peru's North Coast, often next to these *caballitos de totora* (reed horse-boats), and I find Cobo's statement about their open ocean capabilities implausible. Also, in my experience, I have never seen a caballito venture out more than several hundred yards from shore. Caballitos are made from a totora (reed) called *Schoenoplectus californicus*. This totora was readily used to make matting, baskets, roofing, and watercraft at Huaca Prieta four thousand years ago.[17] The paddles for these boats were—and still are—large hollow bamboo shafts that have been cut in half. The bamboo (*Guadua angustifolia*, more commonly named *caña de Guayaquil*) was also found at Huaca Prieta, and images of these cane paddles are prominently displayed on Moche ceramics.[18]

In the late pre-Hispanic era, the northwest Pacific coastal waterways of South America were active with watercraft. In addition to the small reed vessels, fisherfolk used double-hulled inflated sea-lion-hide vessels in the south and eventually balsa wood (*Ochroma pyramidale*) rafts made of seven to nine logs roped together. Sails and oars powered these crafts, which were used to transport cargo.[19] Amazingly enough, these primitive rafts were likely the flotilla for three amphibious invasions. First was the landing of the refined King Naymlap at Chotuna-Chornancap on Peru's North Coast. I will return to this founder of Lambayeque culture (750–1375 CE) and focus on his retinue later.[20] The second was the equally intriguing amphibious invasion by Taycanamo, the founder of Chimú culture (900–1470 CE).[21]

The third naval invasion—by the Inca emperor Tupac Inca—was by far the largest and most intriguing amphibious campaign. After marching his army to the northern city of Tumbez, Tupac Inca encountered some merchants who had come by sea from the west, navigating in balsas with sails. They told him about islands called Avachumbi and Ninachumbi, and they said there were many people there and much gold. The emperor ordered balsas built to accommodate an expeditionary force of twenty thousand men. Then he set off and conquered the islands, which are part of the Galapagos chain. The endeavor took almost a year, and the long absence of the Inca emperor filled the men left ashore with apprehension until his return.[22]

In the conquest and early colonial eras, the waterways of coastal Peru teemed with ships as well as fishing vessels. After the discovery in the mid-sixteenth century of a vast silver mountain at Potosí, Lima became a center for shipping the enormous supply of silver to Spain and, via the Manila galleons, to China. This diffusion of silver continued for more than two centuries and would ultimately change the world economy.[23] At the beginning of Peru's republican era, maritime activity increased during the War of the Pacific (1879–84), which had Bolivia and Peru allied against Chile. Curiously, this war over the coastlines was not for fishing territory but for guano (bird excrement). Guano had been extracted and used as a fertilizer since the pre-Columbian era. The Inca had llama caravans to transport the rich nutrients to their Andean settlements.[24] In the nineteenth century the nitrates from the islands of Peru's southern coast and Bolivia's now lost coastline were a major economic resource. These nitrates were this era's major source of fertilizer and to a lesser extent gunpowder.[25]

The islands' bizarre riches were the impetus for the War of the Pacific, which ultimately led to a loss of coastline for Peru and left Bolivia a land-locked nation.[26] By the beginning of the twentieth century, the futility of the war became apparent because the Haber-Bosch process, which artificially fixes nitrogen in fertilizer, made the guano trade both gratuitous and archaic.[27] In the twentieth century the tension for control of Peru's waterways returned to focus on maritime resources, and it all concluded in 2014 when an international court awarded Peru, over Chile, a rich triangle of Pacific Ocean fishing territory, covering thousands of square miles.[28]

Now let's focus on the fish used for Peruvian ceviche, the finest seafood offering on the planet, and the variations of the recipe in different time and space. I will continue with a discussion of cartilaginous fish, which I will refer to as *tollo,* used to make *sudado,* a staple of Peruvian coastal cuisine. I will close the chapter with observations on the abundant Moche images of stingrays and a small endangered fluvial catfish.

Sublime Peruvian ceviche is a study in simplicity. The indispensable foundation for this dish is the absolute freshest of white-flesh fish. Seven species of cold-water fish have dominated the Peruvian palate for thousands of years. These are (1) *Seriolella violacea,* palm ruff; (2) *Centropomus* sp. (*C. medius* or *C. nigrescens*), Róbalo del Norte or snook; (3) *Anisotremus scapularis,* which is Peruvian grunt or chita; (4) *Paralichthys adspersus,* lenguado or flounder; (5) *Micropogon altipinnis,* Pacific croaker or corvina; (6) *Paralonchurus peruanus,* the Peruvian banded croaker; and (7) *Trachurus symmetricus murphyi,* Pacific jack mackerel or jurel. *Schedophilus haedrichi,* mocosa ruff, is very similar to *Seriollea violacea* and a member of the Centrolophidae family of medusa fishes. But this species was not harvested until the twentieth century when "fishermen started to fish in deeper waters with *espinel de profundidad,*" therefore, *Schedophilus haedrichi* is absent from the pre-Columbian record.[29] These eight fish are the most coveted ceviche fish.

Over the past twenty years I have eaten in many *cevicherías,* and each time I do, I ask what fish is offered. As far as I know, I have eaten six of the eight, only lacking Peruvian banded croaker and Pacific jack mackerel. But by far the most frequent answer, naming the fish of the day, is corvina even though I often doubt that this is the correct answer to my question. The cachet and familiarity of the name *corvina* seems baseline for busy *pituca* (nouveau riche) *cevicherías.* Over the years in our summer rental apartments, I have made ceviche with *Schedophilus haedrichi, Paralichthys adspersus, Seriolella violacea,* in addition to two of the warm-water fish mentioned below.

If you are eating in a coastal *cevichería* dedicated to culinary excellence, south of the North Coast city of Chiclayo, you will most likely be served one of these fish. As the cold Humboldt Current flows away from the coastline in northern Peru and heads west, the warmer waters of northern Peru allow another prized ceviche fish to make its way to the table. *Epinephelus* sp. is known to us as grouper, but in northern Peru it goes by the esteemed name *mero*. I have been sold *mero* in the market of Pimentel, and I have purchased *mero* from caballito fishermen returning to shore in the same town. Some of these *mero* were in fact not grouper but instead snappers (*Lutjanus* sp.). Yet the fishermen sell them under the name *mero*. So *mero* in Peru can be used as a generic name for tasty tropical/semitropical fish in the north.

There is a precedent for this big-tent naming of dissimilar fish in the term *tollo*. I am sure *tollo* is a generic name for any predatory cartilaginous fish. These fish are used almost exclusively to make *sudados* (fish stews), a staple of coastal Peruvian tables. I've bought *tollo* many times in Huanchaco and Pimentel, and the fish are always cut up into pieces when sold. Again, the portions are very fresh, absent any smell of decay, but identifying what species (or for that matter, family) of fish you are purchasing is a task for an ichthyologist.

All the cold-water littoral fish mentioned above, except *Seriollea violacea*, were harvested by ancient Peruvians thousands of years ago.[30] While researching this book, I was astounded by the Peruvian predilection for certain flora and fauna over millennia. You might even say it is an underlining theme for this text. But how were these fish consumed? The essential modern quartet of ceviche—lime (*Citrus* × *aurantifolia*, key lime, *limón sutil*), extremely fresh fish, red onion (*Allium cepa*), and *ají* (*Capsicum* spp., hot pepper)—in the pre-Columbian world lacks lime, the main cooking agent, and red onion. The less essential onion, the *limón sutil*, and the bitter orange (*Citrus* × *aurantium*) all came to the New World via the Spanish, during the conquest era. Mariano Valderrama has pointed out that the bitter orange was widely used in old Lima because the production of limes around the Rímac River, the area around Lima and the namesake for the city, was small. Today the bitter orange is still used to make some ceviches in the Peruvian central coast city of Huacho, but *limón sutil* is omnipresent in *cevicherías* throughout the country.[31]

In lieu of the cooking agent lime, the ancient Peruvians enjoyed pre-Columbian sashimi. Indeed, they were fortunate enough to have varieties of fish that are cherished today by the Japanese Peruvian Nikkei, the most sophisticated connoisseurs of seafood. A tradition of eating raw fish is much older than the arrival of Japanese immigrants to Peru in the late nineteenth century. Valderrama has an excellent list of early colonial references recording the indigenous propensity for eating raw fish.[32] This simple and natural practice is likely as old as fishing itself, and fishing is an ancient tradition on Peru's coast. It is interesting to note that Cobo has a reference to consuming a raw fluvial creature called *chichi*.[33] This *chichi* could be a reference to the Moche *life* catfish, a prominent image in Moche art.

Passiflora foetida (passion fruit, *tumbillo, maracuyá*) has been suggested as a pre-Columbian cooking agent because the fruit is endemic to South America, and faunal remains of *maracuyá* have been found at the Moche site of Huaca de la Luna.[34] While a pre-Columbian ceviche cooked with *maracuyá* is certainly possible, my own experience with *maracuyá* as a cooking agent was not auspicious. Several years ago, I added *maracuyá* to a beautiful *ojo de uva* (*Seriolella violacea*), which I had purchased in the Huanchaco market and served to my wife's family. During and after the meal they were polite but later that day, after a few piscos, we all agreed that the flavor of the *maracuyá* overpowered the delicate taste of the fish. Using *maracuyá* with a darker and stronger flavored fish such as *Sardinops sagax* (sardine or herring) would be more appropriate and an interesting but maybe not a frequent digression from traditionally prepared ceviche. It is impossible to know if this cooking agent was used before the arrival of the Spanish and their *limóns*, but faunal remains of *Sardinops sagax* were also found at the same Moche site as the *maracuyá*.[35]

By the mid-sixteenth century, *limón sutil* (key lime) trees were cultivated in the Rímac Valley near Lima and along the North Coast of Peru.[36] Where the first instance of mixing *limón sutil*, fresh raw fish, and *ají* occurred would be difficult to confirm, but Valderrama has noted that today the North Coast is the principal producer of key limes in Peru and the best fields are in the province of Morropón near Piura and Motupe in Lambayeque.[37] Bearing in mind the ancient fishing tradition of this coastal region, the plethora of excellent ceviche fish, and the indigenous penchant for eating raw fish, and you have a strong circumstantial argument that the first ceviches of lime, fish, and *ají* were made there.

The celebrated Peruvian Japanese Nikkei chef Mitsuharu Tsumura has suggested that the practice of appreciating the taste of fresh fish and quickly marinating the catch in lime juice, comes from twentieth-century Japanese immigrants.[38] Until the 1980s, Limeños let the fish marinate for hours when making ceviche. Certainly, the Nikkei influence changed the cooking time to a quick rinse of *limón sutil*, but outside Lima, particularly on the North Coast, there is little Japanese influence on cuisine.[39]

In Lima the tradition of making ceviche goes back to at least the republican era, after Peru won its independence from Spain in 1821. In his mid-nineteenth-century study of Lima, Fuentes looked down on the *picanterias* of the city, especially the ones that serve *seviches* [*sic*]. He confirms the fact that the fish was marinated for hours, but in this case in bitter orange not *limón sutil*. Fuentes continued by lamenting the addition of potent *ají*, which would bring tears to the diner's eyes. Fuentes's entire chapter on repasts in old Lima has an upper-class Eurocentric bias, and his disdain for *cebiche* [*sic*] and hot pepper is on full display in his record.[40] But his chronicle affirms the positive Nikkei culinary impact on, at least, the ceviches of Lima.

Today's ceviches are a creole quartet with two elements from the pre-Columbian world (fish and *ají*) and two ingredients from the Old World (red onion and key lime). Red onion is not endemic to Peru, but the vegetable has certainly become ubiquitous in modern Peruvian dishes—from the popular Peruvian stir-fry *lomo saltado* to the fish stews (*sudados*). The name *ceviche* is likely derived from escabeche, a fried fish marinated in onions and vinegar that was brought to Peru by the Spanish.[41] Ricardo Alcalde Mongrut's playful yet meticulous ceviche recipe, handed down from bohemian Lima, serves as the standard for the dish. In a snappy dialogue, Alcalde Mongrut (with his alter ego, Compadre Guisao) lionizes the cold-water ceviche fish, while reinforcing my doubt about the reliability of the inescapable corvina label.[42] But again, all the cold-water offerings have ancient bona fides for thousands of years as a coveted maritime resource.

Mongrut disdains any ingredients that take away from the exquisite combination of the finest and freshest fish, select key limes, red onion, and *ají*. Salt is welcomed into the mix, but the addition of cilantro, celery, cumin, *huacatay* (Peruvian black mint), *yerbabuena* (lemon verbena) and *yuyo* (seaweed) is considered insolent.[43] I agree with most of the aficionados' reproach except for the seaweed. After filleting, the fish is washed three times, with the ultimate rinse with salt, and then diced with a very sharp knife. The limes need to be choice, sourced from the North Coast's Chulucanas District in the province of Morropón or the Motupe District in the province of Lambayeque.[44] They should be ripe and fresh. The red onion should be rinsed in water and sliced thin (my mother-in-law soaks the sliced onion in water with a touch of salt for about fifteen minutes). The *ají* (*Capsicum prubescens, Capsicum sinense, Capsicum frutescens,* and possibly the import *Capsicum annuum*) should be cut into thin slices and only partly deveined, in order to preserve *el picor* (the heat) from the fruit. My wife's grandmother always says, *si no pica, no es ceviche* (if it isn't spicy, it isn't really ceviche). Apparently, a small measure of garlic, *ajo* (*Allium sativum*), is permitted without disturbing the Old World/New World balance, but it needs to be ground by hand with a *batán* (a grinding stone). Mongrut, for aesthetic reasons, allows small amounts of two other ingredients brought by the Spanish: parsley (*Petroselinum crispum*) and pepper (*Piper nigrum*), likely in the white version. Finally, after the ingredients are quickly mixed, the dish is then garnished in *estilo limeño* with the fish nested in lettuce accompanied by boiled sweet potato (*Ipomoea batatas*) and *choclo* (*Zea mays*), the large kernel corn so favored in Peru, and quickly served.[45]

In contrast to Mongrut's exacting rules for great ceviche, Valderrama spent time traveling the coast recording the subtle regional variations of the Peruvian dish. For him, the abundance of fish and the simplicity of the dish have an epicenter in northern Peru. The sea around Piura becomes much warmer as the cold Humboldt Current flows away from the South American coastline and heads out into the Pacific, and this enables fishing the tropical *mero* (*Epinephelus* sp.). This fish is held in great esteem in northern Peru, and it is by far the preferred lunchtime repast. Every day in this country, ceviche consumption starts in the morning and ends around two in the afternoon. Peruvians never eat ceviche at the evening meal, and most *cevicherías* either close by four or emphasize other items on their menus. This caution for disdaining ceviche at night is good common sense, because the catch of the day has been hanging around since the early morning, and dead fish do not age well. So be sure to have your *mero* early. I like going to the ceviche restaurants when they open, typically right before noon.

In the north, the accompaniments for a plate of ceviche become complicated, and some sides can be easily explained by history, but one is very unusual. *Lablab purpureus* (commonly called *zarandaja* beans) is an outlier. *Zarandaja* beans do not fit into the underlining theme of ancient Peruvian foodstuffs because they are not endemic to Peru. There are endemic varieties of Peruvian beans that were domesticated thousands of years ago (*Phaseolus lunatus*, commonly known as the lima bean, and *Phaseolus vulgaris*, also known as the common bean), but neither one is a traditional accompaniment for a plate of ceviche.[46]

Beans were an integral part of the enslaved Afro-Peruvian diet, however, and ecogeographic surveys of *Lablab purpureus* show the high probability of occurrence of the species, or endemism, in southeast Africa and Madagascar.[47] Linking *zarandaja* beans with Madagascar is especially interesting, because both Piura and Lambayeque include communities of *Mangaches*, Afro-Peruvians with roots in Madagascar.[48] So this diaspora of foodstuffs and people are reflected in the side dish of *zarandaja* beans for ceviche, which is uniquely popular in these two places. As much as I find this enduring ethnic addition to a regional variation of Peru's most famous seafood recipe fascinating, I am not fond of the seafood and bean combination.

All the other accompaniments have Peruvian archaeological bona fides. Yuca (*Manihot esculenta,* cassava) is a common addition to a ceviche plate on the North Coast, and floral remains go back to at least Guitarrero Cave, several thousand years ago. Also known as cassava, when prepared for ceviche the epidermis of the root is removed, and the cylindric core is quartered into four- or five-inch pieces. These pieces are then boiled in water with oil and salt. Yuca supplements the protein of the fish with carbohydrates, as do both *choclo* (*Zea mays*) and sweet potato. Yuca and sweet potato (*Ipomoea batatas*) also provide a respite from the sharp sting of the ever-present ceviche condiment, *ají.*

In the north, particularly in the area around Trujillo, a prominent addition to the ceviche in this region is the edible seaweed garnish known locally as *mococho*. This is a North Coast term for edible types of seaweed. In other parts of Peru and elsewhere in Latin America, seaweed (or more properly, marine algae) is referred to as *algas marinas*. Along most of the North Coast the idiomatic word *yuyo* is also used for edible seaweed, but it is almost impossible to translate precisely because the word *yuyo* is used in a variety of ways. Perhaps the most accurate interpretation in this context would be "green stuff from the sea." Jose Antonio Salas, in the *Diccionario* of ancient Moche words, notes that *kochkoch* means *yuyo* (seaweed) and *mo* means *este* or "this." So, *mokochkoch* could signify seaweed in this pre-Columbian language.[49]

There are two types of *mococho* harvested on the North Coast of Peru, red and green. The red, the more coveted of the two, gets its name from the reddish-brown tinge on the outside of the blades. Trying to discern the species, or for that matter the family, of Peruvian coastal algae is a daunting task because there are 39 families and 150 species of coastal seaweed, of which 14 are edible.[50] Dillehay has *Gigartina chamissoi* as the scientific name for *mococho;* Peruvian algae specialists list *mococho* as *Chondracanthus chamissoi;*

however, according to the website AlgaeBase, the two names are synonymous.[51] Aaronson has *Gigartina glomerata* as specifically *mococho,* and he notes that both *Gigartina chamissoi* and *Gigartina glomerata* belong in the phylum Rhodophyta (red algae).[52]

Mococho is a fantastic source of vitamins, and many locals chew bits of it in winter to ward off sickness. When consumed in larger amounts, *mococho* has diuretic qualities and is associated with good digestion. Medicinal uses aside, *mococho* has culinary value, too. When *mococho* is washed and served raw as a garnish for ceviche, the strong briny taste of the algae combines well with the lime and raw fish mixture. Typically, in restaurants, a few strands of *mococho* are placed in each serving of *leche de tigre,* which is a milky-white lime-and-fish-juice cocktail served in a glass topped with *ají* and *mococho.* This spicy and salty drink is typically imbibed as an aperitif, its flavor reflecting the freshness of the restaurant's seafood offerings.

In the North Coast city of Chiclayo, *chinguirito* (dried Pacific guitarfish, *Rhinobatos planiceps*) often accompanies the ceviche, but it is also served as an entrée. Faunal remains of this cartilaginous fish were found at Huaca Prieta, so these fish were eaten in the early pre-Columbian era, but they were likely a dietary staple long before this. The *Chiclayanos* also add *cancha* (Peruvian popcorn) and *tortita de choclo* (a corn fritter) to the ceviche. But in most other Peruvian locales *cancha* is placed on the table as *la ñapa* (remember the little bit extra in Quechua). If this calls to mind the obligatory free tortilla chips offered in Mexican restaurants, then you get the idea. Valderrama relays that some ceviches in the city of Huacho are marinated with bitter orange (*Citrus × aurantium*) juice and not lime. Valderrama continues by lamenting the near extinction of the bitter orange tree in Peru.[53] The ceviche I had in Huacho several years ago was made with the more typical *limón sutil,* but when I return to Huacho, I plan to seek out this bitter orange variation, and even though Huacho is somewhat off the beaten path, I would advise any gastronomically interested Peru traveler to make the town a lunch destination following a morning visit to Caral, the oldest city in the Americas.

Equally ancient Peruvian seafood offerings are the *sudados* (fish stews) that are omnipresent table fare for any coastal celebration. The main ingredients for these *sudados* are not the bony fish that are essential for good ceviche but instead cartilaginous fish such as sharks and rays. Sharks and rays inhabit Peruvian coastal waters all year round. The common name for shark meat, or more precisely any meat from a predatory cartilaginous fish, is *tollo*. *Tollo* and small rays are always available in the markets of coastal fishing villages, and this is especially true of Huanchaco and Pimentel, because both hamlets have active caballitos fishing every day except the days with the roughest surf. Solid evidence of ray and *tollo* consumption emerged in excavations at Huaca Prieta, where faunal remains of sharks and rays were recovered dating back to the second millennium BCE. The three major groups of sharks are requiem sharks (*Carcharhinus* sp.), school sharks (*Galeorhinus* sp.), and smooth hounds (*Mustelus* sp.).[54] If you are enjoying a wonderful *sudado de tollo* in a Peruvian coastal town, the fish you are eating is likely from one of these three genera.

Inexpensive ray meat is never referred to as *tollo*, and ray meat has lower status for use in a *sudado*. *Sudado de raya* (ray stew) is such a modest dish that locals are disinclined to serve it.[55] On the North Coast of Peru fishermen generally catch four different types of rays. The smallest and most common ray is the *wira*, which normally measures about one foot in length and is brownish red in color. The *wira* is in the sand skate genus (*Psammobatis* sp.).

The *tapadera* ray (*Urotrygon* sp.) has a longer rounded wingspan than the *wira* and is found in the same sandy-bottomed shallow waters.[56] The *guitarra* (guitarfish, *Rhinobatos planiceps*) derives its name from its distinctly guitarlike shape. Again, this is a tropical fish that frequents the waters around Piura and that is the base for the dish *chinguirito*. It is considerably larger than the *wira* and *tapadera* and it prefers deeper water. Finally, huge oceanic manta rays (*Mobula birostris*), which inhabit deep coastal waters, are accidently caught today on the North Coast by Peruvian fisherman using nylon nets.

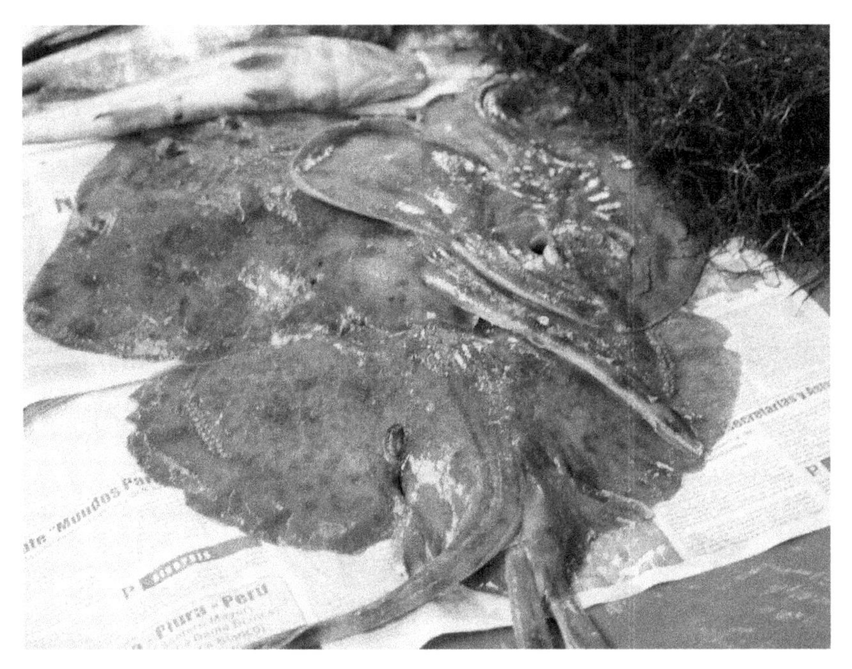

Wira ray (*Psammobatis* sp.) in the Huanchaco market. Photo by Robert Bradley.

As expected, *M. birostris* does not appear in the faunal remains at Huaca Prieta because landing an enormous manta ray with a cotton net would have been an impossible task. But curiously, there is an image of the Moche deity Ai-Apaec landing a manta ray with a cotton fishing line on a pre-Columbian stirrup-spout bottle. Today, the manta rays accidentally caught are salted, dried, and then sold for a price that is hardly worth the effort. The manta ray also has a slow rate of reproduction, so any harvesting has impact on the species. Because of this decline, in 2015 the Peruvian government passed a resolution protecting manta rays.[57] For the other two smaller rays, the effort of line fishing is worthwhile. The fishmongers in the Huachaco market emphasize that line-caught rays taste better than those that have languished and decayed in the fishermen's nets, and this preference for line-caught fish for ceviche is echoed by Ricardo Sulem Wong, the owner of Mococho Restaurant in Huanchaco.

Four main ingredients constitute the pre-Columbian preparation of *sudado*: shark or ray meat, *chicha de jora, mococho,* and *ají amarillo* (*Capsicum baccatum*). *Ají amarillo,* sometimes called *ají verde* or *ají escabeche,* is a mild variety of *C. baccatum,* but the pepper makes up for the absence of heat with intense flavor. This *ají* has been in the diet of Peruvians for thousands of years, as evidenced by floral remains at Huaca Prieta.[58] The dish has changed a bit over time (for example, garlic, which was unknown in the Americas before the Spanish arrived, is now an addition), but these ancient ingredients remain constant. *Chicha* is the corn beer found in many Andean communities. It was the preferred drink of Inca elites, but it predates the Inca; this simple concoction of corn and water has been around for at least four thousand years.

The modern version of *sudado* uses garlic. (Garlic was embraced by indigenous peoples in the Americas after it arrived with the Spanish, but it's likely that in the original preconquest version one or more of Peru's native herbs was used for seasoning—for example, *Mansoa alliacea* or false garlic.) The recipe for this dish is detailed at the end of this chapter, but I want to make a note about *chicha* here. The correct amount of *chicha* depends on the cook and the quality of the available *chicha.* I like to use about a cup of aged *chicha de jora.* The strong aged coastal version of *chicha,* what Valderrama calls *clarito,* has ancient pre-Columbian roots.[59] Finally, any number of Peruvian seafood delights such as the small purple North Coast crabs (*Platyxanthus orbignyi*), sea snails (*Tegula atra*), and *palabritas* (cockles or more precisely *Donax obesulus*). All these additional *mariscos* were found in the remains at Huaca Prieta so they are easily imagined in pre-Columbian fish stew.[60]

Like many *platos típicos* of northern Peru, *sudados* are served with rice. This water-intensive crop is curiously omnipresent on Peru's desert North Coast. It was introduced into Peru by the Spanish, so it was not the original accompaniment for *sudados.* It is likely that the dish was served with the pre-Columbian staples yuca (manioc, cassava) and *choclos* (corn), both of which would add carbohydrates to this protein-rich stew. The *choclos* can be boiled in a separate pot from the *sudado* with the yuca. But be sure to remove the *choclos* soon after the pot boils. The yuca will require more time.

Chinguirito is a typical dish in the area around Lambayeque. It is made in a similar fashion to ceviche, but the dried guitarfish is reconstituted with the addition of lime juice. The side dishes for *chinguirito* are the usual regional variations, yuca, *cancha, zarandaja* beans, and *choclos.* The main ingredient for *chinguirito,* dried and salted guitarfish, is a much humbler main ingredient than the super fresh white-flesh fish in typical ceviches, so restaurants seem to go out of their way to embellish this simple offering.

Before leaving the class of cartilaginous fishes, and finishing with a fluvial curiosity, I want to mention the ray meat dish *tortilla de raya.* The curious main ingredient of this North Coast Peruvian omelet is dried ray meat reconstituted with water and lime juice. The *wira* and *tapadera* rays are the most common main ingredients, but for the past few decades the manta ray has become a source, prompting the 2015 Resolución Ministerial against harvesting this spectacular creature. The ray meat is mixed into a batter with spring onions, *ají,* and eggs, and the cooked omelet is topped with red onion and *ají.* In my favorite variation of this flexible recipe, the edible seaweed *mococho* is also added to the mix.

I would like to close this chapter with a discussion of a river fish, the Moche *life* catfish, because this creature will soon be extinct. Its disappearance will not be caused by harvesting, but by the pollution of coastal rivers by agricultural chemicals. The scientific name for this creature is *Trichomycterus punctulatus,* but it is also classified as *Pygidium dispar,* and I will return to this confusion in a moment. *Life* intuitively seems an English derivative, even though the word has decidedly Spanish pronunciation: in this case both vowels are short and pronounced [lee-fey] not [layhf]. You can find these catfish in the market of Monsefú, about a half hour southwest of the city of Chiclayo.

In Chiclayo they say the Moche live in Monsefú, and this saying validates the ancient traditions of this place. *Lifes* are often the

Tortilla de raya. Photo by Robert Bradley.

subject of pre-Columbian Moche art (as are rays). Some examples can be seen in the catfish pattern mural from the Huaca Cao Viejo in the El Brujo complex, and the greenstone, thorny oyster, and gold wristband motif from the Museo Tumbas Reales de Sipán in Lambayeque. The "Allegory of Fish Reproduction" from Huaca Cao Viejo is an example of ray art. In the mural male and female rays perform a delightful dance in stylized waves. A double tail of the male ray in the mural corresponds to the tail of the small male skate often sold in the Huanchaco market. However, some images of rays and/or catfish are so abstract that positive identification remains elusive—the famous mural of the main Moche deity Ai-Apaec from the Huaca de la Luna, for example. Branching out from Ai-Apaec's ferocious countenance are octopus tentacles, and on the border of the friezes' central diamond-shaped core are stylized geometric forms each with a triangular head and two eyes. In the past, these images were regarded offhand as serpentine, but these creatures are most likely rays.[61] Ultimately, the zoomorphic elements of this mural resist precise identification even though this image is perhaps the Moche icon of record.[62]

An equally enigmatic representation is rendered on a nose ornament recovered in 2003 from the Señora de Cao's tomb at Huaca Cao Viejo. The creature represented on this object is ambiguous and could again be either ray or catfish.[63] Design patterns on many of the Moche ceramic stirrup-spout vessels from Lima's Larco Museum are even more difficult to categorize. However, the most enigmatic and intimate icons of this genre are the ray/catfish tattoos on the mummified hands of the Señora de Cao.

The classification *Thrichomycterus punctulatus* originates from the ancient Greek *trichos* (meaning "hair") and *mykter* (meaning "nose"), and anyone who has seen a catfish understands that this ordering references the barbels of the fish. The scientific naming was initiated by Alexander von Humboldt, but the great French ichthyologist Achille Valenciennes corrected and firmly established the designation for this creature. The Swiss naturalist Johann Jakob von Tschudi illustrated the *life* catfish in an 1844 study of 120 types of freshwater and saltwater fish in the marine environments of Peru. But Tschudi identified the coastal catfish of the northern Peruvian rivers (*lifes*) not with the genus *Thrichomycterus* but instead as *Pygidium* with the species identifier being *dispar*. The explorer took the sample in Peru and added that "the natives [Peruvians] call these fish *Vagres* and make them often because of their very tasty meat."[64] Tschudi's identification of the genus *Pygidium* is obviously in conflict with Humboldt's previous assignment, yet both names are used to identify this species.

I believe the name *life* was initially applied to *Trichomycterus punctulatus* at the end of the nineteenth century because fish expert Carl H. Eigenmann noted that, in Piura, a small catfish was called *bagre, bagrecito,* and *life*. He added that it had been found useful in the control of the yellow-fever mosquito. This comment was published in 1922 in his tome *The Fishes of Western South America: Part I,* but the research was likely conducted decades earlier. So the term *life* is well over a hundred years old.[65]

The Moche certainly consumed *lifes* because excavations at Huaca de la Luna revealed that 27.78 percent of the freshwater fish bones were *lifes*. This archaeological evidence clearly indicates that *lifes* were an integral part of the Moche diet (they are rich in proteins, iron, and riboflavin).[66] Today they are found in dishes such as *panquitas de lifes* or *sudado de lifes* in the town of Monsefú. The ingredients to prepare these offerings affirm their pre-Hispanic origins. The foundation for these dishes consists of *life* catfish, *chicha, ají amarillo,* salt, and herbs. *Lifes* are kept alive until they are ready to be eaten and then are killed when salt is poured directly onto the skin, a process that locks in the flavor of the dish. The second component of the dish is *chicha,* and the third is *ají amarillo,* which adds flavors to sauces. It is added to the preparations for *panquitas de lifes* or *sudado de lifes* in this same manner today.[67] Sea salt has been harvested for thousands of years in Peru as a necessary dietary additive. Today *culantro* (*Eryngium foetidum*), cilantro's more rustic and flavorful American cousin, can enhance the flavors of *life* preparations. But cilantro (*Coriandrum sativum*), the Old World's Chinese parsley, is ubiquitous in coastal Peruvian markets. Spring onion is the final ingredient in the preparation of *lifes*. Scallion was likely first added to *panquitas de lifes* by nineteenth-century Chinese immigrants.[68] But Peru has a plethora of pre-Columbian herbs that could have provided a fragrant substitute. Perhaps the surest way for a visitor to experience the pre-Columbian Moche world is by paying olfactory attention to a cooking pot of *chicha* beer, *lifes,* cilantro, and *ají*. But I recommend that you do this soon before this ancient dish disappears.

Bob's *Ceviche de Pescado*

2 lbs. of the freshest firm white fish you can buy (snapper, grouper, mahi-mahi, etc.)
¾ cup of freshly squeezed key lime juice
1 red onion
½ tsp. *ají amarillo* paste
½ tsp. chopped cilantro
1 tbsp. salt
1 hot pepper

Cut the red onion in half, remove the skins, and slice each half into very thin slivers. If this process makes you cry, soak the slivers of onion in water with a half teaspoon of salt for 15–30 minutes. With a very sharp knife cut the fish into either small thin strips or cubes (*tiradito* or traditional). Put the fish into a large mixing bowl, add the lime juice, and stir vigorously. Add the *ají amarillo* paste and onion and stir. Then add salt so it balances the acidity of the lime. Finish by adding the cilantro and garnish the ceviche with a deveined and deseeded hot pepper.

Bob's *Sudado de Pescado*

2 lbs. *tollo*, cut into portion-sized chunks
4 *ají amarillo* (Anaheim peppers are an adequate substitute), deveined, deseeded, and cut into strips
5 Roma tomatoes, cut in quarters and deseeded
1 large red onion, quartered
1 cup *chicha de jora*
2 cloves of garlic
2 tbsp. vegetable oil

In a large pot fry the garlic in oil. Add the red onion, the strips of *ají*, and the tomatoes and cook for 2–3 minutes, then braise the *tollo* for another 2–3 minutes. Add the *chicha* and simmer over medium to low heat for half an hour.

Chapter 3
Fruit

It is hard to imagine food preparation in Europe and Asia before the Columbian Exchange. Unique and enduring foodstuffs were the great gift sent back to the Old World from the pre-Columbian peoples. The trifling gold and silver of the Mexica and Inca people pale in comparison to the treasure of corn, potatoes, peanuts, tomatoes, chocolate, and hot pepper (or in the Peruvian vernacular, *ají*). Columbus first noted the use and importance of *ají* in the West Indies. Remember, Columbus's mission was not discovery; it was, rather, focused on finding a new trade route to the east that bypassed the Venetians and the Ottomans in order to access luxury goods such as spices. Therefore, when he first encountered hot pepper (in this case it was *Capsicum annuum*), he confused it with *Piper nigrum* (black pepper), a highly valued commodity in his era. Hot peppers are hollow fruit or berries of plants in the family Solanaceae, which includes potatoes, tobacco, tomatoes, and many other floras.[1] There are five domesticated species of *Capsicum: C. annuum, C. chinense, C. frutescens, C. pubescens,* and *C. baccatum.* Although the scientific names help to distinguish the type, generic names for each species abound and are confusing. The names themselves, like many scientific names for plants and animals, are also confusing, because these terms often seem to be meaningless Greek and Latin jargon. Additionally, the names are often misleading, with the most egregious example here being *C. chinense,* because this pepper neither originated in nor was domesticated anywhere near China.

C. chinense, C. frutescens, C. pubescens, and *C. baccatum* were all domesticated from wild plants in South America. I need to point out that *C. chinense* and its semi-wild ancestor *C. frutescens* are closely related, and some scholars believe that from a practical and biological viewpoint there is no reason to separate the two species.[2] Both originated in the forests of northeastern South America. *C. pubescens* originated in the high cloud forests of Peru and Bolivia; this plant thrives at altitude and is somewhat frost resistant. *C. baccatum* was domesticated in the coastal region of Peru.[3] *C. annuum* was first domesticated in Mexico and obviously had made its way to the West Indies before the arrival of the Spanish. *C. annuum* is the most widely distributed hot pepper in the world, and the different varieties of *C. annuum* are well known: Anaheim, ancho, Hungarian wax, bell, cascabel, cayenne, cherry, jalapeño, and so on.[4]

This book is centered on Peru, so I will not concentrate on the myriad cultivars of *C. annuum* but instead will focus on the species of peppers most important to the history of food in Peru: in order from most important to least important, *C. baccatum, C. pubescens, C. chinense,* and *C. frutescens*. I found many inconsistencies in the identification of specific pepper species. The grouping of different varieties or cultivars was, at times, even more confusing. Dr. Jean Andrews's two books on *Capsicum* were very useful, but her latest text is now more than twenty years old; it was written before Peru's culinary traditions aroused the interest of foodies worldwide. I hope to clarify the importance of *C. baccatum, C. pubescens, C. chinense,* and *C. frutescens* in the Peruvian culinary tradition, but more work needs to be done on the specifics of these four species and their cultivars.

Birds have an immunity to the fiery heat of these colorful berries, so migratory birds, after a *Capsicum* pepper feast, spread the seeds of wild *ajíes* throughout the Americas.[5] Curiously, the Quechua (Inca) name for hot pepper (*uchu*) is confined to remote regions of the mountains and rainforests in Peru. Like the complicated appellation *cholo, ají* is a Cariban name for capsicums (hot pepper), brought from the Caribbean to Peru by the Spanish during the conquest era. This was the term, specifically *axí,* first encountered by Columbus.[6] According to the sixteenth-century mestizo chronicler Garcilaso de la Vega:

> Con estas frutas, y aun por la principal de ellas, conforme al gusto de los indios, pudiéramos poner el condimento que echan en todo lo que comen—sea guisado, sea cocido o asado, no lo han de

> comer sin él—, que llaman *uchu* y los españoles pimiento de las Indias, aunque allá le llaman ají, que es nombre del lenguaje de las islas de Barlovento.

> With these fruits—and at the head of them all according to the taste of the Indians—we might include the condiment they invariably take with everything they eat, whether stewed, boiled or roasted. They call it *uchu,* and the Spaniards say *pimiento de las Indias,* though in America it is called *ají,* a word from the language of the Windward Islands.[7]

The first quotation is the 1609 original Spanish text; the second is from Howard Livermore's translation. Livermore has taken some liberties in his English text, likely to make Garcilaso's chronicle more accessible. For example, the term *America* originally applied to both North and South America, but in this instance, it specifically means South America. Also, the Windward Islands are the islands of Barlovento, the southernmost part of the Lesser Antilles.

So, what was this Windward Island language? Although Merriam-Webster has *ají* derived from the Taíno word *axí,* the original language was likely a Cariban tongue brought to the Lesser Antilles by these invaders from north-central South America, well before the arrival of Columbus and the Spanish.[8] The word *cholo* is also a term from this same language pool and is identified as such by Garcilaso, who explains that the word is indicative of a mongrel dog and was used by the Spanish to demean the indigenous population.[9] Oddly, these two Cariban terms, one a pejorative and one for a condiment, traveled north to an island chain and then southwest, back to South America with the Spanish.

But the indigenous Quechua name for one variety of *ají* is still used in Peru. *Capsicum pubescens* (commonly known as *rocoto, locoto* in Bolivia) is listed in González Holguín's early seventeenth-century Quechua dictionary and is defined as a "large hollow *agi* [*sic*], which doesn't burn much" (my translation).[10] I am grateful for González

Rocoto de huerta in Urubamba market. Photo by Robert Bradley.

Holguín's etymology of *rocoto*, but most *rocotos* are in fact extremely spicy. In 2009, Peru's Instituto Nacional de Innovación Agraria (INIA) released a study of *rocotos* in the area around Arequipa, a southern highland city considered the epicenter for *rocoto*-themed cuisine, which listed two hundred different varieties of *rocotos*.[11] In the series *El punto de ají: Investigaciones en Capsicum nativos*, the authors list three different varieties of *rocotos* that seem to be subspecies: *rocoto*, *rocoto de la selva central* (*rocoto* of the central rainforest), and the very curious *rocoto de huerta* (garden *rocoto*). *Rocoto de la selva central* is larger than a normal *rocoto* and always red in color. *Rocoto de huerta* shares the same color spectrum of a regular *rocoto*—green, red, yellow, and orange—but it is intensely hot. It is pointed at the end, resembling a cross-pollinated cultivar of *C. pubescens* and *C. chinense*.[12] The biodiversity of *C. pubescens* implies that González Holguín could have tried a mild variety of *rocoto* or perhaps a mildly spicy cultivar that had been deveined and deseeded.

Rocoto relleno (stuffed pepper) is a famous Peruvian delicacy associated with the colonial centers Arequipa and Cuzco. The origin of this dish was whimsically linked by the Peruvian writer Carlos Herrera to the celebrated eighteenth-century chef Manuel Masías from the Arequipa region and his battle with the devil for his daughter's soul. The origin of *rocoto relleno* could plausibly be the humble colonial era *chicherías*, and later *picanterías*. The complex history and evolution of these simple spaces in the colonial era is meticulously outlined in *Picanterías y chicherías del Perú* and aptly described by Fuentes in his description of Lima in the era of the Republic.[13] The story that these unpretentious locales served small plates with copious amounts of corn beer and a stuffed pepper certainly seems apropos for this type of venue, but I could not find an early colonial reference to this dish.[14]

Curiously, the often-cited earliest example of a stuffed pepper recipe is *pimientos rellenos* from Spain's Basque region. This tapa is made with the celebrated *piquillo* pepper, which is often incorrectly listed as originating in Spain. Of course, all *Capsicum* come from the Americas, and the correct origin of the *piquillo* pepper is likely Mexico because it is a cultivar from the *C. annuum* species. Remember, Columbus brought *C. annuum* back to Spain before the end of the fifteenth century, a very early date for the Columbian Exchange of foodstuffs. But the earliest date for preparing *pimientos rellenos* was two hundred years later, at the beginning of the eighteenth century, which is an interesting colonial time frame.

A digression here is appropriate. I am not exaggerating when I say the establishment of the world's largest silver mine at Potosí, Bolivia (then the Viceroyalty of Peru), in 1545 changed the world. Although entailing a virtual death sentence for the indigenous miners, the silver from this mine funded Spain's wars, opened trade with imperial China, and turned Villa Imperial de Potosí, a cold city over thirteen thousand feet above sea level, into the richest city on earth. Luxuries poured into this decadent town, with the transport hubs of Lima and Arequipa supplying amenities while extracting more silver than ever before imagined.[15] From the mid-seventeenth into the eighteenth century, the citizens of Potosí had an insatiable thirst for alcohol that was mostly assuaged by wine, pisco (a Peruvian brandy), and *chicha*.[16] And in the seventeenth century, this embarrassingly rich city was controlled for a time by a Basque gang called the Vicuñas.

The vicuña is the most feral of the four camelids—llama, alpaca, guanaco, and vicuña. The Vicuñas gang were named for the hats they wore, made of the wool from these animals (which during the age of the Inca was reserved for only the emperor himself). A disproportionate number of Basques thrived in Potosí, likely because of their ability to adapt to the altitude.[17] So, even though the evidence here is circumstantial, could there be a colonial era link between *pimientos rellenos* and *rocoto relleno*? (Certainly, some archival research in Arequipa on this topic could benefit a food studies PhD candidate.)

Finally, in their text *Ajíes del Perú*, Fernando Cabieses, Raúl Vargas, Juan Viacava, and Walter H. Wust mention that the *piquillo* pepper is now commercially produced in Peru; more than one hundred million dollars' worth of these peppers, including paprika, are exported to the United States and Spain annually.[18] The Comisión de Promoción del Perú para la Exportación y el Turismo (PromPerú) confirms the extent of these exports and lists the production site for these peppers as the three North Coast departments of Piura, Lambayeque, and La Libertad. PromPerú states that the *piquillo* pepper cultivar, which is in the *C. annuum* species, was imported into Peru from Spain in the mid-1990s, and cultivation has been so successful it is now exported.[19]

Rocoto relleno arequipeño begins with deveining and deseeding the *rocoto*, then putting them into a pot of boiling water and vinegar. All these steps help neutralize the bite of the fiery *rocotos*. The peppers are then stuffed with ground pork mixed with chopped garlic, onions, peanuts, eggs, crushed crackers, whole peas, and raisins. Oil, salt, and pepper are added to the mix, and then the preparation is put into an oven for fifteen minutes. *Rocoto relleno a lo cusqueño* veers from the first recipe by starting with ground pork and beef

Rocoto relleno a lo cusqueño (foreground) with potatoes and Guinea pig blood sausage. Photo by Robert Bradley.

and adding culantro and *huacatay* (*Tagetes minuta* and *Tagetes graveolens*, Peruvian black mint). The pepper and stuffing are then covered in egg batter and fried.[20]

If the veins and seeds of the *rocoto* are judiciously removed, and boiling completed, the dish is not spicy. And even though *rocoto relleno* is more traditionally associated with Arequipa, Garcilaso mentions how common *rocotos* were in his hometown of Cuzco in the late sixteenth century, the time and place where González Holguín spent twenty years working on his Quechua dictionary.[21] Visual evidence of *rocotos* is on display in Marcus Zapata's iconic eighteenth-century Cuzco School masterpiece *The Last Supper* in the Cuzco Cathedral. Cuzco School artists, and a few of their descendants still active today, added indigenous people, plants, and animals to baroque art. In this case Zapata's flourishes in *The Last Supper* are startling. The main course in the center of the table is a strange animal, which is often called a *cuy* (guinea pig). According to the description in the Cuzco Cathedral, the animal featured as the main course is not a *cuy* but instead a *viscacha* (*Lagidium peruanum*), a rodent in the chinchilla family. I have seen many of these animals while trekking to mountain passes at Salkantay and Ausangate and this identification seems likely to me. The animal on the plate is too big for a *cuy* but, instead, matches the *viscacha*'s frame (think, large rabbit). South American fruits and vegetables are also prominently featured in the image along with representations identified as *ajíes*.[22]

But a close inspection of the peppers reveals that the round orange fruit, at the bottom center of the table and in the bowl to the left of Christ, is a specific *ají*: *C. pubescens, rocotos*. Andrews and Eshbaugh obliquely refers to these *ajíes* as *C. baccatum*, but the *rocoto* identification makes perfect sense if we consider Garcilaso's previous comment that *rocotos* were common in Cuzco and the fact that Holguín listed *rocoto* in his dictionary, which he wrote in the same city.[23] Both observations were recorded more than one hundred years before Zapata created his painting. Also, *C. pubescens, C. chinense*, and *C. frutescens* are common condiments; I have often seen these peppers served on the table, many times with lime and salt, but I have never been served fresh *C. baccatum* in this way. *C. baccatum* is ever-present in the market and in the kitchen, but not on the table. In the kitchen, *C. baccatum* is deveined, deseeded, cut into strips, and put into stews and sauces for flavor, or it is blended into a paste, again to use as a flavoring. *C. baccatum* simply isn't hot enough to serve as a fiery trimming for a meal.

There is a visual precedent for a spicy pepper garnishing the table of Jesus. Luis de Carvajal's *Last Supper with Santa Teresa and the Carmelite Community* (1707), housed in the Templo Santa Teresa de Jesús in Ayacucho, Peru, has two peppers in the lower left part of the table, which are *C. chinense*.[24] One is red in color, but the other is white with a bit of green and red. A fiery pepper enhancing a feast is a common practice, and in Cuzco the *ají* of choice, again according to Garcilaso, was and still is *rocoto*.

Rocotos, known in Mexico as *manzano* peppers, resemble small bell peppers but are about one-third to one-fourth of their size. Because of their shape, size, and black seeds, *rocotos* are easy to identify, and there is no confusion in the literature concerning this species. The color of *rocotos*—yellow, red, orange, and green—are similar too, but the similarity stops on the inside of the fruit because the *rocoto*'s veins and black seeds are fiery hot. And because *rocoto* is rather large for an *ají*, if you want to add heat to a dish, you have a great deal of capsaicin (the molecule that gives hot peppers their heat) to work with when you select a *rocoto* as a spice for your meal. In my preferred *rocoto* recipe, I first remove the seeds but keep some or all the veins, depending on the heat tolerance of my guests. I then cut the *rocoto* into a few pieces, which I place in a blender with salt and the juice of two key limes. I put the mix into a bowl with a small spoon and tell everyone to approach with caution. Finally, preserved *rocoto* paste and whole frozen *rocotos* are available online and in specialty food stores in the United States, but a great deal of flavor is lost in processing and freezing this unique *ají*.

Bob's *Rocoto* Hot Sauce

1 *rocoto* or *manzano* pepper or 2 red jalapeños, deveined, deseeded, and chopped
¾ oz. fresh squeezed key lime juice (about 4 key limes)
Salt to taste

Place all ingredients in a food processor and mix well. Add salt to balance the acidity of the lime juice.

Capsicum pubescens remains have been found at the ancient Peruvian North Coast site of Huaca Prieta from more than seven thousand years ago, and Dillehay has suggested that these *rocotos* were likely traded in from the eastern Andes.[25] An ancient *rocoto* trade network from the eastern highlands is an interesting supposition. The highland origin makes sense, because the *rocoto* plant is cold resistant, but *rocoto* does not travel well. The thick flesh bruises easily, which causes the berry to bruise and rot.[26] The Mexican-grown *manzano* peppers we get in South Texas are encased in plastic like a modified egg container. But even with this added precaution, I have often noticed bruising on many *rocotos* in our local supermarket. Therefore, transporting *rocoto* is not an easy task. Several years ago, while conducting research on the ancient Silk Road network, I was surprised to find that mare's teat grapes were moved great distances while packed in lead containers with ice.[27] The care that went into transporting this commodity, especially considering the antiquity of this operation, surprised me. But another example of a demanding trade network, this time not on the other side of the planet, was the Inca *chasqui* relay runners who could bring the Inca emperor fresh fish from the coast to Cuzco, over two hundred challenging mountainous miles, in two days.[28] Certainly, *rocoto* could have been brought to the coast from the eastern Andes thousands of years ago, but the peppers would have needed to be transported carefully. A hollowed-out bottle gourd with leaf-packing could make the difficult journey successfully. But the Coto de Caza Sunchubamba is an old-growth rainforest area on the western side of the Andes, about forty miles from Huaca Prieta. Transporting *rocotos* from this area would have been a much less daunting journey, even in antiquity. Also, remember the *El punto de ají* authors list three different varieties of *rocotos* that seem to be subspecies. Certainly *rocoto de la selva central* could be grown near the coast of Peru, maybe even very close to the coast if properly irrigated. Regardless, Dillehay has recorded a decrease in *C. pubescens* remains in later settlements at Huaca Prieta.[29]

Categorizing the other frequently used Peruvian *ajíes* is a difficult task because of the conflicting information. For example, in *Ajíes del Perú*, Cabieses et al. have *C. annuum* as the extensively cultivated species of hot pepper widely used today in Peruvian ceviches. The text also uses the ambiguous terms *ají limo, ají lima* in the Andes, and *ají limon* on the North Coast, to categorize C. *annuum*.[30] But this chili is noticeably absent from the plant remains at Huaca Prieta. I used the term *chili* purposefully here because C. *annuum* was first domesticated in Mexico, so it is unlikely this pepper was present in northwestern South America at this very early date, seven thousand years ago.[31] But C. *chinense* and its semi-wild relative C. *frutescens* were both in abundance at ancient Huaca Prieta. Cabieses et al. conflate C. *annuum* with C. *chinense,* which is again confusing, because C. *chinense* was domesticated in the more tropical areas of northeastern South America.[32] Adding more ambiguity, Cabieses et al. also use the generic name *ají limo* for C. *chinense,* while Valderrama and Ugás in *Ajíes peruanos: sazón para el mundo* definitively name C. *chinense* as *ají limo* and list the *ají cereza,* cultivated in the North Coast department (state) of Lambayeque, as the sole Peruvian pepper from the species C. *annuum*.[33] Finally, PromPerú definitively categorizes C. *chinense* as *ají limo* and has the Lambayeque *ají cereza* also in the C. *annuum* species.[34]

To be fair, the confusion here is understandable. C. *chinense,* and its semi-wild ancestor C. *frutescens* are taxonomically closely related to C. *annuum*. Also, C. *frutescens* and C. *chinense* were brought from South America and cultivated in the West Indies long before Columbus's arrival. The same can be said for C. *annuum,* but the pathway was likely from Mexico or Central America. In any case, it was C. *annuum* that Columbus brought back to Europe. From Europe C. *annuum* was introduced to Africa and Asia by the Portuguese and then Europe and the Middle East by the Ottoman Turks.[35] So, did C. *annuum* make its way around the world and then back to Peru over the next few centuries to become the ubiquitous *ají limo,* the most extensively cultivated species of hot pepper widely used today in Peruvian ceviche?

Well, the C. *annuum piquillo* pepper made a journey from the New World (Mexico and the Caribbean) to Spain and then to Peru, but this pepper is exported and has no claim in the Peruvian culinary tradition. Therefore, I don't believe *ají limo* is from the C. *annuum* imported species. I would welcome an extensive biological study of Peruvian *ají,* because with modern scientific methods I believe this would reveal that the spicy *ajíes* used on Peru's coast are *C. chinense* and/or *C. frutescens.* During my research for this book, I was astounded by the Peruvian preference, over millenia, for certain flora and fauna. And *C. chinense* and *C. frutescens* were present and used in food preparation in Peru thousands of years ago.

Additionally, if we go back to Valderrama and Ugás, *Ajíes peruanos: sazón para el mundo,* and PromPerú, these both categorize *ají cereza,* cultivated in the North Coast department (state) of Lambayeque, as the sole Peruvian pepper from the species *C. annuum.* First, Lambayeque is one of Peru's greatest pre-Columbian and gastronomic centers. That is saying a lot, considering Peru's ancient history and culinary bounty. Traditions in places such as Lambayeque are enduring, so it is unlikely that *ají cereza* is an import. Garcilaso offers a bit of circumstantial evidence for this in his chronicle when he describes a potent, small, round cherry-like *ají,* which he calls *chinchi uchu.*[36] Andrews has *chinchi uchu* as a cultivar firmly in the *C. chinense* species, and I believe this categorization is much more likely than placing the pepper from Lambayeque in the species *C annuum.*[37]

Throughout Peru, *C. chinense* is ubiquitous in its dried powder form called *ají panca.* When a pepper is smoked or dried, it becomes a completely different ingredient with a different taste and often a different name. The most common example is when dried jalapeños become chipotles. *Ají panca* is used in countless Peruvian preparations. Think, Peruvian paprika or, more accurately, the less well-known *chinense* predecessor of *annuum*-based paprika, and although it is in the *C. chinense* species, the variety of pepper used to make *ají panca* is not very hot. Also, the peppers are deveined and deseeded before they are dried, which greatly reduces any heat. I love using *ají panca* in a marinade mix with soy sauce and garlic for my rotisserie-grilled chicken, served with salad and French fries, imitating the popular Peruvian nighttime repast. I buy many packets of *ají panca* each season when I visit Peru. Unfortunately, powdered *ají panca* has no distributor in the United States, likely because of the label's female Afro-Peruvian caricature. Images such as these are now considered offensive in the United States (the Aunt Jemima caricature was removed recently as was Uncle Ben), but it is a sign of respect in Peru referencing the revered black cooks, the *Serapios*, from the colonial era.

One of the most interesting *C. chinense* peppers is the green—and, when fully mature, yellow—*mochero ají*, which is frequently used in the ceviches made in and around the Peruvian North Coast city of Trujillo. This pepper is named after the Moche people, who built a civilization in the first millennium of the Common Era in the same North Coast location. *Mochero ajíes* are hot but also flavorful.

I should note that there is also some confusion as to *mochero*'s species. Elmo León has *mochero* classified as *C. annuum*, while Cabieses et al. put it in the group *C. baccatum*.[38] As you can see from my placement of *mochero* in this text, I am inclined to agree with the Peruvian Gastronomical Society's classification of *mochero* as *C. chinense*.[39] Additionally, two different archaeological studies place *C. chinense* at Huaca Prieta, near the modern coastal city of Trujillo, thousands of years ago.[40] Again, I am amazed at how many of Peru's coveted foodstuffs have ancient regional origins, and I believe *mochero* serves as an excellent example.

The best way to try a ceviche with *mochero* is, first, fly from Lima to the city of Trujillo, a one-hour trip. Trujillo's airport is right next to the fishing village and tourist center of Huanchaco, so the cab ride is about five minutes and should cost less than three dollars, depending on your negotiating acumen and proficiency in Spanish. Huanchaco has several *caballitos de totora* fishermen, who still use ancient-style reed watercraft to harvest their catch, but the local market and the plethora of *cevicherías* in the town are mostly supplied with fish caught by trawlers. This catch will still be fresher than anything you can get in even the most upscale markets in the United States.

Huanchaco has many hotels and hostels, and it is a safe and peaceful village, so staying a few days and gaining an appreciation of ceviche with *mochero* peppers will be a pleasant gastronomic experience. Just be sure to ask the restaurant hawker, before you enter, if they are using *mochero ají* for their fish salad. And because the competition for lunch, Peru's main meal of the day, is fierce, if they aren't using *mochero* they will likely send a waiter to the market, a few blocks away, to purchase what you want. But be sure to confirm the *ají* selection by noting the yellow color, possibly with green tinge. The surest way to get a ceviche plate accented by *mochero* peppers is, again, to book a nice room with ocean view in Huanchaco, then hire a driver to take you to the village of Moche the next day. The village is about a half-hour drive from Huanchaco. Along the way you should stop and visit the Moche Huaca de la Luna pyramid and the new museum at the site. Then have a late lunch at the Moche Pueblo. If your driver wants to take you to a restaurant crowded with gringos, kindly refuse. This restaurant will likely be a tourist trap with inflated prices and menu items catering to foreigners. Instead, pick the busiest *cevichería* in the center of the town, no matter how humble the façade. Remember to inquire about their *ají* selection.

Another worthwhile gastronomic and pre-Columbian foray would be to the Norte Chico city of Huacho. *Norte Chico* is a term referencing the ancient population centers in Peru's north-central coastal region. Huacho is somewhat off the normal tourist routes, but fortunately it is less than twenty miles from Caral, the archaeological site of the oldest city in the Americas. Caral has only been open to the public for the last decade, so this ancient site is relatively new (oxymoron intended). A long day trip from Lima with a morning visit to Caral is best, because the site is in an unrelenting desert, and then a late ceviche lunch in Huacho makes a fine break from the heat. Remember, in Huacho some *cevicherías* marinate their fish with the exceedingly rare juice of the bitter orange (*Citrus × aurantium*). And this Norte Chico area is one of the few places in Peru where the *ají arnaucho* is routinely used to spice ceviche.

In *Ajíes del Perú*, Cabieses et al. place *ají arnaucho* as the *C. baccatum* species.[41] But Valderrama and Ugás, in *Ajíes peruanos*, have *arnaucho* as a *C. frutescens* cultivar, and PromPerú identifies *arnaucho* as *C. chinense*.[42] All three species have been cultivated in Peru for thousands of years, so *arnaucho* would seem to have profound ties to this Norte Chico region. *Arnaucho* is a small pepper with a point, and it is very hot. This *ají* can be green, orange, and red, but the green, white, and purple cultivar is the most striking. A long day's visit to a five-thousand-year-old site, then lunching on bitter orange ceviche spiced with the *ají arnaucho* would be both an archaeological and a culinary adventure.

By far, *C. frutescens* is the most prevalent South American species on the world's table. But like the invisible coca in the brand Coca-Cola, the South American and Peruvian links to Tabasco sauce are hidden. Tabasco sauce is made from *C. frutescens*, the same species originating in the forests of northern South America and the same species that was found at Huaca Prieta seven thousand years ago. In *Peppers: The Domesticated Capsicums*, Andrews and Eshbaugh recount the fortuitous origins of one of the oldest and most revered condiments in the United States. The founder's son John McIlhenny said his father gave the fiery concoction the name Tabasco because he found the word "euphonious."[43] My best clarification of this rather archaic word would be that Edmund McIlhenny, the father, found the word "cool." And just like that, the origin and orientation of this sauce moved from South America and Peru to the Nahuatl (Aztec language) named southern state of Mexico, Tabasco. It is also possible that the base peppers for Tabasco sauce came from Peru. As with the word *lagniappe* and its Quechua root *yapa*, if a commonly used term for "a little more" could travel from the colonial markets of Peru to antebellum Louisiana, is it so far-fetched to think that *C. frutescens* wasn't along for the ride through the Spanish colonial ports, and perhaps even through Frontera, the port of the state of Tabasco? Remember, Spain controlled the Louisiana Territory during the Spanish interregnum (1763–1802), before its sale to the United States. Though the argument is only circumstantial, the timeline and hypothesis are interesting.

After all this, however, the one pepper that epitomizes Peru and Peruvian cooking is *C. baccatum*. This *ají* has many common names—*ají amarillo, ají verde, ají escabeche,* and my wife's mother's favorite, *ají de causa*. Fresh *ají amarillo* is universally for sale in every Peruvian marketplace, and this fresh pepper's use in cooking is basically confined to Peru's boundaries. When dried, *ají amarillo* is called *ají mirasol*. Even though it can be called yellow and green, *C. baccatum* is always orange in color. It is commonly four inches long and is more flavorful than hot. It is perplexing to me that many sites on the Internet have *ají amarillo*, specifically *C. baccatum* var. *pendulum*, with the same heat as a serrano. Maybe after more than two decades of working in Peru, I have built up an immunity to capsaicin? But all the *C. baccatum* var. *pendulum* I have tried are not hot like serranos, and my Peruvian friends and family agree. Andrews and Eshbaugh note that when *ají amarillo* is used for mild sauces it is deveined and deseeded, and for hot sauces it is not.[44] But in *Ajíes del Perú*, Cabieses et al. state that, although it is typically deseeded and deveined, the pepper is still not very hot.[45] And finally, in *Ajíes peruanos*, Valderrama and Ugás have *ají amarillo* well below fifteen thousand Scoville Heat Units, the scale that is used to measure a pepper's fire, nowhere near the fifty-thousand level of a serrano.[46]

C. baccatum is the *ají* most frequently used in Peruvian cuisine, and the regular use of this pepper is limited to Peru. *C. baccatum*, of course, has ancient Peruvian bona fides. It shows up early at Huaca Prieta, roughly seven thousand years ago, and in the site's later archaeological phase, about four thousand years ago, it becomes the dominant pepper closely related to feasting and ultimately eclipses all other species.[47] This ancient information makes perfect sense to me because it mirrors what I know about feasting on the North Coast today. In every one of our family fiestas, *C. baccatum* always plays a major role. My wife's mother calls it *ají de causa*, associating it with the famous Peruvian *causas*, which are potato terrines with a wide variety of ingredients, the two essential elements being potatoes and *C. baccatum*.

The antiquity and resilience of certain Peruvian foodstuffs are remarkable, and the importance of *C. baccatum* in the Peruvian culinary tradition certainly is indicative of this ongoing theme. *C. baccatum* is a staple ingredient in the myriad fish stews of coastal Peru and likely has been for a very long time. *C. baccatum* is also a main ingredient in *cabrito norteño*, the famous North Coast Peruvian kid goat stew. *Ají amarillo* is sliced into strips and added to Peru's ubiquitous stir-fry *lomo saltado*. This Peruvian classic is available in infinite variations in almost every restaurant, bus station, and market in the country.

Although fresh *ají amarillo* is not distributed outside of Peru, *ají amarillo* paste in a jar is in stock online and in many specialty markets in the United States and Europe. There are many name-brand pastes and many variations of the basic recipe of deveined and deseeded *ají amarillo*, garlic, oil, and salt. When I'm in Peru, I will typically buy a small bottle to bring home, but with *ají amarillo* paste so readily available these days, I don't think I will continue my self-importation. Besides, I prefer using fresh *C. baccatum*. *Ají amarillo* paste is often used in the ceviches in Peruvian restaurants in the United States. I am a bit of a purist when it comes to ceviche, so although I find the addition of the paste to the fish salad logical, I also find it annoying. And this additive is only plausible because, unlike in Peru, the fish in almost all restaurants and upscale markets in the West are nowhere near as fresh as the offerings in Peru. For example, adding *ají amarillo* paste to a freshly caught *ojo de uva* (*Seriolella violacea*) ceviche would mask the exquisite taste of the fish. The supply chain to most restaurants and markets in the United States simply cannot deliver the fish to table this quickly. If you don't believe me, ask the fishmonger at the most expensive fish market you frequent to let you smell the newest arrival firm white fish. Grouper and red snapper would likely be the most expensive offerings. If the fillets have any smell of fish and do not smell of the ocean, they have a bit of decay. But *ají amarillo* paste hides the faint smell with a tiny bit of heat and an exotic flavor. I must admit I have used the paste this way for my own guests, even though I was serving them red snapper at twenty-five dollars a pound. But although I used this ploy (and felt guilty about doing so), the ceviche was acceptable. Sometimes restaurants will go overboard and have the fish in their ceviche drowning in *ají amarillo* paste, which should give you pause as to what they were working with in the first place.

Ají amarillo paste does work adequately with *causas* and with the famous Peruvian *ají de gallina* (literally translated as "hot pepper hen"), even though today the main ingredient is always chicken. Both famous Peruvian dishes have multiple legendary origins, but the simple and readily available ingredients for each are indicative of their origins as leftovers, and there is nothing wrong with that. In a typical Peruvian *causa,* boiled and mashed *papa amarillos* (yellow potatoes) are layered with (among other ingredients) *palta,* the Quechua word for avocado universally used in Peru, and canned tuna fish. The convenience of having a few cans of tuna in oil in the cupboard reinforces a leftover origin. In my wife's home village, they specialize in the most famous of all *causas, la causa ferreñafana.* This dish is so famous it is considered part of the cultural heritage of Ferreñafe, which refers to the Provincia of Ferreñafe, not just the village. This area is steeped in pre-Columbian traditions and is considered the epicenter of the post-Moche Sicán culture, located on Peru's North Coast. *La causa ferreñafana* is not subtle. The main ingredients are salted fish, chopped onions, sweet potato, corn, potato, parboiled banana, lettuce, and of course, *ají amarillo.* And this traditional dish merits the use of fresh *ají amarillo.* Finally, frozen *ají amarillo* is available in the United States, and these intact peppers are adequate when deveined and deseeded, cut into strips, and added to stews and *lomo saltado.*

I hope this discussion of *ajíes* has been informative and not confusing, but it is clear that the Peruvian government needs to initiate a systematic study of peppers in all parts of the country. Remember, all four South American hot pepper species—*C. chinense, C. frutescens, C. pubescens,* and *C. baccatum*—were being cultivated and consumed in Peru at least seven thousand years ago, and that date is likely conservative. The Cariban term *ají* makes a circuitous journey from northeastern South America to the West Indies and back to northwestern South America. *Rocoto* is a Quechua word, and you will most likely encounter this fiery-hot pepper anywhere you go in Peru, especially in the highlands. Basically, *C. chinense* and *C. frutescens* are the same pepper, and these *ajíes* (not imported *C. annuum*) adorn the delicious ceviche plates of coastal Peru. Go seek out the *mochero* and *arnaucho ajíes;* and if you happen to be near the city of Lambayeque, perhaps visiting the magnificent Moche art collection of the Museo Tumbas Reales de Sipán, look for the *ají cereza.* Coca-Cola is not the only celebrated US food product with links to Peru; Tabasco sauce is another, and it is the most vastly distributed example of *C. frutescens* in the world. Finally, *C. baccatum* epitomizes Peruvian cuisine and has been preferred for thousands of years. *C. baccatum* is always orange in color and only has mild heat, but it makes up for this with its wonderful flavor. *Ají amarillo* is best fresh, but unfortunately fresh *C. baccatum* is virtually unknown outside of Peru's boundaries. However, *ají amarillo* paste and frozen *ají amarillo* are widely available on the Internet and in retail stores specializing in Latin American foodstuffs.

By now you must know that the title of this chapter is whimsical. With the plethora of delicious and exotic South American fruits, I have been disingenuous to concentrate solely on fiery peppers and to neglect, for example, guanabana (*Annona muricata*), pineapple (*Ananas* sp.), passion fruit or *maracuyá* (*Passiflora foetida*), lucuma (*Pouteria lucuma*), and so on. These myriad fruits actually require a separate book, but a chapter so full of heat needs to end sweetly. So we will finish with the fruit that Mark Twain called "the most delicious fruit known to men," the cherimoya (*Annona cherimola* Miller).[48] Twain first tried cherimoyas in Hawaii; they were brought to the islands at the end of the eighteenth century by Don Francisco de Paula Marin.[49] Truth be told, I am not an adventurous fruit seeker like Twain. My taste moves more toward acidic things than sweet things, but I thoroughly enjoy cherimoyas. I had my first taste of this exquisite fruit on Peter and Elizabeth Lerche's farm at Chillo, sixteen hundred feet above the Utcubamba River in northeastern Peru. Peter was an expatriate German ethnohistorian. Elizabeth managed the farm. She prepared the food, virtually all painstakingly from scratch, and almost exclusively sourced from the farm. At the entrance to the front gate they had a large cherimoya tree, which produced fruit with half-inch protuberances characteristic of the *Mamillata* cultivar.[50] Elizabeth offered this strange fruit to me one night after a small dinner. As I said, I rarely have dessert, and strange fruit would typically not be the exception, but refusing her offer would have been ungracious. She easily split it open with her hands and gave me a small spoon to scoop out the white fruit pulp and told me to avoid or spit out the seeds. The flavor was amazing and almost impossible to describe. Imagine a banana and a vanilla-bean ice-cream parfait infused with a bit of pear juice. Then Elizabeth gave me the catch—and with something this delightful, there is always a catch. She told me in Spanish, "Robert, we eat these at night, so we don't see the worms in the fruit pulp." Then I looked at my split cherimoya and identified a few small quarter-inch-long white larvae. Contemplating a little added protein to this feast, I finished the fruit.

Cherimoyas literally live and die by insects. In South America sap-feeding beetles from the Nitidulidae family pollinate the flowers. When cherimoyas were exported to the far corners of the world, they were hand-pollinated, but in several locations such as Israel, Italy (Calabria), and Spain (where it has long been an important crop), Australia, Florida, California, and Mexico, other subspecies of Nitidulidae, or beetles from the Staphylinidae family and bugs from the Anthocoridae family, became proxy pollinators.[51] However, hand-pollinated cherimoyas are superior in shape and size.[52] Our market here in Texas has cherimoyas stocked in April and May. They are pricy, typically costing six dollars per fruit, but worth it for my wife to get a taste of home. However, whereas beetles are the agents of cherimoya fruit production, numerous other insects are intent on devouring the pulp, particularly fruit flies (*Anastrepha* sp.) in South America. In other parts of the world where cherimoyas are cultivated, other pests like the fruit borer (*Bephratelloides cubensis* Ashmead) have devastating effects on the cherimoya harvest.[53] Therefore, the high cost of the fruit makes sense when we take into consideration the need to hand-pollinate each female flower and the volume of predators ready to strike once the fruit is formed. This is why, despite their superb flavor, cherimoyas have never become a market staple like the marvelous New World endemic, the pineapple.

The name *cherimoya* comes from the Quechua language. *Cheri* (*chiri* is the same word spelled differently) means "cold" in the language of the Inca. According to Holguín's early Quechua dictionary, *muya* (same as *moya*) means *huerto o jardin* (orchard or garden). So *cherimoya* is "cold orchard," or perhaps more precisely, "cold fruit from the orchard."[54] What at first seems an incongruous appellation for a South American fruit makes perfect sense. For the past decade, my study abroad Peru trips begin with conditioning hikes in the Sacred Valley of the Incas. These hikes prepare the students for the big mountain treks at the end of the program, Salkantay, Ausangate Vilcabamba, and Choquequirao. There is a small but accessible market in the six-hundred-year-old Inca Sacred Valley town of Ollantaytambo, which we pass on our way to the western slopes across the Urubamba River. After about two hours of trekking we reach a spot with a magnificent view of Nevado Veronica, a glaciered pyramid more than nineteen thousand feet above sea level. By this time the heat of the day has taken its toll, and the students are hot. The western range in this area is in a rain shadow, very exposed to the sun. At this stopping point, I remove a cherimoya, wrapped in my down vest, from my backpack, break it into quarters, and give it to the students. They are always amazed at how the cherimoya is so refreshing and chilled, especially considering the heat of the hike. The name "cold fruit" then is apropos. One word of caution here. If you try this when visiting Peru, be careful with the cherimoya, because they crush easily and can cause an awful mess. That is the reason for using my down vest as packing insulation.

There is a controversy as to the exact location where cherimoyas are endemic but they are endemic to South America, most likely to northwestern South America. Evidence for this origin is the cherimoya diversity in the mountainous area of southern Ecuador and northern Peru.[55] And recently, Dillehay has found flora remains of cherimoya (*Annona* sp.), at Huaca Prieta, dating back to five thousand years ago.[56] Cherimoyas were a staple in the pre-Columbian Andean world. This fruit was illustrated on Nazca ceramics from Peru's South Coast and the Moche and Chimu cultures of the North Coast, both cultures flourishing in the first millennium of the Common Era.[57] Given the great antiquity of cherimoya domestication, the cherimoya is considered an underutilized species, a fact that will hopefully change with more botanical research on cherimoya cultivars.[58] Perhaps someday cherimoyas, the "pearl of the Andes," will be a common and delicious addition to most holiday tables.[59]

Chapter 4
Guarapo, Chicha, and Pisco

In Limeño Manuel Fuentes's 1866 book *Lima; or sketches of the capital of Peru,* he listed aguardiente (here he means pisco), *chicha,* and *guarapo* as the most important national drinks in Peru.[1] Two of these three beverages still hold prominence in Peruvian life. *Chicha* and *guarapo* are fermented beverages that first appear in the Western narrative recorded in colonial documents. Fermentation has been a part of human existence for at least forty thousand years,[2] and *chicha* is the pre-Columbian Peruvian corn-beer staple made famous by the Inca. But I want to begin here with a discussion of *guarapo,* because there is a paucity of documentation about this beverage, compared to sources concerning *chicha.* And *guarapo* is the outlier of Fuentes's original three. Today this sugarcane (*Saccharum officinarum*) beer is an anomaly in Peru, especially when the drink is compared to the ubiquitous presence of *chicha,* which is sold and made in every Peruvian hamlet and town. Offhand, I can think of many recipes that require *chicha,* but I am at a loss to think of even one requiring *guarapo.* Curiously, during the research for this book, I came upon a University of Cuenca (Ecuador) thesis that presented new culinary dishes with *guarapo* as a main ingredient.[3] This text used both fermented *guarapo* and fresh non-fermented sugarcane juice. The non-fermented beverage is sometimes also called *guarapo,* but it is more precisely referred to as *caña de azúcar* in most of Latin America. In their own words:

> The *guarapo* is well known in Latin American countries. In Ecuador, this juice is traditional from tropical and subtropical zones. It comes from the crushing of the sugar cane that passes through the masses of a machine known as *trapiche.* It is usually consumed immediately after its extraction accompanied by ice and lemon juice which makes it refreshing and energizing because of its high

> content of sucrose. The *guarapo* has a short shelf life, after a few days its organoleptic characteristics change, turning a cloudy color and a more pronounced flavor due to the fermentation that takes place. This drink is not used in its entirety since it has not been applied within the gastronomic field; in the present project it has been proposed to use *guarapo* as the main ingredient in the preparation of various salt and sweet recipes applying different cooking techniques such as reduction, baking, emulsification, roasting, deep frying, marinating, stewing, among others.[4]

Here I am using the term *guarapo* specifically for the fermented beverage. The Ecuadorian project seems to be an attempt to elevate the culinary importance of *guarapo* because of the beverage's prevalence in that country, Colombia, Venezuela, Mexico, and Cuba. The key idea from the abstract is that *guarapo* is traditional in Ecuador. But I am doubtful of the overall success of such an undertaking. *Chicha* was a mainstay among pre-Columbian foods in the ancient Andean world. *Guarapo* was not. Catching up on a culinary tradition that was thousands of years in the making will be an impossible undertaking.

Two good friends of mine who have traveled to all parts of Peru, literally from glacial peaks to remote jungle rivers, surprised me by saying they have never had *guarapo*. My encounter with the beer was serendipitous when I had a chance to imbibe many cups of *guarapo* during fieldwork in the remote San Martín department of northeastern Peru. This region has links architecturally and linguistically with northern South America, and the *guarapo* presence here is likely a result of its location.[5] My research was centered on the ruins of the La Meseta tablelands, which were a five-day trek east of the Utcubamba River town of Liemebamba. Our group consisted of three: Joaquin Briones Ortiz, his brother Ernesto, and me. After several days being hosted by Fabian Añasco in Pueblo Añasco, we set off for his brother's village, Canaan. The mission was to survey an Inca fine cut stone building called Puca Huaca, an anomaly for this area. We reached the site after several hours of trekking through one-foot-deep mud. I was exhausted. Ernesto and Joaquin were none the worse for wear, but even with me lagging, we managed to photograph and survey the site.

When we finished, it was getting dark, but David, Fabian's brother and the mayor of the village, invited us all to drink some freshly made *guarapo*. My legs and body were aching; therefore, any source of quick energy and pain relief was greatly appreciated. We stayed for at least an hour drinking many cups of this fine (especially under the circumstances) offering. The *guarapo* was thick and sweet, even sweeter than highland *chicha*. When we finally packed up to leave, I was feeling great as we set off on the trail northwest. After about forty-five minutes we stopped to have a sobering coca chew. I then noticed Joaquin and Ernesto were just as drunk as I was. The coca helped us focus, and we continued our trek back to the village. But night had fallen and now we were following the trail back to Pueblo Añasco using Ernesto's cheap Chinese-made flashlight. My climbing headlamp was an afterthought; I had left it back with my gear in the camp, and from that day on I learned to always carry a headlamp when trekking in the Andes. To make matters worse it began to rain. At first, the rain was light but after a few minutes we were in a downpour. It is impossible to describe the remote eastern slopes of the Andes at night in a rainstorm. Primeval, beautiful, terrifying, lonely, all these words in any combination fall short of portraying the experience. Then the light from the flashlight started to flicker, and I noticed Ernesto and Joaquin's concern. This was an out-of-the-ordinary situation even for these seasoned campesinos, who had homes in this region. They did not like camping out at night, and traveling in this very hostile environment after dark made them uneasy. The concerns were numerous: wild boar running on the trails, puma, jaguar, *víboras*, poisonous vipers, vampire bats, and so on. And if it kept raining this hard, we could get caught in a flow of water and mud, now in full force all around us, which could possibly wash us right off the tableland. But when the flashlight was about to fail, we heard a noise in the distance. Ernesto used it as a beacon to guide us home. Soon we all saw a light, and after several sloppy minutes of deep mud we arrived at the open-air church, a thatched roof on posts, of Pueblo Añazco, where Fabian was conducting a nighttime Seven Day Adventist service with sermon and singing, praying for our return. We were all very grateful for our delivery from the Canaanites. The spirituality and faith of the village permeated the wet forest air. If I did not become a Seven Day Adventist at this moment I never would, but after shaking hands with many of the pilgrims, I went to bed and completely forgot our conversion. This weird adventure was my first, and my last, experience with *guarapo.*

Saccharum officinarum is perhaps the planet's most dynamic early globe-trotting plant. Incredibly, sugarcane is endemic to faraway New Guinea, but over the course of millennia, *Saccharum officinarum* eventually made its way from there to the Far East, Middle East, Africa, and then Europe.[6] Obviously, everyone from kings to commoners appreciated the plant's sweetness just as we do today, but with the physicality of their lives and the lack of modern conveniences, without the threat of diabetes and obesity. Eventually, Portugal and Spain planted *Saccharum officinarum* in the Atlantic islands of Madeira, São Tomé, Cape Verde, and the Canaries.[7] Sugarcane then was brought to the New World by the Spanish and Portuguese. Because of this transport, *guarapo* and *Saccharum officinarum* are inextricably tied to the slave trade. And the frequency and longevity of this beverage coincides with centers for enslaved blacks in the Americas.

Determining the origin of the term *guarapo* is a difficult task, but it probably came to Peru with the Spanish.[8] Peruvian linguist and politician Martha Hildebrandt places *guarapo* in the Cariban or Arawakan lexicon, which seems plausible because of the origin for the term *ají* and the etymology for *chicha.* But the Peruvian food science academic Sergio Zapata Acha has pointed out that in the Quechua language the word *warapu,* a synonym for *guarapo,* signifies aguardiente made with sugarcane.[9] In the parlance of the United States this is sugarcane white lightning. I have had aguardiente many times in Peru, several times in the back of a truck as everyone passed around a shot glass refilled from a plastic bottle. If you are ever in this situation in the Andean hinterlands, after your shot, save a few drops to pour on the ground for Pachamama, the Inca earth mother, and then pass the cup to the next person. Although the intense green taste coupled with the high alcohol content requires an open mind, this spirit will take the edge off a long day of trekking.

I want to point out here that aguardiente in Peru is always made from sugarcane. Even though pisco is technically an aguardiente of *uva* (grapes), it is almost never called aguardiente. Additionally, during my post-pandemic trip to Peru, I noticed a high-end aguardiente called Caña Alta Blue frequenting the top shelves of the best bars and restaurants. This cane liquor was more expensive than some of the finest piscos, even though sugarcane is an exponentially more abundant crop than wine grapes, the source for pisco.

Zapata Acha recorded that daily consumption of *guarapo* and *chicha* in seventeenth-century Lima was *cien mil botijas* (10,000 wine jars) with a capacity of 16 liters (almost 34 US pints) each.[10] That is 160,000 liters (5,440,000 pints) of grog. He continued by reporting that both beverages were consumed by Negroes, *mulatos, indios, zambaigos* (in this instance mixed-race blacks and indigenous people), and mestizos.[11] Obviously, both beverages had huge followings. But I imagine that, although there was cooperation in the production of these beverages, most of the time *guarapo* and *chicha* became signifiers of identity and therefore competition. The historian Sarah O'Toole noted that, in seventeenth-century Trujillo (on the North Coast), indigenous migrants sought out enslaved men to procure sugarcane syrup to produce *guarapo*.[12]

There are also troubling accounts of tension between enslaved blacks and subjugated indigenous people. For example, Felipe Guaman Poma de Ayala's early seventeenth-century chronicle was testament to the virtues of indigenous people and a scathing criticism of colonial era abuse. So much so, that his letter to the king of Spain was disappeared and lost for three hundred years.[13] Thankfully, the complete digitized copy of this manuscript has now been made available online by the Royal Library, in Copenhagen, Denmark, which has expedited research into this masterpiece of the early colonial era.[14] However, the chapter on the black Africans and slaves has been mostly neglected by the academic community. This oversight probably has to do with Guaman Poma's negative depictions of the enslaved Africans, which is in conflict to his celebration of the indigenous Peruvian identity. In his text he often refers to the blacks as *borrachos*, a similar criticism the Spanish reserved for the indigenous population, and he listed many other negative stereotypes. He references the heinous colonial term *bozales* (a worker, but more specifically a muzzled slave, yes, think Hannibal Lecter mask) for the young and powerful enslaved African males, which was, unfortunately, common at the time.[15]

An even more disturbing account from the early colonial period was recorded in a court case between a Chachapoya (a northeastern people conquered by the Inca) leader and the Spanish crown. This trial took place on March 25, 1574, and was presided over by Corregidor (the mayor of Cajamarquilla) Don Diego de Vizcarra. In the proceedings, a Chachapoya cacique (leader or chief) named Guamán made a plea for his land by having the great deeds of his life recounted. But one of the great deeds seemed more appropriate to first-century Rome than sixteenth-century viceregal Peru. Guamán recounted his victorious gladiatorial fight to the death against an African slave, which so impressed Francisco Pizarro that he gave Guamán the honorific name don Francisco Pizarro Guamán.[16] This chilling account of a colonial era reward for barbarity is also indicative of colonial era elites instigating and even fomenting conflict between the enslaved (the Africans) and the colonized (the indigenous people).[17] But certainly, this technique of creating animosity between subjugated groups is not confined to this era. An offhand example is the post–Civil War South in the United States, which for decades had elites pitting poor white sharecroppers against freed African slaves.

The huge consumption of *chicha* and *guarapo* in seventeenth-century Lima was indicative not only of great prowess in alcohol consumption but also of a competition of identity: *guarapo* for the Africans and *chicha* for the indigenous people. This all changed with the coming of independence from Spain and the abolition of slavery in Peru. By the middle of the nineteenth century the consumption of *guarapo* in Peru had evolved. In this later era *guarapo* as sugarcane beer was now called *guarapito,* and it was the preferred beverage of black women. For the men (and here Fuentes used the term *bozales*), the beverage of choice was *achichadito,* which was very strong and made from the cane trash after the syrup had been extracted.[18] Even though Fuentes does not use the term *distillation, achichadito* seems to have been a distilled spirit made from the by-products of fermentation, like Italian grappa, Greek rakija, Spanish *orujo,* and Serbian *komovica.*[19] There was a plethora of stills, and master distillers, in late eighteenth-century and early nineteenth-century Peru, so the production of *aguardiente de caña* was well suited to this environment.[20]

But how did *chicha,* in Fuentes's own words, become the preeminent national beverage of Peru while *guarapo* disappeared? Remember how Zapata Acha pointed out that the Quechua word *warapu* means aguardiente made with sugarcane, so the beer was ultimately forgotten, and the name transferred to sugarcane liquor, which is ubiquitous today in rural Peruvian communities. However, the beer and the tradition for brewing *guarapo* were absorbed by Peruvian culture: *chicha* remained and *guarapo* mostly disappeared. At the beginning of the twentieth century, Mexican philosopher José Vasconcelos imagined the mixing of races in the colonial Americas of Spain and Portugal into a "cosmic race," which he saw as a progressive chapter in human development.[21] But as historian Henry Steele Commager has stated, "Change does not necessarily assure progress, but progress implacably requires change."[22]

In this case, the change that occurred in late nineteenth-century and early twentieth-century Peru was the ebbing of Afro-Peruvian culture. In Peru at the beginning of the eighteenth century the percentage of black and mulatto individuals was approximately 4–15 percent of the population. By the end of that century the percentage had dropped to 0–4 percent, and it remained small at the end of the twentieth century.[23] Of course, there are still remnants of African culture on Peru's South Coast, and both Piura and Lambayeque include communities of *Mangaches*, Afro-Peruvians with roots in Madagascar. Glimpses of this past can still be perceived, for example, in the Peruvian dance the *marinera*, which descended directly from the Afro-Peruvian *zamacueca*.[24] But perhaps the most lingering relic of the Afro-Peruvian past is the fiery aguardiente that campesinos quaff from plastic bottles on their way to the local town's fiesta. A final note, the Caña Alta Blue distillery is in the Sacred Valley of the Inca, and their marketing links the spirit, implausibly, to the Inca world, because early architects of this expensive spirit were Afro-Peruvians.

But while *guarapo* changed and faded away, *chicha* remained omnipresent. I had my first taste of *chicha* beer more than twenty years ago at the house of Dr. Peter Lerche. The brew I tasted was made by Peter's wife, Elizabeth. I remember her description of how to make the *chicha* more than the beer itself, which means I was not impressed by the brew. This had nothing to do with Elizabeth's *chicha*-brewing skills, she was a fantastic cook and extremely knowledgeable about pre-Columbian food and drink. But over the years I have had *chicha* many times with my study abroad students, mostly at the *cuy* (guinea pig) food stalls in Coya, Calca, and Lamay that line the Sacred Valley of the Inca main highway. Drinking highland *chicha* with the students while watching them agonize through their first taste of *cuy* was amusing even though I do not care for the beverage. Therefore, I hardly ever seek out fresh *chicha* from the numerous *chicherías* (local *chicha* bars often serving food) in and around Cuzco. They are marked by a long stick with plastic bag "flag" extending into the air at the house's front. Frankly, I have never relished the sweetness and the viscosity of the highland brew.

Chicha is a fermented beverage made from a variety of plants, but most often it is made from maize. Corn was, and quite often still is, used more like a fruit than a grain in the Andean realm.[25] Of course, maize was also a solid food. In his early colonial record, Father Bernabe Cobo states that maize was the Inca daily bread; he notes that they took maize flour with them on journeys, and he also mentions *humitas,* a type of fresh corn tamale.[26] I think the daily bread assignment is hyperbole, but I have experienced firsthand the utility of traveling with corn flour. But in this case, considering corn as grapes and *chicha* as wine will give you a better understanding of the function of the beverage in the pre-Columbian world.

Curiously, *chicha* is another ubiquitous term in the Andes that was brought to Peru by the Spanish conquest. The Quechua term for corn beer is *açuac* or *accac,* with *aqha* as the most common spelling. In the conquest, then, *chicha* displaced the Quechua *aqha*. The etymology of *chicha* is debated, with some scholars suggesting an Arawakan origin and others advocating Nahuatl.[27] For me, the Arawakan origin is compelling, because *chicha* supplanting the Quechua *aqha* has a precedent with the displacement of the Cariban (a language related to Arawakan) word *ají* for the Quechua word for hot pepper, *uchu*.[28]

There are three basic steps to making the brew. First, the maize is *desgranado* (the kernels are taken off the cob) and prepared. This is an elaborate process that can take weeks, especially if the corn has sprouted.[29] Then the mix is boiled in water, and the cooked liquid is cooled and fermented.[30] This step takes a matter of days, depending on how many times the mixture is cooked.[31] The boiling process sterilizes the wort (the liquid extracted from the first step) and breaks the mixture down so as to release the sugars that are essential for fermentation. In winemaking this boiling is detrimental and would reduce the flavors and terroir (taste of the earth) of good wine. Instead, sulfur dioxide and filtering are used to reduce the contaminants. But recently flash pasteurization has come into vogue; this is heating the mixture to 180 degrees for three minutes.[32] The point here is that fermentation is a messy process. The "good" yeasts are not the only microorganisms that want to eat the sugars, and these other microorganisms often produce flavors and by-products that can ruin wine and beer. Getting the good ones to thrive while suppressing the bad ones is an art, which any brewmaster or winemaker will corroborate.

Back to *chicha*. The initial preparation of the maize diverges with one method of fermenting involving chewed corn and saliva expectorated into the water-and-corn mix. The unsavory details of this process could be mitigated by the fact that, in the Inca world, the ones doing the chewing, spitting, and producing the high-quality *chicha* for the gods and the priests were *acllas* (virgin chosen women). Or perhaps not.[33] During her recording of several *chicha*-making locales in Piura, *chicha* scholar Frances Hayashida notes: "As the *chicha* is worked, small handfuls of mash may also be chewed, and then returned to the pot adding additional enzymes for saccharification (the conversion of starch to sugar)."[34] What is important to note here is not the spitting but the all-important effort to convert the starches to sugars so the hungry yeast can initiate robust fermentation.

The second more hygienic way of preparing the corn is to let it germinate or sprout, but remember, the Piura brewers used both techniques. The malted corn used here is called *chicha de jora* (*sora*). The saliva and the sprouting serve the same purpose: facilitating the process of breaking down starch into sugar.[35] The second process is in wide used today, and I have been told the chewing and spitting preparation is confined to remote regions of the Peruvian rainforest. However, I don't think many people look too closely at each *chichería*'s production practice. In this case, I do think ignorance is bliss. Keep in mind alcohol is a disinfectant.

The sprouting or malting of the *chicha de jora* produces a stronger alcoholic beverage. So much so that the early colonial era Jesuit José de Acosta observed that *chicha de jora* (*sora*) was prohibited by law because of the damage done by indigenous drunks when inebriated from drinking this beverage. In highland communities today, binge drinking of any *chicha* typically results in drunkenness on a Herculean scale. I know this because I have often joined in the revelry. The added alcoholic content of *chicha de jora* likely intensified any of these celebrations. Father Acosta went on to compare *chicha de jora* favorably to wheat beer from Flanders, which evolved into one of the celebrated modern Belgian brews.[36]

Fermentation is a prehistoric process as intimately connected to humans as our first use of tools and fire. Simply, fermentation occurs when sugars from plant material are eaten by yeast and the waste products of this process are alcohol and carbon dioxide gas. The gas disappears into the atmosphere, but the alcohol is greatly enjoyed by us. Often yeasts do not need to be added to a mix to induce fermentation because they occur naturally in the air. In my years as a wine merchant, I was accustomed to having winemakers from France, and some from California, boast how their wines fermented naturally without adding yeast. Yeast will also keep eating the sugars in the mixture until there is no more sugar or until you kill them. One way of doing this with wine fermenting in a tank is to cool the mixture to 50 degrees or below, and the dead yeast will settle to the bottom of the tank. This wine will have what is called residual sugar, which is sugar that has not been consumed by the yeast.[37]

Of the *chicha* I have tried in Peru, 90 percent is the sweet frothy brew I mentioned above. But what if the yeasts were allowed to complete their work and eat every ounce of the beer's natural and added sugar? This would require a longer fermentation than the one to two days most often described in the literature.[38] More than a decade ago, I sampled such a beverage in a *chichería* across from the restaurant Mococho in Huanchaco. I was guided there, along with my study abroad students, by surf-school owner and long-boarder Juan Carlo Huarote Revilla.

The first curious difference between this *chichería* and the many others I have visited in Peru was that the brewer was male. In all the highland *chicherías* I have visited, the owners and brewers were female. Scholars have noted that, in the highland Andean communities, preparing *chicha* is central to the women's identity, and to this day the drink confers considerable social power.[39] Obviously, the *acllas* or Inca chosen women support this statement. But the brewers in the ancient centers of Peru's North Coast were men. This

Huanchaco *chichería* with my daughter, my son, Juan Carlo Huarote Revilla, and study abroad students. Photo by Robert Bradley.

tradition was specified in the early colonial record of the Spanish priest Miguel Cabello de Balboa. In his testimony, gathered from native informants, Cabello de Balboa told the story of a great ruler called Naymlap and his North Coast amphibious incursion. Balboa recorded the great pomp and circumstance of this event including the names of Naymlap's important servants:

> Así como Pita Zofi que era su trompetero o tañedor de unos grandes caracoles, que entre los indios estiman en mucho, otro Ñiñacola que era el que tenía cuidado de sus andas y Silla, y otro Ñiñagintue acuio cargo estaba la bebida de aquel señor a manera de Botiller.[40]

> (Just as Pita Zofi, who was their trumpeter or player of some large conches, which among the Indians they value very much, another

Ñiñacola who was the one who took care of his litter and Silla, and another Ñiñagintue who oversaw that gentleman's drink like a Botiller.)[41]

I cannot stress the importance of this chronicler articulating a Botiller servant, an expert in wine and drinks in the European tradition, Ñiñagintue. Naymlap was the founder of the North Coast Sicán or Lambayeque culture, which thrived for several hundred years between the earlier Moche culture and the later Chimu dynasties, so this ruler and his retinue were of great importance in pre-Columbian history.[42] Naymlap has also been linked to the initial production of *chicha de jora*.[43] The Cabello de Balboa record also speaks to the tradition of male *chicha* brewers in this coastal region of Peru, which I witnessed firsthand with students and that persists to this day.[44]

Additionally, the early colonial era Jesuit chronicler Pablo José Arriaga observed that, although women made the *chicha* in the highlands, there was a tradition of male *chicha* brewers (*chicheros*) in the coastal lowlands.[45] Arriaga's statement has great authority because his chronicle was very different from the rigorous observations of the soldier Pedro Cieza de León or the plea for reform of corruption in the early colonial Peru made by Felipe Guamán Poma de Ayala. Arriaga's project was to eliminate pagan idolatry, and since *chicha* was often used as an offering to *huacas* (sacred places), his ethnohistorical observations have an Inquisitional clarity and focus. In other words, the Jesuit was hell-bent on finding out who the brewers were in order to stop their production and therefore save souls.

Returning to my Huanchaco *chichería*, the brew we had that day was much stronger (higher in alcohol), more flavorful, and more aged, than any frothy highland offering.[46] Hayashida notes that in Lambayeque she was told repeatedly of an aged *chicha* that was fermented until it no longer gave off carbon dioxide (complete fermentation with no residual sugar remaining), was strong and dry, and was like port or wine in flavor.[47] The only exception I have with Hayashida's notes, and what I sampled in Huanchaco, is that

I would compare the Huanchaco brew with an oloroso sherry, perhaps because of the oxidative aging of these olorosos, and perhaps with this *chicha* brew.

Oxidation in brewing beer is generally seen as a negative aspect, because the process can give rise to stale flavors that ruin the beer. However, there are times when controlled oxidation is desired by the brewer. For instance, old ale, strong ale, and barley wine are all bottle aged, and high alcohol ales are subjected to more oxidation than European or American ales. Therefore, these ales can age for long periods of time in the bottle. Another example is barrel-aged lambic beers, which oxidize in the cask for up to two years.[48] What is important here is the brewer's control of the oxidation process. In other words, the brewer uses controlled oxidation to get good flavors and not bad stale flavors. Returning to the wine like *chicha* mentioned by Hayashida, in Lambayeque she was told that some *chicha* was sealed in *cántaros* (large jars), buried in the ground, and aged for up to two years.[49]

Obviously, there is a more complex coastal tradition of brewing that could possibly be linked historically with the arrival of Ñiñagintue, or perhaps an even earlier era. A sign of this complex brewing tradition could be gleaned from among the pre-Columbian coastal ceramics most closely associated with *chicha*, the stirrup-spout bottle. These ceramics were being produced on the North Coast of Peru as early as 1500 BC.

To clarify the talking points here I will use Donnan and McClelland's bottle terminology from their book on Moche fine-line painting. In the Moche ceramic, the top of the bottle is the "upper spout," the symmetrical curves are "the arch," and the area that holds the *chicha* is "the chamber." These ceramics were mass produced in coastal Peru for a period of three thousand years, and their early production precedes by several thousand years the arrival of Naymlap and his retinue. These vessels seem to have had a special purpose, and they were lavished with intricate fine-line painting. Yet scholars still struggle with the function for the stirrup-spout form.[50]

Modern re-creation of a Moche stirrup-spout bottle. Photo courtesy of Tamara Andersen.

I suggest that the unique shape could facilitate longer fermentation with bottle conditioning and oxidative aging. My hypothesis begins with the *chicha* being made in large ceramics, like the *cántaros* used today, in early pre-Columbian coastal Peru. After a fermentation of a few days, the *chicha* was then transferred to a stirrup-spout bottle with a bottle gourd funnel. The fermentation would then continue, perhaps to the point of zero residual sugar. The yeast's carbon dioxide residue would flow up the arch and escape into the air via the upper spout's small opening. While this is happening, the brew in the bottle is less exposed to contaminants entering the vessel because impurities would accumulate at the point where the upper spout meets the arch.[51] The stirrup-spout form also allows exposure to oxygen, but the shape facilitates controlled oxidation. So the stirrup form acts like a cork or a lambic wood barrel, which protects the brew and yet is porous. Certainly, this explanation is just as viable as the suggestion that the stirrup-spout form facilitated transport with a strap.[52] And although there are representations painted on stirrup-spout bottles of Moche people carrying stirrup-spout vessels like this, the stress points of the stirrup shape tend to break, especially over time. I can attest to the breakage because for the past twenty years I have tried to bring back as many beautiful imitation Moche stirrup ceramics to the United States as possible. Most of these have broken right at the point where the arches meet the chamber, even though I spent considerable time wrapping them for protection.

Of course, any hypothesis needs to be tested, and the experiment would involve the purchase of many stirrup-spout bottles, brewing *chicha de jora*, and then a continued fermentation, aging, and controlled oxidation of the different batches of *chicha*. A small National Endowment for the Humanities Grant could expedite such an experiment, may even revive a lost pre-Columbian tradition of *chicha* production, and would certainly help any small family-owned *chicherías* involved in the project. Finally, cotton was abundant on the coast five thousand years ago, and it is also reasonable to assume that the *chicha* brewers could have used a small cotton cap to cover the lip of the upper spout.[53] But I still would like to attempt the long fermentation, aging, and controlled oxidation of the experiential *chicha* production without any cotton covering first, just to determine the effectiveness of the stirrup-spout design.

Distillation is an ancient process and, like fermentation, it is part science and part art. Fermentation has been associated with human beings since before the dawn of civilization, but distillation has a relatively ephemeral link to humans of only a few thousand years. Some of the first hints of the process were seen in the ancient Greek world, but it was the Arabs who recorded distillation in books well before the end of the first millennium of the Common Era. Distillation appeared in Europe in the Middle Ages.[54] The first people making spirits there were not considered the master distillers we have today. Instead, these individuals were counted as the alchemists and doctors of their time. Strong spirits were initially medicine, because it takes a certain dismissal of common sense, or perhaps a great deal of character, for anyone to imbibe quantities of a liquid more than 20 percent alcohol. Of course, we take it for granted today, but early uses of distilled spirits were for chemical purposes such as the extraction of essential oils for perfumes. South Asian archaeologist Raymond Allchin has proposed that production of distilled spirits for human consumption began in India and Pakistan twenty-five hundred years ago, but most scholars attribute the emergence of distilled alcohol for drinking to twelfth-century Europe. Recently, Mexican archaeologists have revealed pre-Hispanic mescal distillation at the Cacaxtla archaeological site in the state of Tlaxcala, but they suggest that the distilled spirit was used in rituals and not for everyday consumption.[55]

One of the largest productions and distributions of distilled spirits in the Americas began in the sixteenth century along the South Coast of Peru. Pisco is an aguardiente of *uva* (grape brandy) that derives its name from the port of Pisco on Peru's southern coast. There are five pisco-producing regions in Peru today, all in the southern coastal area: Ica, Arequipa, Moquegua, Tacna, and Lima.[56] Anthropologist

Prudence Rice and Peruvian scholar Lorenzo Huertas Vallejos tie the first distillation of this brandy to the Peruvian town of Ica in the early sixteenth century, although they both admit the technology used to make the brandy was very crude compared to the complex and expensive *alambique* (alembic) distilling process that became common in the republican era. Also, in the nineteenth century, glass bottles replaced earthenware *cántaros* and animal skin containers used to transport the spirit.[57]

Even without the more sophisticated *alambique* distillation, brandy boomed in eighteenth-century Peru, because of three factors: the winemaking restrictions put on the Viceroyalty of Peru by the Spanish crown; the restraints of shipping wine, a semi-perishable product; and finally, the emergence of what was likely the richest city in the world, Potosí, from the cold and barren Altiplano.[58] Initially, the Spanish crown wanted to control the wine trade and have shipments of wine go from Spain to the colonies. But soon the wine—and more important, the grape vines—were shipped to the colonies from the more proximate Canary Islands.[59] This trade, especially the importation of vines from the Canaries, led to a thriving wine industry stretching more than twelve hundred miles along Peru's coast in the mid-sixteenth century.[60]

The extent of these vineyards became competition for Spanish wine; so much so that when Viceroy Francisco de Toledo was dispatched to Peru by the King Philip II, he was instructed to forbid the planting of new vines in the viceroyalty. But the Peruvian wine trade was difficult to monitor, and shipments to Pacific and Central American ports went underground.[61] This subversive economy also included the smuggling of Potosí's silver to the Chinese through Manila (the Chinese would not trade with the Spanish in their homeland) and the importing of Chinese goods to South America. The silver smuggling was a massive enterprise. Charles Mann has pointed out that a Spanish galleon that sank near Manila Bay in 1654 had under recorded the amount of silver on its manifest by at least two-thirds.[62] By the late eighteenth century, 80–90 percent of the wine produced in southern Peru was distilled into brandy, and staggering amounts of this alcohol were consumed by the Spaniards and the indigenous people at Potosí.[63]

With the coming of the nineteenth century, the silver at Potosí began to run out.[64] This roughly coincided with the independence of Peru in 1824, but a new market for pisco was already emerging, free of the Spanish crown's monopolistic restrictions. Now pisco "spread as wildfire across the Pacific Ocean. [And] one of the places set ablaze was California."[65] At the beginning of the nineteenth century, California was a remote and isolated part of the viceroyalty of New Spain and then, after Mexican independence, a remote and isolated part of Mexico. The Treaty of Guadalupe Hidalgo awarded this territory to the United States in 1848. But by then the pisco market in this politically mutable region was already firmly established. The Englishman William E. P. Hartnell in 1822 was recorded as the first documented pisco importer to the region.[66] After California became part of the United States, pisco imports to the region boomed, particularly imports of the preferred pisco made from the Italia grape varietal during the California Rush of 1848–49.[67]

I need a moment here to discuss the grapes arriving from the Canary Islands that were (and still are) cultivated in southern Peru. Pisco grapes are divided into two categories: aromatics and nonaromatics. The four aromatic grape varieties are Torontel, Italia, Albilla, and Moscatel, and the nonaromatic varieties are Quebranta, Negra Criolla, Uvina, and Mollar.[68] As it sounds, the aromatic grapes are the most coveted for a *puro* (pure) sipping pisco, but 80 percent of all Peruvian pisco is made solely with or includes the nonaromatic grape Quebranta.[69] This by no means signifies that the Quebranta variety is mundane and should be avoided. Indeed, the Quebranta grape is considered the national *uva* (grape) of Peru and is especially prominent in Ica.[70] But, more important, all Peruvian pisco is special because the brandy must be distilled to proof. In other words, you cannot distill the spirit to a higher proof and then add water to bring down the alcohol level. And pure flavors of pisco must not be obscured, so it is illegal to age pisco in wood.[71]

Again, the Peruvian pisco maker must use their *alambique* copper still in a technique that is part art and part science. The distiller Johnny Schuler uses the image of an animal to describe the process of distilling. The first and last distillates, the head and the tail, are separated out to get to the heart of the distillation, pisco.[72] Keep in mind that pisco is made from wine, which is a much costlier spirit to distill than a liquor such as Italian grappa. Grappa is distilled from the must left over from fermentation, the discarded by-product of winemaking, whereas every bottle of pisco requires three bottles of wine to distill.[73] I loved pisco from the first moment I tried it in Peru. I have always had an affinity for the taste of grapes, so twenty years ago I knew pisco was special. I also think Peruvian pisco is economically priced, and I believe the cost of pisco will rise considerably in the not-too-distant future.

Of the four aromatic grape varieties, my favorites are Albilla and Torontel. In Argentina, Torontel is called Torrontés, and in the country it is an extensively cultivated dry white wine. In Italy this grape is known as Moscato Bianco and it is also widely grown.[74] I match Torrontés wine with spicy food, and I especially enjoy this wine with ceviche. In many ways Torrontés reminds me of the dry Alsatian wines that are coveted by wine merchants. Torontel pisco obviously has some of the great flavor elements of the wine. A real treat is a *leche de pantera* made with Torontel pisco. Remember that *leche de tigre* is the residual marinade drained from ceviche, a milky-white cocktail of lime and fish juice, served in a glass topped with *ají* and *mococho*. Peruvian *leche de pantera* is made in the same fashion but with a shot of pisco added. I recommend adding a delicious shot of Torontel pisco to the mix and even your most impressive hangover will quickly fade like the sun going down on the ocean. You can easily find Torontel and Moscatel in the upscale restaurants and department stores in Lima, and maybe even the fruity and complex

Albilla aromatic pisco, but the aromatic you will encounter most often in Peru's hinterlands is Italia. And be assured, a good bottle of pisco made from this aromatic grape, like Biondi Pisco Italia, is an exceptional spirit. Keep in mind that Italia pisco became a name brand in mid-nineteenth-century California.

There are three categories of pisco. The first is the pisco *puro* (pure) made from a single grape variety. Typically, the sought-after *puros* are distilled from aromatic grapes that are the top of the line, so Italia, Torontel, Moscatel, and Albilla will be featured prominently on the label. *Mosto verde* is made from wine that has not fermented completely, and this requires more grapes per liter and more work.[75] Remember, if it takes three bottles of wine to make one bottle of pisco, then imagine four or five to make one bottle of *mosto verde*. Again, Italian grappa, which tends to be pricy, is made from the residue of winemaking. But here the pisco distillers are instead using several bottles of wine to make their spirit and—with *mosto verde* doing this with sweet wine, which has not completed fermentation, requiring even more juice. This type of distilling does not seem like a sound business decision. I truly believe good pisco is one of the most undervalued liquors in the world, and I hope it stays that way. But I am sure the world will come to appreciate good pisco just like it has come to appreciate Peru as a culinary destination. The final category is *acholado*, which is a blend of two or more *puros* or two or more *mosto verdes*, and each pisco house or brand can only produce two *acholados*.[76]

Most of the piscos just discussed should be lovingly sipped neat from a clear snifter. Please forgive my decadent use of Torontel in the *leche de pantera*, but I want to end here with the two most famous pisco cocktails: pisco punch and the pisco sour. Pisco punch is less well-known today, but from the mid-nineteenth century until Prohibition it was a sensation that made the San Francisco bar called the Bank Exchange, located where the Transamerica Pyramid towers today, the mecca for the cocktail aficionado. The punch was popularized by Bank Exchange bartender Duncan Nicol, who served the famous cocktail for decades until the Volstead Act (Prohibition) in 1919 closed the celebrated bar for good. Nicol died in 1926, supposedly taking the famous recipe for the cocktail with him to the grave.[77]

However, William Bronson's detective work in the 1970s recovered the missing recipe from the notes of a man named John Lannes. Bronson's article presents compelling evidence for the authenticity of this recipe. He also noted that the gum syrup was not made at that time, but in his article he added a formula re-creating this syrup. According to Bronson the gum syrup gave the cocktail an appealing texture and bite. Looking at the recipe (given below), one might think "What is all the fuss about?" but I only need to quote writer Rudyard Kipling's exclamation after drinking his first pisco punch. He said the cocktail was "compounded of the shavings of cherub's wings, the glory of a tropical dawn, the red clouds of sunset and the fragments of lost epics by dead masters."[78]

The punch was so formidable that two cocktails were the limit. If some luminary pressed Nicol for another round, they were directed to walk around a long city block and then make an appeal for another punch when they returned. McDonnell and Abiol in their book *Drinking the Devil's Acre: A Love Letter to San Francisco and Her Cocktails* suggest another possible addition to the pisco punch, coca. They erroneously rule out cocaine as an ingredient because it did not exist at the end of the nineteenth century (but it did, cocaine was first synthesized in the 1860s), and they suggest Vin Mariani as a possible secret ingredient. Nicol could have added cocaine to the gum syrup in the basement of the Bank Exchange, and this perhaps might explain his notorious secrecy concerning the recipe. He would not have needed coca wine, because if he had steeped coca leaves in pisco, the cocaine in the leaves would also be activated. This step would create a very interesting infusion for a cocktail.[79]

There is no evidence that Nicol added cocaine or made this type of concoction, but whatever happened in those celebrated days, the era of the pisco punch ended with Prohibition, devastating West Coast pisco culture. The compromised shipping routes from South

America to the United States during World War II added to this loss even after the Twenty-First Amendment made it legal again to drink alcohol. Finally, during the war, tequila flooded the US market, which then secured the twilight of pisco punch and the dawn of the margarita.[80]

Sours are a category of cocktails that are the hallmark of a good bartender. The combination of sweet and sour should be in harmony but not finish sweet because this sweetness will ruin the appetite.[81] One of the most exemplary examples of a sour is the pisco sour. And after reading the passages about pisco punch, it should come as no surprise that the inventor of the pisco sour, Victor V. Morris, migrated to Peru from the Bay Area. The Morris Bar operated in the center of Lima from 1915 until it closed in 1933. The bar specialized in the type of cocktails served in the United States (and here the emphasis is on San Francisco) from the end of the nineteenth century. The pisco sour developed out of the tradition set by Bank Exchange's pisco punch. A good way to imagine the irony here is that Peru gave San Francisco the major element for the pisco punch, and someone from the Bay Area (Morris was from Berkeley) brought the custom of making an exquisite cocktail from pisco back to its place of origin, Peru.[82] Like a pisco punch, an exceptional pisco sour takes some preparation and no shortcuts. (My very popular recipe is below.)

Either the common nonaromatic Quebranta pisco or a blended *acholado* pisco is a perfect spirit for this cocktail. Simple syrup is necessary, and I suggest that you make your own. You do this by mixing equal parts white sugar and purified water in a pot and then boil it until the mixture is reduced by half. You want the final mixture to be syrupy but not too thick, so I would suggest you measure the mix before and after, when you do the reduction for the first time. Squeeze the key limes yourself into a bowl with a strainer to collect the seeds. A pisco sour should be vigorously shaken by hand with about three or four ice cubes, for about five minutes, to get the proper consistency. Of course, a vigorous dry shake with no ice first will begin the process toward a perfect sour.[83] The bottom three-fourths of your glass should be pale green with the top fourth a crown of milky foam. Most of the pisco sours you will try in the States or in Peru will be made with a blender. This technique is not as special as hand-shaken (yes, I am being a little James Bond here), and if you let the blended mix settle for a few minutes it will somewhat resemble the hand-shaken drink. Additionally, the ice is not pulverized when you shake the drink by hand. A blended pisco sour will be slightly watered down by the ice. The Museo del Pisco bars in Peru turn the shaking of their pisco sours into performance art, which is hypnotic to the observer (at least to this observer). Finally, the white foam crown of the cocktail is topped off with a few brown drops of Angostura bitters forming a foamy Rorschach test. I will return to the pisco sour, in the guise of the coca sour, in the chapter on coca, because I believe the coca sour is the next evolution in the pisco punch–pisco sour–coca sour triad.

Lannes's Pisco Punch

Take a fresh pineapple. Cut into pieces about ½ by 1½ inches. Put these squares of fresh pineapple in a bowl of gum syrup (below) to soak overnight. This serves the double purpose of flavoring the gum syrup with the pineapple and soaking the pineapple, both of which are used afterward in the pisco punch.

In the morning, mix in a big bowl:
8 oz. gum syrup flavored by
pineapple as above
16 oz. distilled water
10 oz. lemon juice
1 bottle (24 oz.) Peruvian pisco

Serve very cold, but be careful not to keep the ice in for too long because of dilution. Use 3- or 4-oz. punch glasses. Put one of the pineapple squares in each glass.[84]

Gum Syrup

Crush one pound of gum arabic (if not already in crystal form), and soak for 24 hours in one pint of distilled water. (Gum arabic can be purchased at some confectionery supply houses and health food stores.) Add the gum arabic solution to a syrup made of four pounds of sugar and one quart of water boiled to 220° F. As the mixture continues to boil, skim off impurities and then let it cool to room temperature. Filter through cheesecloth and store in bottle.[85]

Bob's Pisco Sour

5 oz. pisco
1½ oz. simple syrup
1 egg white
2 oz. freshly squeezed key lime juice
Bitters for garnish

Place all ingredients in a shaker with four ice cubes and shake vigorously for 3–4 minutes, then strain the sour into a glass and top off with several drops of bitters. Makes two 8-oz. cocktails.

Simple Syrup

16 oz. distilled water
16 oz. white sugar

Combine and boil the mixture until reduced by half.

Chapter 5

The Mutant and the Clone

Choclos and *Papas*

To the casual observer, Mint Museum Randolph in Charlotte, North Carolina, houses an odd pre-Columbian relic. The object in question is an Inca-era golden corncob.[1] This corncob was most likely part of a celebratory golden maize field at the sacred Temple of the Sun in Cuzco.[2] Obviously, corn (*Zea mays* L.) had elevated status in the Inca Empire because of *chicha,* which was consumed throughout the Inca world. But there are and were other uses for *choclos* (cobs of corn) in ancient and modern Peru, and I would like to give a brief history of the origin of the food that was the organic foundation of many New World civilizations.

Zea mays L. is one of the world's largest crops; it is also the most extensively researched plant on the planet. Scholarly articles about maize abound, and the debate about the ancestor of maize, although mostly settled, still attracts intense scrutiny. In simple terms, *Zea mays* L.'s wild progenitor was the grass-like plant teosinte (*Z. mays* ssp. *parviglumis*).[3] If you look at the two plants and compare them, however, their placement in the same scientific genus defies logic. Teosinte is an unassuming grass like wheat. The seedpod top of the plant contains only two entwined rows of small well-armored kernels, with the sum averaging about ten kernels, compared to the almost thousand-kernel average of a corncob. These two plants are so unalike, nineteenth-century botanists placed teosinte in the genus *Euchlaena* rather than in *Zea* with maize.[4]

The domestication of maize—or, maybe more accurately, the human-manipulated mutation of teosinte—took place in southern Mexico over thousands of years.[5] Notice I avoided the word *evolved* because the changes of the plant's physiology have destined *Zea mays* L. to extinction, along with its human caretakers.[6] When we are gone, who will cultivate and protect this genetic monster, which shed its small well-armored kernels, from the numerous predators who are ravenous for its exposed thousand-kernel bounty? And keep in mind, human manipulation of corn continues today. According to the FDA, most of the corn grown in the United States is genetically modified (GMO), so there is no reason to believe the modifications to *Zea mays* L. will cease any time soon.[7] And why should it? We have been the Dr. Frankenstein enabler for this plant from the beginning when ancient Native Americans combed the hillsides around the Balsas River or Oaxaca looking for promising teosinte pods.[8]

Guilá Naquitz Cave in the southern Mexican state of Oaxaca has yielded the earliest macrofossil evidence for the domestication of maize, which dates to 6,250 years ago.[9] This is the spot where the first corncobs were archaeologically recovered. But macrofossil remains that are not corncobs show that maize spread south out of Mexico earlier than that. For example, maize arrived in Panama 7,600 years ago. But most important for this study, 6,000 years ago maize was well established in northwestern South America.[10] Maize was documented at the coastal archaeological site of Huaca Prieta, so the presence of maize in Peru more than 6,000 years ago is secure.[11] In the past decade or so, an intense debate has developed over multiple domestications of teosinte, but a recent article by a celebrated group of maize scholars suggests that a semi-wild race of teosinte (a term for a maize cultivar) made its way to South America very early on and was dispersed by ancient peoples in this region.[12]

Zea mays L. was the crop responsible for the flourishing of pre-Columbian Mesoamerican civilization. In the Early Pre-classic Mesoamerican timetable, roughly three thousand years ago, the Maya people of Mesoamerica began processing maize to make foods such as tamales.[13] By this date the Maya had somehow discerned that if maize was to be a dietary staple, it required alkali processing. Perhaps the Mayan familiarity with quicklime as a building material expedited their ingenious adaptation of quicklime to enhance maize. But if the ancient Mesoamericans did not process corn, "there would be a considerable degree of malnutrition in societies where corn is a major part of the diet."[14] Therefore, the alkali processing of maize (called nixtamalization) was and is a vital conclusion to the extensive maize agriculture in Mesoamerica. Nixtamalization (from the Náhuatl *nixtamalli*) happens when maize is soaked in a vessel containing water and quicklime.[15] This alkali processing of maize is essential in preparing corn for human consumption because it releases lysine and tryptophan and, most important, niacin. Without these, when the primary dietary staple is unprocessed maize, the result would be malnutrition and, in extreme circumstances, a horrible disease called pellagra.[16]

Yet nixtamalization is unknown in pre-Columbian South America, a region with thousands of years of substantial evidence of extensive maize cultivation.[17] What is the disparity between these two regions? Anthropologist John Staller has suggested that although maize is consumed as a grain in Mesoamerica (it is the region's daily bread, so to speak), in the Andean realm of South America it is used as a vegetable. I would add, not a vegetable per se but, instead, more precisely as a fruit. The vegetable or fruit component of maize takes the form of *chicha* beer in South America, at once an ever-present refreshment, offering of tribute, and centerpiece of ritual feasting and exchange.[18]

But *chicha* was and is not a dietary essential in South America. In Mexico maize was and is indispensable. Imagine Mexican food, past and present, without corn tortillas, tamales, and hominy for posole and menudo.[19] All these foods use processed maize. In contrast, in South America, there is a plethora of crops that easily fill in when alkali-processed maize is removed from the diet of pre-Columbian civilizations. For instance, Moseley's waning but relevant "Maritime Hypothesis" has the ancient coastal Peruvian civilizations thriving on fish protein.[20] But research has also pointed to the diversity of nutritional Andean crops such as potatoes, manioc (cassava), quinoa, *tarwi*, and so on, which could easily have provided the carbohydrates and calories necessary for the rise of civilizations both on the coast and in the mountains of South America.[21]

The incongruous development of the diet in the ancient centers of Mexico and Peru has been on full display for the past decade in my study abroad Peru course. The UTRGV is a Hispanic serving institution with a more than 90 percent Latino student body. My study abroad Peru trips often mirror the university's demographic, so most of the student travelers are of Mexican American or Mexican ethnicity. At the orientation for the trip, I always tell the students they will be hard-pressed to find tortillas in Peru, because a tortilla in Peru is, as in Spain, an omelet. They seem to listen, but each year, after a few weeks in Peru, I always have a student complain about the lack of what is daily bread in south Texas and Mexico. A type of ancient tortilla, and for that matter tamales called *humitas*, were made in pre-Columbian Peru, but with corn flour, which, I am certain, was not processed.[22] There was no need to process the flour because these foods were only one part of a rich and complex diet.

The tradition of making these ancient tortillas has disappeared, much to the chagrin of my study abroad students, but the tradition of making fresh corn *humitas* has survived. There are several reasons that these Peruvian tortillas have disappeared. The tortilla tradition was likely not as widespread nor as vital or as nuanced as that of ancient Mexico. Upon arriving in Mesoamerica, the Spanish noted not only the essential role of tortillas in the ancient Mexican diet but also the plethora of different kinds of tortillas made for elites and commoners.[23] I am guessing here about a lost tradition, but I am sure there was not a similar complexity of tortillas in pre-Columbian Peru.

Also, according to the chronicler Cieza de León, by the time of the early conquest wheat fields were already extensively planted throughout Peru.[24] Any visit to a Peruvian town or village provides evidence that in the colonial era bread-making was embraced with a passion. Two times each day in all Peruvian hamlets, villages, and towns, young men stand on corners or ride bicycles around town hawking freshly baked bread. Enter any Peruvian market and you will encounter baskets full of fresh breads. Several years ago, I was delighted to be sampling the breads sold on the street in the highland city of Cajamarca. My personal favorite was the delicious Pan Árabe. But here I need to remind you that although bread complements breakfast and the late-night repast, the afternoon meal from twelve to two is served with a *cancha* complement. Finally, the abundant adobe baking ovens throughout Peru are a testament to the evolution of bread-making skill from the colonial era, and one recent manifestation of this prowess is the exceptional pizzas in the highland tourist centers. A good pizza crust is essential for great pizza, and my study abroad students are always impressed with pizzerias in Cuzco and the Sacred Valley such as La Bodega 138 and Incontri del Pueblo Viejo.

One of the forms in which maize was consumed in ancient Peru besides the ever-present *chicha* was as corn flour. The Jesuit chronicler Bernabé Cobo observed that the Inca would take a ration of maize flour on their journeys.[25] On an expedition into the highlands of Chachapoyas near the town of Atuen, I was saved from severe dehydration by a maize-flour-water mixture. After an exhausting two weeks in the field, my friend and guide Joaquin Briones Ortiz and I crossed the thirteen-thousand-foot Ulillen Pass and trekked down to Atuen. The time in the mountains had both conditioned and acclimatized me for the journey back to Leymebamba, which would still require a few days on foot. My newfound vigor also gave me misguided hubris because, with the trip's end in sight, I smugly decided that I would drink water only when Joaquin drank. This was unwise. When I showed signs of dehydration, Joaquin immediately found a source of fresh water. Then he mixed some brown sugar and cornmeal into the water and had me drink two pint-sized bowls of this wonderful liquid.

Later, as we walked into the campsite, I asked Joaquin about the sugar and cornmeal mixture. He called it *sheve* and said he never went on a journey into the mountains without it. He added that an Andean hiker could climb these mountains with just *sheve* and coca if she or he could find water, and Joaquin was an expert at finding potable water in the mountains. He also told me that I needed to become accustomed (*acostumbrado*) to water rationing. Keep in mind, when hiking in the mountains, water will likely be the heaviest thing you carry. I never asked for the spelling assigned to this mixture, but Holguín's early seventeenth-century Quechua dictionary has the *chillpi* as maize flour.[26] Of course, there was no sugar in the Andes before the arrival of the Spanish, but the water and maize flour would provide ample carbohydrates and hydration for mountain trekking, even without the glucose.

Then *humita* was and is an Andean treat. In his record of Inca customs from 1653, Cobo mentions *humitas* being small cakes of maize cooked in a pot. González Holguín lists *humitas* as similar to tamales in his early seventeenth-century Quechua dictionary and has the term coming from the Quechua (Inca) language.[27] The major difference between tamales and *humitas* is that tamales are made with processed corn and *humitas* are made with fresh corn. Today most tamales involve an addition of lard or butter to the masa (corn flour), a decidedly unhealthy addition to the pre-Columbian recipe recorded by the Spanish during the conquest.[28] "Basic *atolli* involved taking eight parts of water, six parts of maize, and lime and cooking them together until the maize softened. This is the standard process of nixtamalization, the way to prepare maize for the manufacture of dough for tortillas and tamales, and it tremendously enhances the nutritive value of the maize. The softened grain was then ground and cooked until it thickened."[29] Although this passage refers to making the masa for tamales, I imagine that the preparation was the same for the pre-Columbian *humita*, only omitting the quicklime for nixtamalization. At present, milk is added to the masa when making fresh corn *humitas*, and obviously this is a postcolonial addition to the pre-Columbian recipe.

The tamale is traced back to the Maya people of pre-Columbian Mesoamerica, with representations of tamales appearing on ceramics. Justin Kerr and Michael Coe's *The Maya Vase Book* contains a delightful image of a ruler being served tamales likely covered in a chocolate sauce.[30] This sauce would be the pre-Columbian antecedent of mole, which is still common in Mexico today. Indeed, the sheer variety of tamale types and tamale ingredients recorded by the Spanish during their conquest of Mexico is astounding. Just a sampling of ingredients include turkey, fish, tadpoles, mushrooms, chili, gopher, fruit, rabbit, beans, *axolotl* (salamander), and so on.

Unfortunately, there seems to be scant evidence for myriad types of *humitas* in the pre-Hispanic Andean world. The ancient recipe was likely a simple mix of fresh sweet ground corn mixed with water (mirroring the process described above), and the most common ingredient added to the corn cake would be kernels from the cob (*choclo*). After the conquest, many variations of *humitas* developed in Peru, albeit with many Old World food additions. For example, sweet *humitas* with raisins; *humitas* with fresh cheese; *humitas* de Cajamarca with cheese, butter, and pork; and *humitas de manjar blanco*, thickened milk with sugar.[31]

Holguín's early seventeenth-century Quechua dictionary defines *choclo* (his spelling is *chokllo*) as corn on the cob.[32] The most common place to find *choclos* in Peru is on a plate of ceviche next to a slice of sweet potato. Typically, the corncob is steamed and cut into quarters with perhaps one or two quarters plated, depending on the restaurant. Very fancy *cevicherías* will cut the steamed kernels from the cob. Most Peruvian corn has big white kernels, and it is far chewier than our bicolored and delicate super-sweet corn. But this texture pairs well with the heat from the ceviche's *ají*. Note that recently the Peruvian government extended a ten-year ban on GMO crops for another fifteen years.[33] But more than ten years ago, when I was eating *choclo* in the remote northeastern village of Chilchos, I was offered an ear of bicolored super-sweet corn. Perhaps this crop's influx started the ban in the first place?

Going back to Holguín, *mutti* (*mote* is the common spelling today) is cooked corn, cooked wheat, and cooked peanuts.[34] Holguín's ambiguity here is only part of the problem, because he mixes in an Old World crop (wheat) in the Quechua definition. Of course, Holguín's dictionary was written after decades of Spanish colonial rule,

Giant kernels of mote drying in the field below the Inca site Pisac.
Photo by Robert Bradley.

which ushered in a drastic upheaval of the pre-Columbian world. But the confusion of what *mote* really means is compounded with the observation of the famous nineteenth-century naturalist Johann Jakob von Tschudi that *mote* are maize kernels taken off the cob and boiled in water with wood ash.[35]

By Tschudi's definition, *mote* is hominy or processed, nixtamalized, corn. Holguín mentions the consumption of wood ash only once in his dictionary where he refers to gummy balls of ash that act as an alkali and release the cocaine in coca leaves into the chewer's mouth.[36] But in Holguín's record there is no mention of boiling *mote* in an alkaline solution. Holguín mentions a *mote* stew (spelling it *mutti ppatascca*) as does Father Cobo (he spells it *motepatasca*), but no wood ash.[37] Therefore, I believe the tradition of adding wood ash to the preparation of *mote* came with the Spanish to Peru from Mexico sometime during the colonial era. And the Peruvian tamale tradition likely came along the same route.[38]

Now let us conclude this section on maize with *cancha*, the delicious Peruvian popcorn that no visitor to Peru will be able to avoid. Almost every Peruvian restaurant, from the most unpretentious *picantería* to the most frequented and expensive *cevichería*, will place *cancha* on the table at the main noonday meal, in the same way bread is served in European-style restaurants. Again, although there is ample bread-making in Peru, this baking is for breakfast and the late-night meal. Curiously, the origin of the term *cancha* for toasted maize is elusive. The consensus places this toasted corn nut in the Quechua language, but Holguín's listing for *mayz tostado* (toasted corn) in the Inca lexicon is *hamcca*. He has the word *cancha* defined as a patio or a corral.[39] But the term *cancha* unequivocally refers to toasted corn today, so sometime in the late colonial or early republican era in Peru, the word's meaning shifted.[40]

Types of corn are referred to as races, and in Peru the most popular races of corn for *cancha* are Chullpi, Huayleño, and Paro, which are all linked to an ancient ancestor called Confite Chavinese.[41]

Chavín culture thrived in highland Peru three thousand years ago, so the Peruvian *cancha*-making tradition is likely ancient. Perhaps at some point *cancha* was served at so many courtyards in colonial era haciendas that the word became associated with toasted corn? Or *hamcca* could be a homonym that linguistically drifted into *cancha*? In any case, enjoy this simple offering when in Peru and remember requests for refills are expected.

Are there any examples of pre-Columbian solid gold potatoes like the solid gold corncob? No. A search of the Mint Museum or any other institution in the world for a golden potato will result in failure. However, there are images of potatoes sculpted into Moche ceramics.[42] But the Moche people had a taste for odd representations in this medium; examples include graphic sex scenes (human, bestial, and necrophilic), images of deformed and diseased individuals, and representations of fruits and vegetables, to name but a few. I believe the pre-Columbian Moche people had a perverse sense of humor in depicting the everyday-things category of their ceramics. They had other types of religious and martial ceramics, which are very different, but certainly their representations of the lowly spud fall into the everyday-things group.

In Peru, as in many other parts of the world, potatoes are called *papa*. The term is supposedly from the Quechua language, but González Holguín's dictionary curiously has *papas* as both a Spanish and a Quechua word, which somewhat obscures its etymology.[43] Very few people like eating potatoes. No, you really do not. We like the things we put on potatoes to give them flavor: butter, sour cream, chives, bacon bits, olive oil, hollandaise sauce, truffles, caviar, and so on. All these additives are what makes you fat, because the unadorned slow-burn carbohydrates of the potato are an exceptionally healthy source of calories and are, in fact, not fattening. Basically, *Solanum tuberosum tuberosum* is a bland tuber packed with nutrients. And almost the whole potato can be eaten, not just some small grains as in the cereal crops. The carbohydrate-to-protein ratio of potatoes, along with the essential vitamins and minerals, more than satisfies an active individual's daily energy requirements. To be specific, a potato is a giant swollen piece of stem and bud set apart from the plant's underground system. This bizarrely inflated stem facilitates reproduction for the potato even if the plant withers aboveground. Writer and photojournalist John Reader, who has written a compelling and thoroughly documented history of the potato, has noted that this tuber is essentially a clone of the original plant. Therefore, when humans began manipulating the plant, the flower and seed reproduction aboveground was ignored as attention focused on cultivation of the tuber.[44]

There is one glaring problem with the initial human consumption and domestication of *Solanum tuberosum tuberosum* and its ancestors: toxic glycoalkaloids. These alkaloids are the plant's defense system, and they are particularly abundant in wild varieties of potatoes and in the seeds and flowers of domesticated plants. Again, the seeds and flowers of domesticated potatoes are an evolutionary afterthought, particularly when humans began reproducing the plant vegetatively by cutting up and planting sections of the tuber itself.[45]

When potatoes were first domesticated in southern Peru and northern Bolivia from approximately six thousand to ten thousand years ago, how did the ancient Andean people filter out the toxins in the first place?[46] A 1986 study of the Bolivian highland Aymara people provides some insight into this dilemma. In their analysis, anthropologist Timothy Johns and biologist Susan L. Keen noted that the Aymara could distinguish between different potato tastes, bitter and nonbitter, even at extremely high glycoalkaloid levels. In other words, the Aymara in question had a high resistance to the toxins in *Solanum X ajanhuiri* Bitt, a semi-wild hybrid potato used in their study.[47] In a different study, Johns noted that geophagy (in this case the consumption of potatoes with small amounts of different clays) absorbed the toxins in the potato.[48]

Ancient Andean people also neutralized the toxic and bitter aspects of semi-wild potatoes by making *chuño* (freeze-dried potatoes). In the early sixteenth century, conquistador Pedro Cieza de

León first observed the process of making *chuño,* and he noted that these freeze-dried potatoes were held in high esteem because they could be stored away and used when other crops failed. He went on to mention that some Spaniards became rich just by selling *chuño* to the miners of Potosí.[49] There are two types of *chuño,* called *tunta* and *moray,* and both are made with bitter potatoes.[50] The potatoes are spread out and allowed to freeze. Then people walk on them to squeeze out all the moisture. This process allows the freeze-dried product to be stored for considerable time, until the *chuño* is rehydrated when it is used to thicken stews and soups.[51]

Like the human manipulation of teosinte into maize, over millennia ancient Andean people tasted and selected the least toxic potatoes. And like the story of teosinte's change to maize, the potato—which is one of the world's top food crops, *Solanum tuberosum tuberosum*—will disappear when human beings are no longer around to tend and work this crop. This continuously cloned plant has lost its capacity for survival by having its natural defenses (glycoalkaloids) and genetic diversity neutralized by human intervention. Indeed, potatoes are not only one of the world's top food crops; they are also the world's most vulnerable food crops. The cost of protecting cultivated potatoes, specifically with fertilizers and pesticides, exceeds more than two billion dollars annually.[52]

Potatoes were first domesticated in the southern Andean highlands between six thousand and ten thousand years ago, emerging from thousands of varieties of wild potatoes. Potatoes then became "widely distributed in the Americas from the southwestern United States to southern Chile."[53] Today, six species of potato are grown in the Andes, most notably *Solanum tuberosum andigena,* and from these, and especially *Solanum tuberosum tuberosum,* there have "evolved" thousands of cultivars or potato landraces. But it was *Solanum tuberosum tuberosum* that was brought back to the Old World, and this prolific variety has now spread to 130 countries worldwide.[54] When you enter the fruits and vegetables section of your supermarket, you are looking at *Solanum tuberosum tuberosum,* the world's greatest Andean crop, on full display in all its colorful and varied sizes and shapes.

Cieza de León was a keen observer of the Andean world and likely the first Spaniard to take notice of the humble spud. His account was recorded in the early days of the conquest but, unfortunately, was not published until the nineteenth century.[55] "Of the native foodstuffs there are two which, aside from corn, are the main staples of the Indian's diet: the potato, which is like a truffle, and when cooked is as soft inside as boiled chestnuts; it has neither skin nor pit, any more than the truffle, for it is also borne underground."[56] The second important crop Cieza de León mentions is quinoa. It is curious that Cieza de León initially compares the potato to the celebrated Old World fungus, the truffle. Foraging for truffles is the stuff of legend with the olfactory abilities of dogs and pigs leading the human hunters to their treasure—fungi worth more than their weight in gold. As every Peruvian potato farmer knows, the effort of carrying a forty-kilo bag of potatoes to market is hardly worth the price. But many scholars note that when *S. tuberosum tuberosum* was introduced to Europe, the humble potato ended famine and changed the course of history by fueling the rise of the West.[57] This was something the rare truffle could never accomplish.

The migration of the potato from its Andean home to Europe and then to the rest of the world began a few decades after the conquest of the Inca Empire. Unlike the potato, maize, Capsicum (hot peppers), cassava (yuca), and sweet potatoes were all recorded by Columbus and taken to Europe before the end of the fifteenth century. But there is little specific documentation concerning early potato agronomy in Europe. And confusion between the tropical sweet potato (*Ipomoea batatas*) and the potato (*S. tuberosum*) muddies this paucity of information. The durable potato superficially looks like the sweet potato, but the limited climatic conditions and altitudes for growing *Ipomoea batatas* stopped it from becoming a worldwide dietary staple. Also, in the sixteenth century, Spanish Empire potatoes were called *patatas* and sweet potatoes were called *batatas*. The similarity in spelling added a great degree of difficulty to scholars' efforts at archival research focused on handwritten sixteenth-century records. But the exacting work of J. G. Hawkes and J. Francisco-Ortega and others lead to shipping manifests from 1567 and 1574, which listed potatoes sent from the Canary Islands to Antwerp in November 1567, and to Rouen, France, in 1574. Hawkes and Francisco-Ortega estimated that it would have taken about five years to have a sufficient supply of potatoes to export. Therefore, with some certainty, potatoes had been planted in the Canary Islands by at least 1562. These scholars also used archives from the Hospital de la Sangre in Seville to prove that potatoes were grown in that area from 1570 onward. Finally, Hawkes and Francisco-Ortega concluded that the Canary Islands were the intermediate point for potatoes' entrance into Europe, because direct shipments from South America to Europe would have resulted in tubers far too shriveled and sprouted to use for growing.[58]

With the Canary Islands as an intermediate point, *S. tuberosum tuberosum* spread to Spain, Italy, France, England, and the Low Countries.[59] In a statue that stood in southern Germany, Sir Francis Drake was immortalized as the individual who brought the potato to England. Unfortunately, the Nazis destroyed the statue during the night of Kristallnacht.[60] In fact, this monument celebrating the British navigator conflicted with another narrative that has Sir Walter Raleigh delivering the potato. Both stories are legendary, based solely on circumstantial evidence. The potato was supposedly featured as a stage prop symbolizing lasciviousness in early English theater—but in this case, the tuber causing the randy behavior was *Ipomoea batatas*, brought to Europe a hundred years earlier by Columbus.[61]

By the seventeenth century, *S. tuberosum tuberosum* was well on its way to securing Europe's worldwide hegemony. Indeed, the potato has been credited with changing the world's history by feeding populations decimated by famine. For example, between the tenth and eighteenth centuries, the French people suffered through no fewer than eighty-nine widespread famines caused by grain harvest failures.[62] The potato eliminated this constant threat of misery, filled their bellies, and made people productive. In a way, then, perhaps the potato was indeed an aphrodisiac because sex and starvation are an ill-suited pair. However, war and potatoes are a better suited couple. From 1778 to 1779, Prussia and Austria fought the War of the Bavarian Succession, in which both hungry armies scoured the countryside for potatoes until the spuds ran out, which ended the conflict.[63]

At first Europe's masses were reluctant to accept the potato. Their daily bread was literally made from grain, and bread was not only a food but also a profound symbol of faith in Christian Europe. The misshapen and oddly colored spud recalled the dreaded biblical disease leprosy, and the potato was for a time thought to cause this horrible affliction. Therefore, it took 250 years for the potato to become Europe's "most widely consumed, cheap and nourishing food."[64] And the pathway for *S. tuberosum*'s ascendance as the nemesis of European famine was often made possible by coercion and trickery. Coercion was applied by Frederick the Great in 1744 when he threatened to have the ears and noses cut off Prussians who refused to eat the free potatoes he supplied.

Trickery was used by the French pharmacist Antoine-Augustin Parmentier, who was captured by the Prussians during the Seven Years War while he was serving in the French army. As a prisoner Parmentier thrived on a potato diet for three years before being released. This experience made Parmentier a potato advocate, but what made him a brilliantly successful advocate was his use of the "mass follows class" sales technique. Parmentier lobbied the French aristocracy, particularly Louis XVI and Marie Antoinette, and soon the royals became enamored with *S. tuberosum*. However, Parmentier's real genius was manifest when he had soldiers patrol and guard a large field of potatoes at Les Sablons, near Neuilly. The peasants took note, and when Parmentier ordered the soldiers to withdraw, the locals stole the potatoes. If potatoes were worth guarding, they were worth eating, and after this event eating potatoes became routine in France.[65]

Ireland was a land completely transformed by the potato. After adopting the potato into their diet, famine disappeared in the country, and 40 percent of the Irish ate no other solid food except potatoes. In 1839 a British inquiry implied that Irish laborers ate an astounding twelve and a half pounds of potatoes a day. Even if that unbelievable number was partially British hyperbole, people consumed more potatoes per capita in Ireland than in any other European country. And this sustenance caused the population of the Emerald Island to grow from 1.5 million to 8.5 million in two hundred years. The sheer size of the potato fields in Ireland and the uniformity of the single productive cultivar there (Lumper) would make the crops especially vulnerable to the devastation that was to come. In hindsight, the ensuing Great Hunger of 1845 (the Irish Potato Famine) seems almost a fait accompli. *S. tuberosum*'s introduction to Ireland was highly transformative, but it still was an invasive species from a profoundly different ecosystem a world away. Add to this the fact that a single cloned cultivar dominated the vast fields of Irish potatoes, then what could possibly go wrong?[66]

What ensued was the Great Hunger, a human catastrophe of epic proportion. At least one million Irish died of famine, and another million fled the deprivation by emigrating.[67] The cause was a highly contagious water mold (*Phytophthora infestans*) equipped with an army of zoospores that used the vascular system of the potato to devastate the plant. *P. infestans* came from the New World; some scholars point to an origin in Peru because of the potato diversity there, and others suggest Mexico because of that country's diversity of *P. infestans*.[68] The delivery system for the blight is more certain. *P. infestans* entered Europe in shipments of guano (bird excrement) that were sent there as fertilizer.[69] Guano had been extensively used as fertilizer in the pre-Columbian world, and guano extraction from Peru's southern islands was a major industry in the nineteenth century until synthetic fertilizers were invented using the Haber-Bosch process. Unfortunately, especially for the Irish, the invention of this process was about fifty years too late to save their vast fields of Lumper potatoes. To put this scourge in perspective, if a famine of this same scale hit the United States today, forty million people would ultimately die.[70]

The nineteenth century was the era when the bill for the enormous botanical bounty from the Columbian Exchange finally came due. Blights and bugs seem to have awakened toward the end of the century, aroused by large-scale farming practices. For example, the boll weevil entered the US antebellum South from Mexico, and the aphid phylloxera, native to eastern America, devastated the vineyards of Europe. Adding to the devastation, in the late nineteenth century, potato crops were destroyed by a second scourge: *Leptinotarsa decemlineata,* also called the Colorado potato beetle or Murphy's beetle. And what was the major weapon to combat these menacing pests? Toxic chemical pesticides, with arsenic and copper sulfate leading the charge. This was the beginning of a war that continues to this day, driving a toxic treadmill of pesticides and fertilizers that makes some farmers wary of even letting their children walk around their potato fields because the fields are saturated with fumigants, fungicides, herbicides, and insecticides.[71] The strategy of the Bolivian Aymara, experimenting and tasting a wide range of bitter semi-wild potatoes to increase crop biodiversity, is prescient when compared to the toxic treadmill.

This strategy is completely at odds with our modern industrial farming practices, however. Indeed, the monoculture that caused the Irish potato famine is in play today with the Russet Burbank cultivar filling the role of the Irish Lumper. This is the preferred variety for the world's beloved French fries, and the vast fields of these potatoes in places such as Idaho can only be sustained by mountains of fertilizers and pesticides. In the 1990s Monsanto genetically engineered a Russet Burbank with a gene from a bacterium that produced its own pesticide, which kills the Colorado beetle. But public outcry about GMO foods forced Monsanto to discontinue making this hybrid shortly after its introduction.[72]

I am a French fry lover, as I am sure many of you are as well. I would never turn down any piping hot fast-food fries, even knowing about the pesticides. However, I do not eat them every day. French fries that you could, in fact, eat every day, and remorse free, are the *Papas Fritas Huayro* from the famous Peruvian restaurant chain La Lucha Sangucheria Criolla. French fries are a modern import to Peru, but *huayro* potatoes are a cross between *"piquiña" Solanum stenotomum* (believed to have an ancestral relationship with twenty-two modern potato cultivars and thought to be a potential source of resistance against disease) and *S. tuberosum* from the primitive Andigenum group.[73] These potatoes were relished in the pre-Columbian era.

My first encounter with this cultivar took place almost twenty years ago, again with Joaquin Briones Ortiz. We had trekked to a remote eastern town in the Peruvian department of La Libertad searching for Chachapoya ruins. The Chacha were a pre-Hispanic cloud forest people conquered by the Inca before the arrival of the Spanish. The structure we wanted to investigate was on the land of a potato farmers' cooperative in the valley below the massive mountain of Cajamarquilla. The farmers were extremely helpful and after we chewed some coca, they offered us lunch, which of course consisted of potatoes. The potatoes were boiled, not my favorite spud delivery system, but turning down this lunch would have been rude, so I dug in. The potatoes had purple skin and a few purple veins running through the interior. It took me years to find out that these delicious potatoes were *huayro.*

I want to end this chapter with a discussion of Peru's most accessorized and famous potato recipe, *papa a la huancaína.* This is my wife's favorite potato dish, but my expertise in cooking potatoes ends with preparing French fries or baking new and Russet potatoes. Much to the chagrin of my spouse, my heart is more into making perfect ceviche than garnishing spuds. But she loves my ceviche too. However, I reached out to Chef Cecilia Ríos of the Restaurant Pueblo Viejo in Miraflores, because my wife says she makes the best *papa a la huancaína*. Full disclosure: I have enjoyed many meals in her North Coast themed venue, and besides being an excellent cook, Cecilia is also my wife's favorite aunt. Her list of ingredients is as follows.

Chef Cecilia Ríos's *Papa a la Huancaína*

3 lbs. yellow potatoes
4 hardboiled eggs
1 lb. fresh cheese[74]
1½ cups soda crackers
7 *ají amarillo*
1½ cups milk
1¾ oz. vegetable oil
Salt
Pepper
Lettuce, thoroughly washed
1½ cups black olives

The combination of milk and potatoes is extremely nutritious and was the mainstay of the Irish diet before the potato famine.[75] And high-quality fresh cheese is readily available throughout Peru. *Ají amarillo* (*C. baccatum*) has moderate heat but adds a lot of flavor. Adding soda crackers might seem mundane, but again, they are an item you will find in every bodega in Peru.

Tía Cecilia continues as follows:

1. Wash the potatoes and boil them; press the potatoes once boiled, knead them with oil, salt, and pepper, until compact potato balls are formed.
2. Remove the seeds and devein the *ají amarillo* and blend them in a blender along with the milk.
3. Strain the liquid milk and *ají amarillo* into a bowl.
4. Add the soda crackers and cheese and blend again. Then add the oil in a thread to give it texture, then add salt and pepper to taste.
5. Serve two kneaded potato balls accompanied by one hard-boiled egg, halved or quartered, on a lettuce leaf.
6. Pour the cream on top of the potatoes and egg; garnish with olives.
7. Enjoy

Papa a la Huancaína is a nutritious and filling recipe to end a chapter on two of the most popular foods in the world, which now are literally part of the global human experience. One last note, if you think my last sentence is hyperbole, consider that today China is the largest producer of potatoes in the world.

Chapter 6
Superfoods

In the early sixteenth century Pedro Cieza de León wrote what is likely the first description of the worldwide health food staple quinoa (*Chenopodium quinoa*): "There is another very good food they call *quinoa*, which has a leaf like the Moorish chard; the plant grows almost to a man's height, and produces tiny seeds, some white, some red, of which they make drinks and which they also eat boiled, as we do rice."[1] Cieza's keen observation would not be published for three hundred years, but the conquistador certainly had a knack for documenting important foods. Recall his description of the potato. Also unfortunate, and completely misguided, was the Spanish belief that Incan crops were inferior to wheat and barley.[2] In the case of quinoa, this assertion is laughable, because the seeds of the plant contain all nine essential amino acids and up to 20 percent protein. Add to this the fact that the plant can thrive in poor soils up to fourteen thousand feet in altitude, and you have a candidate for perhaps the world's greatest crop. There are more than three thousand different varieties of quinoa, which gives it a biodiversity rivaling that of the potato.[3] The greatest variety of cultivars is in the area around Lake Titicaca, making this region the likely site of domestication, which occurred roughly five thousand years ago.[4]

After the conquest, quinoa really did become a "lost crop of the Inca," with its production suppressed in the Viceroyalty of Peru. Part of this was disdain for indigenous crops, but quinoa also played an important role in rituals and rites that were outlawed by the Spanish.[5] Production of quinoa did continue in the high Andean communities that resisted the *reducciones*, the sixteenth-century colonial doctrine that forcibly moved highland communities down to more governable sites near rivers and roads. And for four hundred years, quinoa remained a little-known highland crop. Garcilaso took quinoa to Spain after his exodus from Peru, and there was some interest in the plant in several European countries, but quinoa never became an extensively cultivated crop like the potato.[6]

Western interest in quinoa grew in the mid-twentieth century, and quinoa really started on the road to becoming a global commodity in the 1980s when two North American impresarios started to export Bolivian *Quinoa Real* to health food stores throughout the United States. Consumer interest in quinoa grew in the 1990s and into the new millennium, with Peru's production and export of quinoa ultimately exceeding that of Bolivia. The growth of quinoa as a worldwide crop culminated in 2013 when the United Nations declared that year the Year of Quinoa.[7] Of course, as the price of quinoa soared, the seeds became priced out of the reach of the Peru's urban poor and even the highland farmers themselves.[8]

High-quality Peruvian products that become too expensive for your average Peruvians is a norm repeated with olive oil and coffee. Peru's southern desert coast has olive trees that were planted by the Spanish in the early sixteenth century. These trees produce wonderful olive oil, which for centuries was reserved for the upper classes or exported. This all began to change in the late twentieth century. At this time a movement began, spearheaded by chefs Gastón Acurio and Virgilio Martínez, to promote Peru's fantastic olive oils, and now Peru is one of the largest producers of olive oil in South America.[9] When I first started traveling to Peru in the late 1990s I was greeted with a tin of Nescafe instant every morning at breakfast, even though I knew Peru produced some of the best coffee in the world. A few decades ago, you had a better chance of getting fresh roasted whole bean Peruvian coffee at a Starbucks in New York City than in Peru. Again, market forces destined Peruvian coffee for export. This has changed in the past decade, as Peru is experiencing the growth of a fledging coffee culture. Today Starbucks serves Peruvian coffee not only in Lima but also in the gritty northern city of Chimbote, and the Peruvian coffee shop Puku Puku serves some of the best coffee I have ever tasted. But there are still plenty of Nescafe tins on tables at breakfast throughout the country, especially in remote regions.

Additional disparities occurred with the rise of quinoa's popularity. For example, anthropologist Emma McDonell has investigated the practices of the campesino quinoa producers in the highland Peruvian town of Puno. Her research emphasizes the farmer's efforts to maintain the biodiversity of different cultivars of quinoa: "Prior to the quinoa boom, typical highland agriculturalists cultivated four or five varieties of quinoa each year, each of which had a unique purpose (i.e., use-value) to them. Some quinoa varieties are resilient to droughts, others to frost or pests and the per acre yields of some quinoas are triple that of others. It was the cultivation of multiple varieties of quinoa that provided a sure harvest in such extreme highland environments and the often unpredictable climate."[10] Keeping in mind the potato farming practices of the highland Aymara, the efforts of the Puno farmers to ensure biodiversity is not at all surprising. It will also come as no surprise that after 2013, when quinoa became a globally traded commodity, there was a propensity to restrict quinoa production to a single uniform quinoa: in other words, to force the implementation of a monoculture.

McDonell rightly highlights that the expansion of uniform quinoa production to the prolific farms of coastal Peru and other regions of the world led to the quinoa bust of 2014, in which highland farmers lost their share of the worldwide quinoa market.[11] Economic impact aside, what is worrisome here is the inclination toward monoculture. In the twenty-first century, we should know better. Again, what could possibly go wrong with extensively planting only one cultivar of quinoa, a crop foreign to most of these new highly productive farms, worldwide? Someday we might find out.

Kiwicha (*Amaranthus caudatus*, amaranth seeds) is a relatively unknown cereal that is even more nutritious than quinoa. According to a National Research Council study from 1989: "These seeds are one of the most nutritious foods grown. Not only are they richer in protein than the major cereals, but the amino acid balance of their protein comes closer to nutritional perfection for the human diet than that in normal cereal grains."[12] Several species of *Amaranthus* were widely cultivated throughout the Americas thousands of years ago. The Spanish first encountered it in their conquest of the Aztecs, who grew *Amaranthus* for tribute in their floating gardens called *chinampas.*[13] The *Amaranthus* endemic to the Andean world, *Amaranthus caudatus,* is a stunningly beautiful crop with colors of purple, red, and gold blanketing the mountain fields where it is grown.[14] The name *kiwicha* is from the Quechua language of the Inca still spoken today throughout the Andean region.[15] *Kiwicha* is best when it is toasted and popped. This crunchy white popcorn can then be added to milk or honey and used as a breadlike batter for chicken or fish. In highland communities, it is also added to *chicha* beer and to the purple corn jello-like dessert *mazamorro morado.* With 13–18 percent protein, *kiwicha* turbocharges the nutritional value of any food to which it is added.[16]

Father Bernabé Cobo differentiated *kiwicha* from quinoa (both are beautiful plants with similar characteristics) and called it *bledo. Kiwicha* made the journey to Europe and was recorded in a publication by the great botanist Carolus Clusius in 1601. Curiously, the plant migrated to Asia where it was planted in the foothills of the Himalayas.[17] But *Amaranthus caudatus,* once a staple of the Inca Empire, became an afterthought after the conquest and remained that way until the 1980s when Peruvian scientist Luis Sumar Kalinowski started a *kiwicha* renaissance in the Inca Sacred Valley near Cuzco.[18] In terms of nutritional potential and worldwide distribution, however, *kiwicha* is still an afterthought.

Amaranthus deflexus L. is a separate species in the same genus as *kiwicha* (*Amaranthus caudatus*).[19] In the highlands of Peru, *Amaranthus deflexus* L. is commonly referred to as *yuyo.* Recall that, in coastal Peru, *yuyo* was a generic term used for edible seaweed. However, in the highland market stalls, *yuyo* is *Amaranthus deflexus* L., cooked with diced potatoes and corn kernels and garnished with *ají. Amaranthus deflexus* L. (*yuyo*) is a type of pigweed. It is called pigweed because in many parts of the world, plants from this genus are used as pig fodder, proving once again how smart pigs are, because *yuyo* is packed with vitamins A, C, and folate, as well as calcium. It is considered a weed because it typically grows between food crops such as corn and potatoes and competes for the nutrients in the soil. In the Andes the weeding was done by turning pigweed into a crop. Indeed, different species of pigweed have been consumed for hundreds of years in different parts of the world such as Jamaica, India, Guatemala, to name just a few.[20] To prepare *yuyo* for consumption, it is first washed, then boiled. The boiled *yuyo* is made into balls, which are then fried with oil and a bit of water. Corn kernels and diced potatoes are added, and the dish is served with rice and/or *cancha* with an *ají* dressing.

Spinach is used as a less exotic substitute for *yuyo,* which I find intriguing because my favorite easily prepared recipe uses spinach. But soon I want to make this dish with *yuyo.* Years ago, I became enthralled with Hedy Giusti-Lanham and Andrea Dodi's cookbook *The Cuisine of Venice & Surrounding Northern Regions*. The recipe for broccoli *"strascinati" all'olio d'oliva* (dragged broccoli with olive oil) was particularly intriguing, and it became a staple in my kitchen.[21] I first made the dish with broccoli raab (*Brassica rapa*), which was readily available in the New York metro region because of the large Italian American population. This type of turnip was well-known in the classical Greek and Roman eras. But as I moved to different regions of the United States and the world, broccoli raab became harder to find, so I substituted spinach. In my preparation I first add the olive oil and then lots of garlic. I cook the garlic until it starts to burn a bit, then add the spinach, stirring rapidly, and then finish with salt and pepper to taste. Over time I started substituting Thai fish sauce for salt, and I added it to the spinach as it started to fry and then covered the pan. The spinach was then both fried and steamed with the fish sauce adding a pungent flavor. The ancient Greeks and Romans used a fish sauce condiment called *garum* in their cooking, so perhaps this dish is a nod to some ancient recipe?[22] At least I would like to think so, and every time I serve this "dragged spinach" with fish sauce I receive rave reviews. I am sure that substituting *yuyo* would be another tasty evolution for the dish, merging ancient Old World and New World traditions. Finally, this treatment of the *yuyo* makes more sense because frying preserves the nutritional content of the leaves better than boiling them for a long time in water.

I would not be exaggerating in classifying *tarwi* (*Lupinus mutabilis* Sweet) as one of the best foods you can put into your body. *Tarwi* is a legume in the plant family Fabaceae, and it is a distinctly separate New World species from the cherished Mediterranean legume *Lupinus albus*.[23] *Tarwi* seeds contain more than 40 percent protein, as much or more than the world's best protein crops, and the protein in *tarwi* is high in the essential amino acid lysine.[24] Evidence for consumption of *tarwi* in the Andean realm goes back about fifteen hundred years, or roughly to the Moche and Wari eras. *Tarwi* designs were used in the decorative pattern of the south coast Wari people, and remains of *tarwi* were excavated in several North Coast Moche sites.[25] *Tarwi* was favorably described in Garcilaso's early seventeenth-century chronicle *Comentarios reales de los Incas*. In the record Garcilaso says the Inca *tarui* [*sic*] is whiter and softer than the Spanish *chochos*.[26] Holguín goes further and lists *chochos* and *altramuzes* (the Spanish word for lupin) as a synonym for *tarui* [*sic*] in his seventeenth-century Quechua dictionary.[27] Both men were obviously comparing *tarwi* to the Mediterranean legume *Lupinus albus*, which had the common name *chocho*. This name is important, because today the most famous *tarwi* dish in the highlands of Peru is called *ceviche de chochos*, and it is interesting to note that the name *chochos* came from a colonial Spanish term for lupins. But *tarwi* will not become an international commodity like quinoa any time soon.

Tarwi is a perfect food in every way except one: it is loaded with bitter toxic alkaloids. *Lupinus mutabilis* Sweet is a cultivar specifically grown because this variety is low in alkaloids. However, two problems arise with *Lupinus mutabilis* Sweet. First, *tarwi* cross-pollinates easily, and in any Andean field bitter and wild varieties are always nearby. The second problem at this point should be abundantly clear. When you reduce *Lupinus mutabilis* Sweet's alkaloids, the plant becomes susceptible to insect predators.[28] In fact, alkaloid-laden *tarwi* is so powerful it is used as an insecticide for other crops.[29] The solution to depending on the persnickety cultivar *Lupinus mutabilis* Sweet is also problematic: lots and lots of water. In the central highland Peruvian town of Huaraz, eating *tarwi* is a way of life. But before most seeds make their way to the market, they are boiled, then rinsed in the river for three days.[30] In a place like Huaraz, which is replete with streams and rivers fueled by the snow peaks surrounding the town, water is not an issue. But planting *tarwi* on Peru's desert coast, for example, would be problematic because of the lack of water. Additionally, other cultivated lupins have specific soil and temperature requirements, which would limit *tarwi* from being developed as a crop in different ecosystems.[31] León points out that *tarwi* can grow at 2,600 feet above sea level, but it thrives at an altitude of ten thousand feet.[32] Therefore, *tarwi* seems poised to remain an exotic Andean superfood.

Ceviche de chochos is also called *ceviche serrano*. *Cevichocho* is a mixture of *chochos* and sliced fish.[33] Peruvian *chochos* are also available from many online Latin American food specialists, so buying them is not a problem. *Ceviche de chochos* is a relatively simple dish to make once you prepare the *chochos*. But detoxifying the *chochos* is a time- and water-consuming proposition, which, it seems from my own survey of online reviews by customers who bought the *chochos*, most consumers hate. I bought fourteen ounces of dried *chochos* online for the ridiculously exorbitant price of $10.00. In Cuzco's San Pedro Market a kilo of dried *chochos* (thirty-five ounces) cost about $2.50. However, I did not return the pricy *chochos* because I wanted to detoxify them myself. I boiled the dried *chochos* in water for two and a half hours, almost burning them in the process. I then soaked the *chochos* in cold water for eight days changing the water in the morning and in the evening. I appreciated doing this once for the experience, but I cannot imagine doing this detoxification often. You can buy detoxified jarred *chochos* in brine online, which are ready to eat, but they will be salty.

In Peru detoxified moist *chochos* are a staple in highland markets. Again, in Cuzco's San Pedro Market they are $1.25 a kilo, which at first seems odd, but keep in mind the water adds a great deal of weight to the *tarwi,* so you get a lot less *chochos* per kilo. After water-treating the *tarwi,* I added chopped parsley, chopped cilantro, and key lime juice to taste. I garnished the ceviche with sliced red onion and chopped tomato and added a pinch of salt. The *ceviche de chochos* can be paired with rice and/or *cancha.* And it would not be ceviche without a small plate of hot pepper on the side. In this case I used *ají mochero* (*C. chinense*), which I grew in my garden. To me *ceviche de chochos* is worth the effort if you are an aficionado of food preparation. Is the dish equal to a ceviche of fresh *ojo de uva*? No. But if you are a vegetarian and are fond of the hot and citrusy flavors of ceviche, which I certainly am, then *ceviche de chochos* is an excellent choice.

If *ceviche de chochos* is a superfood, then *ceviche de chocho y cushuro* is a super-duper-food. *Cushuro* is a generic term, with myriad spellings, for several species of the genus *Nostoc* from the phylum of cyanobacteria or blue-green algae: *Nostoc commune, Nostoc parmeloides, Nostoc pruniforme, Nostoc sphaericum,* and *Nostoc verrucosum.* These algae take the form of gelatinous balls varying in size from a pinhead to a large marble. The terms *elullucbcha, kocba-yuya, llullcha, crespito, and murmunta* are just a sampling of some other common names used for the edible *Nostoc* in the Andes.[34] *Cushuro* is omnipresent in towns and villages in the high Andes, and it is listed in Holguín's early seventeenth-century Quechua–Spanish dictionary under the name *llullucha,* a synonym for *chusuro.*[35] *Cushuro* was likely consumed in the pre-Columbian Inca era although archaeological evidence is lacking. However, there is extensive evidence of marine algae consumption from pre-Columbian coastal cultures, which would hint at the prevalence of freshwater algae consumption in the highlands.[36]

Also, keep in mind the coast is much more intensely investigated because of the difficulties of highland work due to altitude and access. *Nostoc* is an excellent nutrient that adds protein, calcium, phosphorus, iron, and vitamin A to the Andean diet.[37] Today, *cushuro* is consumed in two distinctly separate spaces: the humble restaurants and food stalls near the Andean town's central market and the expensive haute cuisine restaurants in Lima and Cuzco. I first tried *cushuro* at the Nikkei-style (Japanese Peruvian) restaurant Limo in Cuzco. The small blue-green balls complemented a plate that can only be described as a fusion of ceviche and sushi. At that time, even though on the coast I routinely sought out edible seaweed for my ceviche, I did not know about the edible freshwater algae consumed in the highlands. When I asked the waiter if the tiny balls were fish or frog eggs (my best guess), he politely told me they were algae. I have to add that, when I returned to Limo post-pandemic, *cushuro* was absent from the dish.

Virgilio Martínez, the internationally acclaimed chef and owner of the fourth-best restaurant in the world, Central, proudly incorporates *cushuro* into his finest offerings, as does Peru's other international celebrity chef, Gastón Acurio. But food studies scholar Emma McDonell has criticized Virgilio Martínez, specifically for his *Chef's Table* episode on Netflix. She rightly pointed out that identifying Martínez as the discoverer of exotic foods like *cushuro* is disingenuous at best, which is often how Martínez is represented in mainstream culinary magazines and certainly how is he presented in the *Chef's Table* program. To put it simply, *cushuro* is a staple in any highland market and has been one for hundreds of years.[38]

What these chefs (and I am referring particularly to Martínez) are doing here is discovering *cushuro* for the elite neoliberal world—via, of course, a Netflix series. This framing is less offensive and more precise. But what bothered me most about this *Chef's Table* episode was how Chef Martínez harvested the *cushuro* from a mountain pool. In the program, he spent some time picking the *Nostoc* from the pond while showing his assistant which ones were good enough to be served at his table. I am confident someone with multigenerational wisdom guided and/or instructed Chef Martínez in the finer points of harvesting *cushuro*, because some species of Andean

A $2.50 platter of *cushuro* and *chocho* in the restaurant Super Chocho, Huaraz. Photo courtesy of Gladys Jiménez.

Nostoc have neurotoxins. Think mushroom hunters. Years ago, I was a guest of vineyard owner Pete Seghesio on a mushroom hunt near Willits, California. Everybody in our group only picked two types of mushrooms, because they knew these were not poisonous. This was multigenerational wisdom, as the Seghesios have been in Sonoma, California, making wine for five generations. Earlier in the episode Martínez does mention guides and the fact that he spent a year in the Andes and Amazonia learning from locals, but his cavalier collecting of *cushuro* seems at best misleading.[39] There was probably some highlander off camera who guided Chef Martínez to this pool, and I wish that Andean villager was in front of the camera instead.

This criticism is about as grumpy as I will get, because I believe Virgilio Martínez is an excellent ambassador of Peruvian cuisine to the elites of the Western world. These elites and their media promote an aspect of Peru other than Machu Picchu, which is assailed each year by an increasing multitude of tourists. Also, I hope a small percentage of these students of Virgilio Martínez's epicurean classrooms, which is what his restaurants really are, do their homework by visiting some of Peru's more modest restaurants and markets where these exotic offerings are commonplace. In the end, I admire Chef Martínez's genius, because it is no small feat to get the international haute bourgeoisie to pay the equivalent of a week's worth of groceries for a Peruvian family to eat pond scum.

Chef Martínez's audacity does not end with *cushuro,* because he has created an astonishing plate that combines *cushuro* with *tocosh,* a waterlogged fermented potato, which after processing smells rotten. *Tocosh* is made by leaving potatoes (maize and *ullucus* are also treated in this manner) in cold high-altitude pools, protected by straw or mesh bags, for periods ranging from six months to two years. This fermentation goes back to at least the Inca era and is remarkably indicative of a pre-Columbian medicinal knowledge.[40] Researchers using next generation DNA sequencing not only securely identified bacteria in *tocosh* that produce antibiotics but also bacteria that are probiotic. This detailed sequencing also left open the possibility for further study of the beneficial effects of *tocosh* on the body because 50 percent of the bacteria species in *tocosh* have not yet been identified.[41] What Chef Martinez does to *tocosh* is culinary alchemy:

> We first drain the potato for two days, because it's actually very smelly. Then we dry the potato, cover it with three high-altitude aromatic herbs—muna [*sic*], huacatay, and paico—and bake it. A crust forms with the stems of the herbs, and the smell is nice; they [the stems] have a meat aroma. We remove it from the oven, then we add a sauce made from the tree tomato, which grows in the Andes. Next, we cover the potato with the cushuro. The potato skins are also dried and then put on top just to cover. Finally, we add some herbs, and it's finished. This is just one course in the eighteen-course tasting menu and one of two vegetarian dishes on our menu.[42]

Let me try to decipher Martinez's wizardry a bit. *Muña* (*M. mollis, M. tomentosa, M. diffusa,* and *M. andina*) is typically used to make an Andean mint tea, which is said to provide protection from fungi, bacteria, and insects.[43] *Huacatay* (*Tagetes* spp.) is Peruvian black mint.[44] The plant has a very strong flavor and is often used with *rocoto* in highland hot sauce preparations. It is also used in roadside *cuy* (guinea pig) food stalls. *Paico* (*Chenopodium ambrosoides* L.) is a native Peruvian plant that has been associated with antiparasitic properties.[45] The tree tomato (*Solanum betaceum*), or the red *tamarillo,* is in the same nightshade family as the tomato and the potato. The fruit is bitter but packed with vitamins.[46] What Virgilio Martínez has created here is a cocktail of organic drugs and proteins. However, serving this dish at the fourth-best restaurant in the world seems incongruous when the *tocosh* and *cushuro* plate would be better suited to a cafeteria in a hospital ward specializing in the treatment of amoebic dysentery. His creativity and exotic ingredient selection, at least to those unfamiliar with highland markets, is exactly what the acolytes making the pilgrimage to his culinary classroom want. And Chef Martinez will not disappoint his followers.

I want to end this chapter with a decidedly unexotic superfood that was once extremely popular but has now fallen out of favor in the United States. Before doing so, I would like to make clear that the subject of this chapter (superfoods) merits an entire book. Here I just picked out some of the more interesting superfoods, both known and unknown. The Peruvian superfood that is best-known to us is the peanut. In South America and Spain, peanuts are called *maní.* This word, like the term *ají,* is a Cariban word, brought to Peru from the islands of Barlovento by the Spanish.[47] In Mexico and here in South Texas, peanuts are called *cacahuate,* which comes from the Nahuatl (Aztec) word *tlalcacahuatl.*[48]

Peanuts (*Arachis hypogaea*) were domesticated in South America very early on, and the center for this domestication is debated. Southern Bolivia, lowland northwest Argentina, and the Matto Grosso area of Brazil are all advanced as candidates because of the abundance of wild species in these regions. Peanut shells were recovered archaeologically at the North Coast Peruvian site of Huaca Prieta in an area dated to approximately five thousand years ago. *Arachis hypogaea* was also found at several other sites on Peru's north and central coasts.[49] Indeed, by 500 BCE, peanuts were so common at sites in coastal Peru that, according to archaeologists, the floors of some excavated structures resembled unswept baseball stadiums.[50] The finest artistic rendering of this legume (peanuts are not nuts but, rather, legumes like *tarwi*) is the pre-Columbian gold and silver necklaces from the Moche culture. Celebrated Moche specialists Walter Alva and Christopher Donnan aptly describe this beautiful metalwork during their salvage work at the partially looted tombs of Sipán:

> a necklace unlike *any* we had postulated was before us. It consisted of two strands, each with ten beads—five of gold and five of silver. The gold peanuts began over the right shoulder of the wearer and continued to the center of his chest. There the silver beads began, and they continued up over the left shoulder. The beads on the lower strand were larger than those on the upper strand. In this way each large peanut bead was paired with one of the same metal, but of smaller size. Between each pair of beads was a metal spacer bar which connected the two strands and held them in position. The result was a magnificent necklace, balanced in elegant harmony, each side forming the complement of the other.[51]

Such was the esteem in which this legume was held in the pre-Columbian era. And for good reason. The peanut has one of the highest amounts of protein of any vegetable, right up there with its Fabaceae cousin *tarwi*. Peanuts store healthy monounsaturated oil, not starch, with the oils comprising about 50 percent of their weight.[52] From this it is apparent that pre-Columbian people were extremely wise in domesticating the peanut as a food choice, and

I greatly appreciate this domestication because anytime I embark on a trek in the Andes, I visit the highland markets and buy many packs of freshly roasted peanuts for the field.

During the pre-Columbian era, peanuts had already made their way to the Caribbean and it was from there that they first entered Europe. In 1569 peanuts were mentioned in a text written by the Seville physician Nicolas Monardes.[53] In fact, there are more than twenty written records referencing the peanut—beginning with the Bartolomé las Casas's preconquest description from Hispaniola (now Haiti/Dominican Republic) and ending with Jean Baptiste Labat's excellent report from French Antilles of what he called *Pistaches des Isles* in 1697.[54] Although peanuts did not reach France and England until more than a hundred years after the Spanish first encountered them, the Spanish brought them to Asia via the Manila galleons and the Portuguese dispersed them throughout Africa's tropical coast. Indeed, in the 1560s, the Portuguese explorer André Alvares de Almada noted a great quantity of peanuts growing off the coast of what is today Guinea-Bissau. Peanuts spread so quickly throughout Africa that early botanists believed they were endemic to the continent.[55] The occasion of an endemic South American plant thriving in Africa has a modern corollary in chocolate (*Theobroma cacao*), which now has two African nations—Côte d'Ivoire and Ghana—producing over half the world's chocolate![56]

The introduction of peanuts to the North American colonies was even more curious, because the legumes entered as a by-product of the slave trade, where they thrived in the sandy soils of the southeastern United States.[57] Peanuts nourished enslaved people on the ships that carried them on their harrowing journey into bondage and were an integral crop in New World plantations from Brazil to Virginia.[58] In the nineteenth century peanuts were on their way to becoming an established food source in the United States, with the last decade of that century being vitally important because of the invention of peanut butter. And the legume's position as a mainstay "American" food was secured at the beginning of the next century when the recipe for the peanut-butter-and-jelly sandwich was recorded in 1901 by Julia Davis Chandler in the *Boston Cooking-School Magazine*.[59] From then on, for more than one hundred years, children's lunch boxes were often filled with PBJs. Also, in the twentieth century, the great American scientist George Washington Carver (a man who was born enslaved) detailed more than a hundred recipes for the nutritious legume and applied the peanut and its oil to myriad industrial uses.[60]

But the attitude toward peanuts started to change toward the end of the twentieth century, and it hit a free fall of decline in the twenty-first. "By the 1990s, however, the AAAAI's (American Academy of Allergy, Asthma, and Immunology) attitude toward food allergy could not have been more different. Far from being a topic to be snubbed, food allergy was a major public health issue, with the association taking a major role in raising awareness of and taking action about it. Of course, it was not just any food allergy the AAAAI had in mind; it was IgE-mediated, anaphylactic reactions to peanuts and a small number of other foods."[61]

The once celebrated legume is now banished from schools and playgrounds. Warning signs need to be posted if even a small part of the peanut and its oil happens to be on the menu. And this even though Harvard physician Nicholas A. Christakis noted that in the United States in 2008 only 150 people (children and adults) died that year from all food allergies combined, while 50 died from beestings and 100 from lightning strikes in the same year.[62] Historian Matthew Smith finds Christakis's statement hyperbolic but offers a comparison of peanut allergies and asthma. Asthma, which kills several thousand people annually, has far more mortality and morbidity than peanut allergies, yet the condition is far less addressed, likely because pharmaceutical companies make so much money from selling profitable drugs and inhalers. In any case, the growing propensity for parents to have their children avoid peanuts altogether "actually would result in more peanut allergy because large numbers of children would never be exposed to them."[63]

This propensity toward a complete ban on peanuts would be a great shame and a loss for the United States. Peanuts are a food that has appealed to the most diverse groups of human beings in the history of the world. They were celebrated and consumed with relish in the pre-Columbian era, were fed to Spanish and Portuguese sailors, provided nutritious protein that likely saved countless enslaved Africans, made their way to Japan, India, and China (now the world's largest producer) in the early sixteenth century, were championed by perhaps the most famous African American scientist, sustained soldiers in wars, fed spectators at the circus and the games, and were part of an integral lunch for children in the United States for more than a hundred years. And peanuts, like most legumes, replenish the soil, adding back the nitrogen that most plants remove.[64] I hope people heed Christakis's call for an end to the peanut ban cycle of increased anxiety, draconian measures, and preoccupation with nut allergies.[65] If not, the consumption of peanuts, an integral part of US history, could literally come to an end.

Bob's Dragged Spinach/Broccoli Raab/*Yuyo*

16 oz. greens (spinach, broccoli raab, or *yuyo*), patted dry
4 tbsp. olive oil
4 cloves of crushed garlic
2 oz. high-quality fish sauce

In a large frying pan or wok, fry the garlic in olive oil until the garlic burns a little, brown not black. Add the greens and sauté until they start to wilt, then sprinkle with fish sauce and cover. After a minute, stir again and serve. The total cooking time is less than five minutes.

Ceviche de Chochos

8 oz. detoxified *chochos*
¼ cup fresh key lime juice
1 chopped Roma tomato
1 tsp. chopped cilantro leaves
1 tsp. chopped parsley
1 *ají*, chopped, deveined, and deseeded
Salt to taste

Mix the ingredients together and serve with a starch, like a boiled sweet potato, to cut the pepper's heat.

Chapter 7
Not So Superfoods

Considering the myriad plant domestications in the pre-Columbian Andean world, the animal domestication list is surprisingly short. Two high mountain camelids—alpaca (*Lama pacos*) and llamas (*Lama glama*)—are the most utilitarian of the Andean domesticates, followed by a large duck (*Cairina moschata*, Muscovy duck) and finally a small edible rodent (*Cavia porcellus*).[1] I will start with this rodent. Feasting on rodents is a decidedly non-Western thing, and the Old World lacked the New World's plethora of large tasty creatures from the order Rodentia. Among the three I am most familiar with, the first is the smallest *cuy* (*Cavia porcellus*), by far the most abundant Rodentia food source in Peru. In the States we call *Cavia porcellus* guinea pigs. These creatures have been found in archaeological excavations dated nine thousand years before the present day, and they were domesticated several thousand years later. For the earlier dates, guinea pig remains often are charred and with cut marks indicating they were butchered for feasting. However, "after 2500 BC, guinea pig remains appear in contexts suggesting ritual use."[2]

Holguín has the word *cuy* coming from the Quechua language but oddly spelled as *ccoui*.[3] Cieza de León was something of a conquistador foodie savant, but his remarks about *cuy* are negative because he saw many of these animals, along with others, sacrificed in what he called *exorcismos diabólicos* (demonic rituals).[4] Arriaga also had disdain for *cuy*'s ritual use, but because of his role as inquisitor, he records the details of these ceremonies.[5]

Fortunately, Garcilaso had a different agenda, which was to glorify the Inca world, and his assessment of *cuy* resonates with my experience in the highlands. Garcilaso notes that many of the highland commoners did not have cattle, so the guinea pigs were a valuable source of protein that they could raise in their homes.[6] Several times when invited into even the humblest Andean home, I observed a muddle of guinea pigs grouped in a corner near the wood-burning stove. These *cuys* feed on kitchen scraps, which makes raising them convenient. When there is a special occasion, in this case the presence of a visiting gringo, the woman of the house grabbed a *cuy*, snapped its neck, flayed it, and spread it out on the frying pan. I must emphasize that because of the lack of animal protein in the Andes, being offered a plate of guinea pig is a real honor, and you are obliged to eat what you are served. Not doing so would be rude. And by the way, to me *cuy* tastes like chicken wings.

Guinea pigs were imported to Europe early in the conquest era, and they were likely brought to the Caribbean by the Spanish and then brought on to Spain soon after the conquest of Peru. In 1554 the Swiss doctor Conrad Gessner described the guinea pig in his Renaissance natural history opus the *Historiae animalium*. Guinea pig remains from the late sixteenth century were recovered at the town of Mons, in Belgium, and these residues indicate that the animals were kept as exotic pets, not as a food source.[7] Today the Western tradition of treating guinea pigs as adorable pets is sacrosanct in the United States and Europe, so much so that when most tourists see the animals being butchered and eaten, they are aghast. A Peruvian doctor friend of ours told us when her colleague in Maryland went to a pet store to buy several guinea pigs for a feast he was planning, the clerk and the store manager would not sell the *cuys* when they found out the animals would be eaten.

The fried guinea pig experience I described is typically confined to remote areas and humble restaurants not frequented by tourists. Most tourists might try *cuy* in an upscale restaurant in Lima or Cuzco, and the dish will be ridiculously overpriced. I imagine the majority will do this once and then move on to alpaca steaks. Alpaca (*Lama pacos*) is a species of camelid (think, short-legged high-mountain camels with no humps). They are generally grouped with their other domesticated cousin, llamas (*Lama glama*), and their two wild relatives, guanaco (*Lama guanicoe*) and vicuña (*Vicugna vicugna*), even though they are all separate species. Alpaca steaks are a much

Coya guinea pig stall with study abroad students. Photo by Robert Bradley.

better choice for a healthy meal because the meat is very lean. On the contrary, *cuy* meat is oily, and the skin, which is very fatty, is considered by many as the best part of the meal. An Andean farmer or rancher walking all day ten thousand feet above sea level could eat guinea pig daily with no ill health effects, but a Cuzco tourist with cholesterol or cardiac issues should probably avoid *cuy* altogether. If tourists are seeking exotic fare, I recommend they substitute *ceviche de chochos* for *cuy*. However, my recommendation for the healthy and adventurous Cuzco travelers is to try the *cuy al palo* (grilled guinea pig on a stick) in the Sacred Valley of the Inca towns of Coya, Calca, and Lamay.

The Sacred Valley is located right below Cuzco, and it is a must-see when visiting the region because the climate is lovely, the views are magnificent, and the ruins at Ollantaytambo and Pisac are spectacular. Coya, Calca, and Lamay are towns all located less than twenty minutes from Pisac and a little over an hour from Cuzco. These towns specialize in *cuy al palo* with many restaurants (some with large dancing-guinea-pig sculptures) and many roadside stalls. If you visit these towns, don't be put off by the simplicity of the stalls, because many of them serve excellent *cuy al palo*.

For *cuy al palo*, the *cuy* is marinated, then impaled on a stick, and roasted over coals. Next the *cuy* is cut up and served with potatoes and *huacatay* hot sauce. *Huacatay* (*Tagetes* spp., Peruvian black mint) is used as a flavoring throughout Peru, especially in the highlands. The herb is typically blended with *rocoto*, salt, lime, and oil, and sometimes with either evaporated milk or mayonnaise.[8] Grilled *cuy* is less greasy than fried *cuy*, and if it is grilled correctly the skin and meat will be crisp and tasty. Some stands and restaurants serve a side dish that the late great Anthony Bourdain would have relished: guinea pig blood sausage with *huacatay* wrapped in rabbit intestine. Eat the sausage with lots of hot sauce and chase it down with *chicha* beer, which is readily available in both towns.

After missing his mark on *cuy* the conquistador Pedro Cieza de León returned to form as keen observer when he detailed our second rodent. The northern *viscacha* (*Lagidium peruanum*) is one of several species of mountain *viscachas* living in rocky enclaves at high altitudes in Peru, Bolivia, Argentina, Chile, and Ecuador.[9] They are large rodents in the chinchilla family (Chinchillidae), the size of a hare, with a thick warm coat and a bushy tail. They are communal, and they make whistling sounds as a warning when threatened. I have seen many of these animals while trekking through mountain passes at Salkantay and Ausangate. There is a wall of rocky crevices at Salkantay, about an hour before the pass, where they can be easily spotted peeking out of crags. *Viscacha* remains, eaten and skinned, have been archaeologically recovered in numerous coastal and highland sites dating back to almost the end of the last Ice Age.[10] In the early colonial era, Cieza de León noted that their wool made excellent blankets and that they were good to eat.[11] Proving the point, Marcus Zapata's iconic eighteenth-century Cuzco School masterpiece of the last supper in the Cuzco Cathedral has a *viscacha* as the main course of Christ's last meal. According to Garcilaso, the luxurious wool from these animals was specifically used to make clothing for the Inca elites, which mirrors the function of the wool from the *vicuña* (except *vicuña* wool was reserved exclusively for clothing the Inca emperor, upon pain of death).[12] You can buy *vicuña* clothing today, but it must be ethically sourced, the *vicuñas* are corralled (not killed) in an event called a *chacu* and only shorn every two years. Peruvian government paperwork is a requirement for leaving Peru with *vicuña* clothing.[13]

Today the mountain *viscachas* are curiously not a source of clothing or food. This is fortunate for the *viscacha*; its two Chinchillidae cousins *Chinchilla lanigera* and *C. brevicaudata* were hunted almost to extinction for their thick soft fur. *C. brevicaudata*, the short-tailed *chinchilla* has the softest fur, so it is the closest to extinction. *C. lanigera* is domesticated as both a pet and a fur source, but the harvesting of *C. lanigera* for its pelt has not been without controversy.[14] Knowing the *chinchilla*'s fate, I am puzzled as to why the *viscacha*, a known source for food and clothing in Inca and colonial eras, thrives today in numerous herds. The fate of the plains *viscacha* (*Lagostomus* spp.), a delicacy on the menu of fine restaurants in Buenos Aires, adds to the mystery of why the fine-furred mountain cousin remains unmolested.[15] The plains *viscacha*, notably a separate genus from the mountain *viscachas*, inhabits the easily accessible lowlands of Argentina, Bolivia, and Paraguay and is considered a pest. In contrast, the northern *viscacha* (*Lagidium peruanum*) thrives in the frozen and unpopulated Andean highlands above fourteen thousand feet. Andean farmers and herdsmen frequent these heights, so hunting and harvesting the northern *viscacha* for food and its pelt would seem plausible. Yet I have never eaten one, nor do I know of a highland restaurant that serves northern *viscacha*. I am certain some opportunistic and hungry Andean campesinos might pick off a *viscacha* or two when leaving the high country, but there seems to be no tradition of harvesting these animals.

Textile scholars Elena Phipps and Caroline Solazzo have noted images of *viscachas* in both colonial tapestries and books continuing into the eighteenth century. They have also pointed out the many references to the mountain *viscachas* in early colonial documents. Yet "in spite of these numerous references, very few preserved textiles with viscacha hair have been identified."[16] Why? Perhaps the *reducciones* were a factor?

These edicts were enforced by Viceroy Francisco de Toledo in the late sixteenth century. When Toledo took control, the viceroyalty was in chaos. The conquest of Mexico was a devastating event for the Aztec and their Triple Alliance, but it was a disciplined military campaign for the Spanish. In contrast, the conquest of Peru was a fiasco. First, the Spanish executed the Inca emperor without the king's permission, and then a blood feud broke out between different factions of conquistadors. After Spanish success in the initial battles, the Inca launched a protracted guerilla war that went on for decades. Finally, in 1558, the Spanish were horrified to find out that the descendants of the Inca kings were still practicing their old religious beliefs in secret. Viceroy Toledo arrived in 1569 to crack down and bring order to this important colony. He ended the civil war by capturing the jungle redoubt of Vilcabamba in 1572, and he instituted the policy of *reducciones,* which forced Andean people down from their high-altitude ancestorial homes to the more accessible valley towns near roads and rivers. This forced resettlement was put in place so the Spanish could more easily control the native population.[17] If the conquest had destroyed most of the pre-Columbian way of life, the *reducciones* razed the traditions that had endured after the conquest. But the *reducciones* could have saved the *viscacha* from decimation by moving traditional population centers away from the high-altitude crags where these valuable animals thrive. Then the imagery of the *viscacha* in the late colonial era could be nostalgic, explaining the paucity of textiles with *viscacha* hair.

Cuniculus paca (Linnaeus, 1766), commonly referred to as the lowland paca, is a neotropical, opportunistic nocturnal rodent that inhabits broadleaf forests from Mexico to Paraguay at altitudes up to sixty-five hundred feet above sea level.[18] In Peru, the lowland paca is called the *picuro* or *majáz*. *Picuro* is the term used in the high northern forests of Peru and in the southern Manú National Park area, while *majáz* is the term for *C. paca* in the lowland department of Loreto and the city of Iquitos. The lowland paca has white spots on its brown fur, which resembles the coloring of a white-tailed deer. The paca can weigh up to twenty pounds. Because of its size and tasty flesh (it tastes like pork), this animal is one of the most hunted species in Latin America. The harvesting of their populations by hunting led to the domestication of *C. paca*, but these breeding farms are hampered by the fact that *picuro* female only gives birth to one offspring every two hundred days.[19] The lowland paca may be in the Rodentia order, but they do not reproduce prolifically.

Cuniculus paca and its close cousin the highland paca (*Cuniculus taczanowskii*) are not recorded in the documents chronicling the Viceroyalty of Peru. This omission makes sense, because these animals live in the cloud forest and jungle, areas that it took the Spanish decades to understand and explore. Even the Inca had problems in the high jungle, having suffered their worst defeats to the ethnic groups inhabiting these forests; and yet, during the guerrilla war, the Spanish were stymied several times when the Inca disappeared into the jungle.[20] The lowland paca was recorded by the Spanish during their conquest of Mexico. The Nahuatl term for *C. paca* was *tepezcuintle*, which the Spanish would ignore. Instead they used the term *perro* (dog) for this large rodent.[21]

I first tried *picuro* near a village in the remote southwest corner of the Peruvian department of San Martín. We were four days from the town of Leymebamba on the Utcubamba River on our way to the Chachapoya (a pre-Columbian cloud forest people conquered by the Inca) structure called Huaca La Penitenciaría de la Meseta.[22] As we made camp on a remote river, the sun started to go down quickly as it inevitably does in these deep mountainous river valleys. After dark, Milver, a member of the community of Chilchos, vanished into

Milver Hidalgo Briones with a freshly killed *picuro*. Photo by Robert Bradley.

the forest with a single-barrel shotgun, a small bag of corncobs, and a flashlight. He returned an hour later with a freshly killed *picuro*.

His technique for hunting the paca was simplicity itself. He baited the trail with corncobs and then waited a few feet away in the dark. When he heard the *picuro* eating the cobs, he shone the light in the animal's eyes, causing the *picuro* to freeze, and then shot it. Milver told me this way of hunting *picuro* was so effective that there were very few left near his village, but since we were deeper in the forest, he knew they would be plentiful after dark. Of course, flashlights are a modern invention that no *picuro* hunter would have had access to until the beginning of the twentieth century. Pre-Columbian settlers to the Americas would have used the snare, a very ancient hunting device, and possibly bows and blowguns to bring down the *picuro*, and certainly, their hunting success would be diminished compared to Milver's deadly flashlight and blast.

Our preparation of the *picuro* was also not complicated. After the paca was dressed and skinned, it was cut into pieces, put in a pot with river water and potatoes, and then boiled over a fire for about forty minutes. In the southern Peruvian jungle towns around Manú National Park, *picuro* is typically prepared *asado* (grilled), and in the northern city of Iquitos, located on the Amazon River, *majáz* is made escabeche-style—that is, cooked with garlic, onions, vinegar, and so on.[23] To me the *picuro* meat tasted like pork. Even with this no-frills treatment, the meal was outstanding. The next time I have *picuro* meat, however, I will use the recipe for *cabrito norteño*.

Cabrito norteño (northern-style kid goat stew) is one of the most famous dishes coming out of the celebrated gastronomic center of North Coast Peru. The recipe's pre-Columbian bona fides are manifested in the use of *chicha*, *loche* squash (*Cucurbita moschata*), and *ají amarillo*. We have already seen lengthy discussions of *chicha* and *ají amarillo*, so here the focus will be on the ancient *loche* squash.

I mean *ancient* because this squash was first domesticated by the hunter-gatherers who built some of the first human structures ten thousand years ago in the Nanchoc Valley in northwestern Peru.[24] Interestingly, *C. moschata* was found near Huaca Prieta during the archaeological Phase V, dating to approximately four thousand years ago. I say "interestingly," because for several summers during the first decade of the millennium, my wife and I stayed in different apartments in the fishing village of Huanchaco, about fifteen minutes north of the city of Trujillo and about a forty-five-minute drive to the Huaca Prieta archaeological site where the remains of *loche* were found. During our summer stay, my wife's mother would often come down to visit and help us with our infant daughter, Gabriella. Every time she came by bus from Chiclayo, a coastal city three hours north of Trujillo, she carried a *loche* with her because she could not find the squash in either the Huanchaco or the Trujillo market.[25]

To Sonia, my mother-in-law, making *cabrito norteño* without *loche* is a sacrilege. Sans *loche*, she says, the stew sauce tastes like water. Sonia told me the addition of *loche* gives the stew a sweet-and-sour

Loche squash (*Cucurbita moschata*) on a bed of peppers. Photo courtesy of Jim Sykes.

aspect, which is the reason *cabrito norteño* is considered one of Peru's greatest gastronomic offerings. Chef Ricardo Sulem Wong says in his opinion "*loche* flavor is rich and intense with hints of coconut, carrot and lucuma" (*Pouteria lucuma*, a favored fruit of the Moche people).[26] And Sonia's taste for *loche* is not surprising, because towns around Chiclayo such as Lambayeque, Monsefú, Puerto Etén, Reque, Ferreñafe and Mórrope are famous centers for growing *C. moschata*. Indeed, the department of Lambayeque (Peruvian departments are like our states) includes all these towns and is the epicenter for *loche* production in Peru.[27] Cucurbitaceae botanists (squash specialists) have noted that *loche* is a high-quality landrace (cultivar) of *Cucurbita moschata* Duchesne that is grown only on the North Coast of Peru and is practically unknown elsewhere.[28] *Loche* was lionized in high-quality Moche ceramics, and a fine example of a Moche *loche* bottle is in the Metropolitan Museum of Art's pre-Columbian collection.[29]

The main ingredient of *cabrito norteño* (kid goat stew) obviously arrived with the Spanish, as did the red onion and rice that always accompany the dish. Although these imports are now part of this recipe's DNA, the meat source for a pre-Columbian antecedent was most likely dog or deer.[30] The second ever-present side dish served with *cabrito norteño* are Mayocoba beans (*Phaseolus vulgaris*), also known as "Canary beans" or "Peruano beans." These beans also have solid pre-Columbian bona fides, likely having two areas of domestication: Mesoamerica (Mexico) and the Andes.[31] Plant remains of *P. vulgaris* were recovered from the Nanchoc Valley in northwestern Peru dating back at least seven thousand years ago.[32] And indicative of the permanence of *P. vulgaris* as a pre-Columbian foodstuff, the beans were recovered from the archaeological investigation at Huaca de la Luna, on the outskirts of the modern city of Trujillo, dating approximately fifteen hundred years ago.[33] So these beans have been a staple of the North Coast diet for thousands of years. The beans are soaked overnight and then cooked for an hour and a half over low heat. The ceviche complement boiled yuca (*Manihot esculenta*) is also a common side for *cabrito norteño*.

The side of rice on a platter of *cabrito norteño* is a foreign import that came to Peru with the Spanish, but on the North Coast rice figures prominently in almost every meal—except for ceviche. Rice is mostly grown in northern Peru, an epicenter being the hot and humid valley town of Bagua. With its abundance of rice paddies and plethora of *motos* (three-wheel motorcycles with a rear enclosure), Bagua seems more like a southeast Asian locale than an Andean one. But I must add that the *flor* rice from my wife's North Coast village of Ferreñafe has been called the best rice in the world.[34]

I cook Peruvian-style rice almost every day for my family. First, I fry a chopped clove of garlic in oil, then I add rice and water, and boil with salt. Simple but delicious. The red-onion hot-pepper side on a plate of *cabrito norteño* serves more as a condiment than as an accompaniment. The onion is sliced very thin and is often soaked in salted water to take out the sting. The pieces are then mixed with key lime juice, hot pepper, and salt with the heat and acidity of the garnish complementing the meaty richness of the stewed goat. My wife calls this relish *sarza,* but if you look online it is referred to as Peruvian salsa criolla.

Muscovy duck (*Cairina moschata*) is a silly name right up there with *Capsicum chinense,* because the duck's origin has nothing to do with Moscow, just like the South American hot pepper *C. chinense* has no relation to China. There is much conjecture as to why the fowl is called Muscovy, but the following explication seems plausible. "A host of theories have been advanced as to how this native American became known by a Russian name. A reasonable suggestion that is logistically possible maintains that these birds were transported to England by the Muscovite Company during the 1500s. Since it was a common practice to attach the importer's name to products it traded, it would have been an easy transition from Muscovite Duck to Muscovy."[35] I am inclined to believe this explanation because of the misnaming of our favorite holiday bird, the turkey. Turkish traders brought large fowl from Africa to Europe, so the English named the birds turkey after the merchants. Then when the pilgrims arrived in Massachusetts, they applied this appellation to the large bird found there, *Meleagris gallopavo* (Linnaeus, 1758).[36] But there are other possibilities for the name Muscovy: perhaps the name is because of its musky smell (*moschata* from the Latin *moschatus,* "musky"), or perhaps it is a reference to the *muysca* Indians of Nicaragua's Mosquito Coast. Additionally, the first part of the duck's two-part scientific name is *Cairina,* meaning Cairo, which is also confusing.

Cairina moschata was first recorded on the island of Guadeloupe during Columbus's second voyage with the fowl dispersed throughout Europe during the early sixteenth century.[37] Today wild Muscovy ducks are found throughout the neotropical Americas from Mexico through Central America, western Peru, and down to Argentina and Uruguay.[38] *Cairina moschata* is a very large forest duck that nests in trees near bodies of water. In the wild, males can reach up to ten pounds, females seldom reach five pounds, and domesticated males and females are a few pounds heavier.[39] Several regions have been suggested as the domestication site for these ducks, including the Central Andes, the southern Caribbean shore, Paraguay, the Argentinian Chaco, and the Amazon.[40] Regardless of the origin, the Muscovy ducks' mating and eating habits incline the fowl toward domestication, where they thrive.[41]

The archaeological record of *Cairina moschata* is poorly known, and this deficiency is compounded by the difficulty of differentiating between wild and domesticated remains.[42] However, a body of artwork from the pre-Columbian Moche people reveals the prominent role these ducks played in Moche culture. The Moche specialist Christopher Donnan recorded thirty samples of art related to the Muscovy duck, but he noted that there were probably three hundred more samples in private art collections.[43] *Cairina moschata* was also recorded in the early colonial record. Garcilaso noted the indigenous people had ducks that were smaller than geese but larger than the ducks in Spain. They called them *ñuñuma,* which he postulated came from *ñuñu* (meaning to suck), because when they ate, these fowl appeared to suck down their food. Holguín confirms this identification in his Quechua dictionary, stating that *ñuñuma* was the term for the domesticated duck.[44] I need to mention here that a cross between *Cairina moschata* and the Asian Peking duck (*Anas platyrhynchos*) produces a sterile hybrid mule or mulard duck, which is a meat source for pâté de foie gras.[45]

Today, one of the most famous dishes from the North Coast gastronomic center is *arroz con pato* (rice with duck). This is a famous signature dish like *cabrito norteño,* closely associated with the North Coast city of Chiclayo and the surrounding towns Lambayeque, Monsefú, Puerto Etén, Reque, Ferreñafe, and Mórrope. There are many variations of the special recipe (typical ingredients and preparation are given below). I have several comments concerning the various recipes for *arroz con pato* that are available on the Internet. First, as per my discussion of *ají amarillo,* you likely won't have access to this fresh pepper outside of Peru. In some preparations the dried version of *ají amarillo* (called *ají mirasol*) is used, which is readily available in a jarred paste form. This paste is added to the pot with the duck drippings, along with the garlic and onion. On the positive side the paste probably gives the dish a smoky flavor. The downside is that the paste comes from a jar, and I imagine it is supposed to substitute for *loche* but I am sure by now you understand—there is no substitute for *loche*.[46]

Héctor Solís, the head chef of Chiclayo's most famous and most expensive restaurant, Fiesta, fries grated *loche* with the duck, onions, and garlic before removing the duck to make the rice. He also uses *chicha* instead of black beer.[47] The fully fermented and aged *chicha de jora* would be best for this dish. The blended mix of cilantro (leaves only) and spinach included in my mother-in-law's recipe gives the rice flavor and the greenish color associated with *arroz con pato*. But the next time I have access to a kitchen in Peru, I would like to substitute *yuyo* (*Amaranthus deflexus* L). This would keep the green but add nutrition and another interesting pre-Columbian ingredient.

I started this chapter with exotic animals and ancient recipes, but I want to go from sublime to ridiculous by ending with Peruvian fast food. The golden age of modern fast food commenced during the peaceful years following World War II. In 1949, as Ray Kroc launched McDonald's and Glenn Bell started Taco Bell, two Swiss Peruvians named Roger Schuler and Franz Ulrich observed a local cook at La Hacienda de Santa Clara in Chaclacayo cooking whole chickens.[48] The cook had impaled the chickens on a spit, which he cranked by hand to turn the birds over a wood fire. Schuler and Ulrich must have been inspired by the same fast-food muse as Kroc and Bell because they soon opened a restaurant called La Granja Azul and started selling whole chickens for five Peruvian sols (about a dollar and a quarter). Ulrich was the engineering partner with his contribution being the invention of a *rotombo*, a six-bar rotisserie oven that could hold up to eight young chickens on each bar. The original rotisserie burned *algarrobo* firewood (the most traditional fuel) or charcoal made from *algarrobo*. Ulrich's colleague Heriberto Ruiz went on to advance the oven's design to use charcoal and gas and, in the process, became the largest manufacturer of these ovens.[49] The name Schuler should be familiar from the master distiller and pisco impresario Johnny Schuler. Roger was Johnny's father, and it is apparent that business acumen and marketing genius ran deep in the Schuler family, because the father was the force behind Peru's famous fast food, and his son promoted the pisco industry and the seventeenth-century Caravedo Pisco distillery. Today, Caravedo (Pisco Portón) is the most widely marketed and most expensive pisco available in the United States.

On any given day in Peru, *pollerías* throughout the country are busy serving *pollo a la braza* (grilled rotisserie chicken) from a six-spit grill. The *pollerías* are active during the main lunchtime meal but become even busier in the evening with dine-in and takeout. The traditional wood for grilling chicken comes from the coastal desert mesquite trees *Prosopis pallida* and *Prosopis limensis*, which are in the same legume family (Fabaceae) as *tarwi* and peanuts.[50] These trees (carobs, or more precisely, *algarrobas*) have fruit that is made into flour and syrup, which are then put into smoothies, cocktails, and bread. For good reason, because the fruits are full of sugar and proteins, including the essential amino acid lysine, and vitamins E, C, and potassium.[51] *Algarrobo* trees have shaded the coastal deserts of Peru for millennia; their remains have been identified in Phase I archaeological context at Huaca Prieta dating to at least ten thousand years ago.[52] Fortunately, and unfortunately, *algarrobo* trees also make excellent firewood, which has led to gross overexploitation of the trees on Peru's thin strip of desert coast. One study alone has *algarrobo* charcoal from rural locations on Peru's North Coast being sold to large urban centers like Trujillo and Chiclayo for use in *pollerías*.[53] A trip to northwestern Peru's Bosque de Pómac Historic Sanctuary can give you some inkling of how magnificent these *algarrobo* forests once were. But in other parts of the world's dryland ecosystems, *P. pallida* thrives to the point that it is sometimes considered an invasive species, and is hence denied any protected species status.[54]

A recent study determined that 37.3 million grilled chickens were sold each year in Peru—that is, more than ten *pollos a las brazas* for each Peruvian on an annual basis.[55] That number even seems a bit conservative to me, because in one taxi drive from Lima's Jorge Chávez International Airport in Callao to the ritzy Miraflores barrio you will pass a mind-boggling number of *pollerías*. And this density of chicken restaurants is repeated in every coastal city. Even the small villages and towns on the coast and in the highlands have several busy *pollerías* from which to choose.

Pollo a la braza is served with french fries, salad, and different sauce condiments, the most important being the *ají* sauce. Roger Schuler never marinates his chicken, and he insists they are delicious with just salt, but each *pollería* chain and each mom-and-pop *pollería* has a different marinade recipe made from myriad seasonings like rosemary, *huacatay*, dark beer, cumin, soy sauce, *sibarita/ají panca*, and so on. The *ají* sauce typically showcases local ingredients, and the quality and taste of this condiment is just as important as the chicken entree.[56] Often the salad is lettuce with a ranch-style dressing, but my favorite is the beet, carrot, and avocado offered at restaurants like the upscale *pollería* Pardo's Chicken. Beets and carrots are ancient Old World plants brought to Peru by the Spanish, but avocados are from the Americas. Most scholars believe that avocados originated in highland Mexico, but avocado remains have been uncovered at Huaca Prieta dating back to Phase I (from 14,000 to 7,500 years ago).[57] In Peru, avocados are called by the Quechua name *palta*; not *aguacate*, which is from the Aztec *āhuaca-tl*.[58] Cieza mentions the fruit *palta* several times in his early conquest era record.[59] Holguin's early seventeenth-century Quechua dictionary has *palltay* meaning *la palta* (either the tree or the fruit).[60] Peruvian *palta* tend to be larger and creamier than avocados from other places.

My recipe for *pollo a la braza* has evolved over years of making the dish for my family. First, I wash the chicken and cut off excess fat, skin, and the fleshy tail protuberance. I break the chicken's breastbone to keep the ribs from stretching out and drying the breast meat.[61]

Then I marinate the bird for a day. Here in South Texas I grill with either charcoal briquettes containing shavings of mesquite wood or mesquite charcoal from Mexico. Using the briquettes is much easier because they don't burn as hot as the mesquite charcoal (more on that in a minute). I have a Weber kettle grill with the rotisserie kit that includes a motor, a skewer or shaft with a wooden handle, two spit forks, and a ring that elevates the rotisserie. The last item is very important. I want the skewered chicken elevated because I do not use a drip pan and the dripping grease will cause flare-ups that can burn the outside of the chicken if it is too close to the coals.

At the bottom of the kettle, I evenly place one layer of coal. Then I tie the chicken with string in two places: one around the breast and wings and one around the legs. Next, I impale the chicken with the shaft and secure it with spit forks at either end. After lighting the coals, I wait about fifteen minutes and then place the shaft end into the motor and the other end into the ring support. Next, I turn on the motor and put the lid on the grill. I check the grill temperature and chicken temperature, with a meat thermometer, every fifteen minutes. I like having the temperature for the grill high at first, 500 degrees plus, then have it gradually decrease. After forty-five minutes I check the chicken temperature every five minutes because I do not want the chicken to cook past 165 degrees. I take mine off the grill at 160 because the bird will continue to cook a bit after it is removed from the grill. When cooking, the flare-ups will cause the grill to smoke. Therefore, I have a long extension cord for the motor, so the grill is always away from the house and back patio area. Finally, my cleanup is easy because the grease burns in the fire.

Using lump mesquite charcoal is much more difficult, but if it is done correctly the skin is cooked to perfection, slightly charred and crispy. The chicken must be higher above the charcoal. To do this, I first place another ring I have for making grilled pizzas on the kettle, then I stack the rotisserie ring on top of that. This elevates the chicken about six inches higher, with a total distance from the flame being about eighteen inches. After lighting the charcoal, I wait from twenty to twenty-five minutes because charcoal takes longer to reach the optimum burn. When my mesquite is grey and shooting sparks, I know it is ready. With lump mesquite, I check every ten minutes because the size of the mesquite charcoal pieces varies. But the process is the same. I want a higher temperature at first to char the skin, then a slow reduction in temperature toward the middle and end of the cooking cycle.

Finally, I have tried many different hot sauces for the chicken including *sarza* or Peruvian salsa criolla; the previously mentioned *ají,* salt, key lime, and oil with evaporated milk; and my own hot mayonnaise (made of egg yolk, *ají amarillo* paste, salt, and lime all blended while gradually adding vegetable oil). But my favorite condiment is *rocoto* (peppers, key lime juice, and salt mixed in a food processor, see the recipe for Bob's *Rocoto* Hot Sauce in Chapter 3). Again, how many veins and seeds you leave in the mix depends on your guests' tolerance for hot foods. Sometimes, here in South Texas, we get *manzano* peppers (*Capsicum pubescens*) grown in Mexico, but the *rocoto* paste sold in Latin American markets and on the Internet is a somewhat satisfying substitute.

Of course, black pepper (*Piper nigrum*), garlic (*Allium sativum*), and cilantro (*Coriandrum sativum*) are not native to Peru. However, they are so commonly used in Peruvian cooking it seems as if they were endemic. *Sibarita* or *ají panca* is a dried mild variety of habanero, sold in packets in every bodega in Peru.

Sonia's *Cabrito Norteño*

2 lbs. kid goat
1 package *sibarita* (*ají panca, C. chinense*)
4 tbsp. cilantro
Two cups of aged *chicha de jora*
4 fresh *ají amarillo* (*C. baccatum*)
¼ *loche* (*Cucurbita moschata*)
Half a red onion
Two cloves of garlic
Black pepper
Salt

First the cabrito is cut into pieces, scored (my preference is *deshuesado*, or deboned), and put into a bowl. My mother-in-law then grates about half the *loche*, skin and all. The other half is diced into small pieces. Finely chopped cilantro, grated *loche*, deveined and deseeded *ají amarillo* cut into 3-inch strips, pepper, chopped garlic, salt, and the *chicha de jora* are all added to the cabrito in the bowl and mixed by hand. The ingredients are then left to marinate for an hour. Later, she heats the chopped onions and diced *loche* in a large pot with oil, then cooks the marinated cabrito over low to medium heat for an hour and a half. Be careful with this dish, because if you have a taste for stews, you will find *cabrito norteño* addictive.

Sonia's *Arroz con Pato*

4 duck legs and thighs
2 cans black beer or a strong *chicha*
½ cup vegetable oil
1 cup red onion, chopped
4 garlic cloves, chopped
1 tsp. ground turmeric
1 tsp. ground cumin
1 cup cilantro leaves
1 cup spinach leaves
½ cup grated *loche* squash
Salt and pepper
3 cups long grain white rice
1 *ají amarillo* (*C. baccatum*)[62]
1 red bell pepper, diced
1 cup green peas
Salsa criolla (*sarza*)

Fry the duck first with the garlic, onion, and *loche* until it is browned. You can also marinate the duck in the beer and/or *chicha* for a time if you like. Other versions of this recipe use a pisco/*chicha* mix, which I find a bit odd because pisco has strong flavors that would conflict with the *chicha*. The duck is then put aside. In the same pot with the duck drippings, Sonia puts in the peas, the garlic, and the chopped cilantro leaves and spinach that have been blended with a cup of water. This mixture is then fried. After it is fried, she adds 1 cup of water and 3 cups of black beer and boils the mix for 15 minutes. Then she adds 2 lbs. of washed rice. Finally, she places thin cut strips of *ají amarillo* and red bell pepper on top.

Bob's Rotisserie Chicken Marinade

1 whole chicken, cleaned
5 cloves of garlic
½ cup of soy sauce
Juice of 4 key limes
Sibarita/ají panca or paprika

Chop the garlic and mix the ingredients. Put the chicken in a large Tupperware bowl and pour the marinade over the chicken. Use your hands to rub the marinade into the body cavity. Place the lid securely on the bowl, then shake and turn the bowl upside down. This will ensure that the marinade covers the whole chicken. Place the bowl in the refrigerator overnight.

Chapter 8

Everything You Always Wanted to Know about Coca but Were Afraid to Ask

For the past ten years I have included a session on coca chewing in my Peru study abroad course. Coca chewing is a perfectly legal and common practice in Andean nations, yet even when I relay this information to my students, they approach this exercise like some clandestine adventure. Ultimately the undertaking is woefully disappointing, because 99 percent of my student travelers are repulsed by chewing coca. Many visitors to South America, like my students, become acquainted with coca chewing on their quest to experience the Andean world. On any given day, the parking lot of Cuzco's Alejandro Velasco Astete International Airport, the main launching point for Machu Picchu, is crowded with Quechua-speaking women hawking small bags of a dozen or so leaves to hotel-bound foreigners. When the tourists conclude their business of scoring coca, they typically retreat to their rooms and chew the leaves in private because the practice has a feel of illegality to them, probably reminiscent of their first line or their first toke. This touristic experience is completely spurious, because the vendors almost never sell the foreigners *cal*, quicklime (CaO), or the little balls of quinoa ash, gum, and lime called *llypta* (*llipta, llujt'a, ilipta* and *torca*).[1] Quicklime is a strong alkali that liberates the alkaloid cocaine from the leaves.[2] But ash is also used as a processing agent, because approximately one-third of the chemical composition of wood ash is CaO.[3] The availability of wood ash in almost every human circumstance seems to indicate that cinders were the more primitive precursor to quicklime, which is more difficult to manufacture, but in Peru the use of *cal* is more common in the north and the use of *llypta* in the south.

Without these alkalis, chewing coca leaves has very little effect on the human body and is therefore a placebo just like the *mate de coca* tea served in upscale Cuzco establishments. But be prepared, even though the boiled water solvent only releases small amounts cocaine into your system, the *mate de coca* will still cause you to flunk a urine analysis test back home, if you return to the States and test within twenty hours of teatime.[4] The vendors, of course, know that a ball of *llypta* should complement any purchase, free of charge, but at the Cuzco airport most sellers will feign ignorance if they are challenged for not freely providing this catalyst. Imagine if the store that sold you cigarettes refused to give you matches. To a certain extent the reluctance of these merchants is reasonable, because giving a complementary lesson on masticating coca leaves with a strong alkali in one's mouth would be a daunting task for any campesino intent on making a few easy sols for the day. Also, imagine the fear the vendors would create for the tourists if they pulled out a pressed chemical ball of some white powder *cal* to seal the sale? But two and a half miles away from the airport, a *libra* (one-pound bag) of coca leaves can be purchased in the San Pedro market, with complementary *llypta,* for approximately the same price as the small green plastic packages of leaves at the airport.

The cost for the airport's small bags can be fifteen sols (five dollars) or more, which is an outrageous price that only remains viable because of the naivety of the visitors steadily flowing into the region. In other areas of Peru—the upper Marañon in the northeast, for instance—a *libra* bag of *tupa coca* leaves, available there but not in Cuzco, will cost about fifteen sols, *cal* (CaO) included. However, small bags of coca leaves are common in other southern Andean regions. In La Paz, Bolivia, for example, street hawkers sell coca in small packets like those sold at Cuzco's airport, but these bags have a ridiculously low retail price (in cents) and come with a ball of *llypta.*[5]

Unlike the solitary chewer alone in a luxury hotel room and without alkali, in Andean communities coca chewing is a social practice that reinforces communal relations.[6] When an Andean coca aficionado chews coca, the leaves are masticated in the mouth, and the chewer can then either bite off a pinch of *llypta* or add small amounts of CaO from a lime gourd to the masticated leaves lining their inner

A one-pound bag of coca leaves with four balls of *llypta.*
Photo by Robert Bradley.

cheek.[7] An elegant lime gourd is a small container typically finished with horn at the top and accented with a horn-handled pin, which fits snugly to the top of the gourd. The two-inch pin could be more succinctly described as a spoon. Imagine a small pin that fits into a bottle-shaped sheath. The chewer licks the metal spoon and dips the metal into the gourd to extract lime. Getting the right amount of quicklime on the end of the spoon requires practice. Also, the quality and causticity of the quicklime will vary greatly according to where it is sourced. Biting off small amounts of *llypta,* while lacking the elegance and ceremony of the lime gourd ritual, is more suited for the beginner. The *llypta* or quicklime activates trace amounts of cocaine in the leaves and puts the drug, and nutrients, into effect.

Coca-chewing session in the remote village of Chilchos.
Photo by Robert Bradley.

Prowess in chewing is an acquired skill focusing on the right mixture of macerated leaves and lime. The juice from the process should be kept in the mouth as long as possible, before the inevitable spitting. Repeated swallowing of the juice is not recommended because of symptomatic loss of appetite and diarrhea, but this would only occur after swallowing quite a bit of juice. A quid of coca leaves can pleasantly last for a half hour or more depending on the variety of coca and the amount of leaves the chewer can add to the mash in the cheeks without triggering the gag mechanism. Ultimately the quid becomes stale, and the entire ball of leaves needs to be expelled. The process is then repeated. In Andean communities these chewing sessions, typically beginning around dusk, can last well into the night and are often accented with a few cigarettes, a great luxury in Andean villages, and a bottle of aguardiente.

Despite the mystique associated with coca chewing, most foreigners (and my students) are typically revolted by the experience. Chewing coca can be compared to chewing tobacco. Developing a proficiency in dipping smokeless tobacco is also an acquired skill. The chewer must keep the proper amount of tobacco in their mouth and then expel the tobacco and spit at the right time and in the right place. Like chewing coca today, this practice is more suited to a rural environment where freedom of the hands for hard work is often required. Specifically, both chewing tobacco and chewing coca provide a respite for the agricultural worker. The cosmetics of tobacco chewing have kept this custom from gaining popularity in the modern world, even during the tobacco industry's twentieth-century product offensive. Similarly, coca chewing also entails practice. Spitting is also required, and it is interesting to note that the habit of expectorating is not considered rude in Andean villages as it is in the States. The green mash on the lips and teeth, necessary by-products of the process, also presents a cosmetic barrier to most Western travelers. Therefore, they are not open-minded enough to acquire the skill necessary to become a *coquero*. Finally, the Western travelers who have been instructed correctly and given coca with the proper alkali are almost always disappointed by the mild effect of the leaves. Westerners coming from the land of fentanyl, OxyContin, and Prozac will consider the "high" from chewing coca as hardly worth the considerable effort. Or to paraphrase the anthropologist Enrique Mayer: chewing coca is like going through the Andes on a donkey whereas using cocaine is like streaking through the region in a jet airplane.[8]

Coca chewing is also frowned upon by the upper classes in western South America. To the Eurocentric elite of Peru's coastal cities, chewing coca is anathema because the practice is most indicative of the indigenous working class. Take, for example, this provincial Andean paradigm. In the northern highland capital city of Chachapoyas, a group of small business owners who have worked their way up from their humble campesino origins chew coca in secret. The current prosperous state of these burghers has forced them to be clandestine so that they are not seen as regressing to their previous role as country bumpkins.[9] But coca chewing was once indicative of high status in the pre-Columbian Andean world, and ceramics displaying elite Moche figures enjoying coca are a fine example.[10]

There are more than two hundred species of coca throughout the Americas, which throughout history have been largely ignored. Instead, human beings have focused, and domesticated, two species of Erythroxylum. Why? Because the two species *Erythroxylum coca* and *Erythroxylum novogranatense* contain cocaine.[11] Recently, Dillehay et al. have published archaeological evidence that coca chewing took place eight thousand years ago in the Nanchoc Valley (Zaña River) about fifty miles southeast of the North Coast city of Chiclayo. They identified the coca leaf in this archaeological find as *Erythroxylum novogranatense* var. *truxillense*.[12] Curiously, Erythroxylum only appears late at the Huaca Prieta archaeological site, about four thousand years ago. The species and variety excavated as plant remains was *Erythroxylum coca* and not *Erythroxylum novogranatense* var. *truxillense*. Granted, the Nanchoc Valley site is about sixty-five miles from Huaca Prieta as the condor flies, but it is still worth pointing out that a more flavorful variety was already being cultivated on Peru's North Coast thousands of years earlier.

Previous archaeological research has confirmed that ancient coastal Peruvians used bottle gourds and Mytilus shells to hold their quicklime.[13] But Dillehay et al. showed evidence that the earliest example of coca chewing at Nanchoc was practiced using *llypta* (in this case quicklime powder mixed with water, ash, and salt) as the alkali.[14] Certainly, in this ancient time, bottle gourds were likely valuable because the myriad uses for them would range from simple containers to floaters for fishing nets.[15] Dillehay et al.'s evidence of *llypta* as the prototypical caustic agent for coca chewing is interesting because this crude method of quicklime delivery seems to precede the use of a gourd.

Coca acts as a mild stimulant and helps ward off fatigue, hunger, and thirst, which might be the reason it was cultivated thousands of years ago by ancient South Americans. The term *coca* comes from an Aymara word for "bush" or "tree," but in the pre-Columbian era, each variety of coca had its own unique indigenous appellation. Botanist Timothy Plowman was responsible for isolating the four varieties of the two previously mentioned Erythroxylum species, which contain cocaine, and in particularly the most important of the four—*tupa coca.*[16] *Tupa* is the Quechua word for "royal," and it is spelled many ways (remember, Quechua was never meant to be written, at least not in any way we can imagine). The most familiar spelling of *tupa* for Westerners is *tupac,* the first name of the famous deceased rapper. But this appellation of high esteem was also used in the name of the greatest Inca conqueror Tupa Inca.

The term *tupa coca* defines a special type of coca with small and tasty leaves. It is first referenced in the early seventh-century Quechua dictionary of Jesuit Diego González Holguín, and the good priest emphasizes the flavor of the leaves.[17] Plowman also identified the two species of *Erythroxylum, Erythroxylum coca* and *Erythroxylum novogranatense.* He further classified each species of plant into two varieties. *Tupa coca,* the focus of this study, is scientifically classified as *Erythroxylum novogranatense* var. *truxillense.*[18] This variety of coca was preferred by the Inca nobility.[19] *E. novogranatense* var. *truxillense* is named after the Peruvian North Coast city of Trujillo or, more specifically, the parched region that typifies this part of northwestern Peru. All species of coca flourish in consistent temperatures, from 50° F to 90° F, and like three of four related varieties, Novo *truxillense* thrives in altitudes of from sixteen hundred feet to five thousand feet above sea level, although the altitude range of Novo *truxillense* extends upward another thousand feet to about six thousand feet above sea level. But, in contrast to the other three varieties, *E. novogranatense* var. *truxillense* grows in the dry mountain foothills of coastal Peru.[20] Wintergreen oil (methyl salicylate) is found in the leaves of *E. novogranatense* var. *truxillense.* This essence has made the leaf popular with the campesinos who chew the plant on a daily basis.[21]

Tupa coca has always been cultivated for its taste. *Tupa coca* is so aromatic that the Peruvian historian María Rostworowski has even suggested it was used as an ingredient in pre-Columbian food preparations.[22] Indeed, the process of chewing coca mimics the ancient method of making corn tortillas (also hominy for posole and menudo), which are the daily bread of the Mesoamerican world. I want to be clear here, I consider coca a food.[23] Nixtamalization (from the Nahuatl *nixtamalli*) is a technique in which maize is soaked in a solution of quicklime (CaO), just as coca is soaked in a solution of quicklime and saliva in the chewer's mouth. Quicklime is produced when calcium carbonate ($CaCO_3$) is heated in a kiln.[24] The chemical reaction is $CaCO_3$ (Calcium carbonate) plus heat equals CaO (calcium oxide or quicklime) plus CO_2 (carbon dioxide). The source of calcium carbonate in this decomposition can be myriad: pulverized limestone, chalk, travertine, marble, marl, seashells, and coral.[25] Seashells are a very pure form of calcium carbonate, and this organic material was utilized extensively by pre-Columbian people as an agent.[26] Besides breaking the corn down and making it physically easier to work into tortillas, the quicklime-and-water mixture releases niacin and vitamins in the corn and reduces incidents of protein deficiency. A coca chewer also processes the coca with the strong lime alkali, and in the mouth of the chewer the trace amounts of cocaine are extracted along with the vitamins B_1, riboflavin, and vitamin C.[27]

In northern Peru the *puros* or *caleros* are commonly used in the practice of chewing coca. There are many pre-Columbian examples of lime gourds but often the archaeological spoons are made from precious metals that are likely indicative of the chewer's elite status. In the pre-Columbian era, then, coca chewing was defined by the use of the *puro*.[28] Many scholars believe coca chewing was restricted to elites in the pre-Columbian world, but others, including John Murra, suggest that the ordinary activity of coca chewing drew interest from both peasants and lords in the pre-Hispanic era.[29] After the arrival of the Spanish, the population of aboriginal

South America was decimated by disease, and the remaining indigenous populations were given coca for stamina to perform the back-breaking labor required in the colonial age.[30] Coca was the balm of choice for the indigenous workers in the silver mines of Potosí, Bolivia, undergoing some of the most extreme working conditions the world has ever seen.[31]

Today the tradition of using *puros* to hold the quicklime for coca chewing continues in the northern part of Peru and Colombia but not in the former Inca imperial core around Cuzco. Artisanal-style gourds made in the Utcubamba River Valley of the department of Amazonas are unknown in Cuzco and La Paz, Bolivia. A few years ago, a woman selling coca leaves at the bottom of the salt mines at Moray, just outside of Cuzco, was amazed by the artisanal gourd I showed her, but she seemed completely unfamiliar as to its use. When asked for an alkali to accompany the coca she produced *llypta*. Similarly, a woman in La Paz, Bolivia, selling inexpensive bags of coca leaves was enthralled by the carved artwork on my northern Andean *puro* but was unaware of its function. The gumlike ball of *llypta* she provided me had a rather sweet taste indicative of sugar as a flavor additive, likely to offset the bitter taste of the Huánuco coca. Keep in mind, *Erythroxylum novogranatense* var. *truxillense* is not planted in southern Peru and Bolivia, so the coca produced in these regions does not have the exceptional flavor components of *tupa coca*. Also, in the southern Andes some ritualized elements of the pre-Columbian tradition for chewing coca with quicklime appear to have been lost.

This is curious because the city of Cuzco was the "navel of the universe" for the greatest pre-Columbian state in South America, the Inca Empire. One would expect the tradition of chewing coca with elite paraphernalia (*puros*) to have endured in this place. But perhaps the inclination to associate coca with workers, which developed out of the colonial age, made the practice socially impractical for the mestizo aristocracy. Indeed, *puros* are not used by *coqueros* in and around the north-central Peruvian town of Huaraz. This Andean town is located near the three-thousand-year-old pre-Columbian center of Chavín de Huántar and less than one hundred miles from the Inca provincial hub of Huánuco Pampa, near the city of Huánuco, the namesake for Huánuco coca.[32] The region figures prominently in the history of at least two pre-Columbian population centers, yet *puros* are mostly absent from the coca-chewing tradition in this area. Therefore, a vital question for future study must be "At what geographical point going southward in Peru does the *puro* become a forgotten pre-Columbian heirloom?" Perhaps this investigation could be tied to a comprehensive survey of the type of calcium carbonate used in the pre-Columbian manufacture of CaO. For example, quicklime containers (gourds) and spatulas could be examined for shell and travertine.

Human manipulation of coca, leading to the variety known as *tupa coca,* could have begun in the Upper Marañon Valley of northeastern Peru.[33] I have worked in this region for more than a decade, and during my research I learned to appreciate the importance of coca chewing to the farmers of the northeastern Andes. Any discussion about the direction of a particular pre-Columbian trail or the location of an important ruin was always prefaced by a long period of *chac bola*: coca chewing.

The area that Dillehay et al. implied was the point of origin for *tupa coca* likely corresponds to the coca-growing region west of the Yumal Pass, which leads into the Marañon River Valley district of Cocabamba. The coca from this valley is celebrated for its delicacy and flavor, and certainly this description is consistent with pre-Columbian references concerning *tupa coca* or more precisely *E. novogranatense* var. *truxillense*.[34] The Cocabamba coca price is about thirteen Peruvian *nuevo soles,* or a little less than five US dollars for a *libra* (pound) of coca leaves—at least that was the price in the Utcubamba Valley when I worked there at the beginning of this millennium. The price is likely a bit higher now, but probably not that much. To a tourist in Cuzco buying a small bag of coca leaves for several dollars this price might seem like a bargain, but to the cash-strapped farmers of Chachapoyas this cost is dear. The leaves are indeed a luxurious necessity for their daily labor. I must add that from experience I know *E. novogranatense* var. *truxillense* dissolves faster in your mouth when chewed. Again, the leaves are more delicate and flavorful, and perhaps this makes the archaeological traces of the practice of chewing *tupa coca* more difficult to uncover?

There are two locations in Peru associated with *E. novogranatense* var. *truxillense,* but I need to point out the regions that produce the coveted *tupa coca* used for coca chewing account for only 3 percent of the total production of coca leaves in all of Peru. Although the data I am using here is from a 2008 Peruvian government survey, I would imagine the statistics are similar today, except for an expansion of production in the VRAEM.[35] The major Peruvian coca-growing regions involved in supplying *narcotraficantes* are detailed in this study—that is, the Apurímac-Ene and the peripheral La Convención–Lares areas, today defined by the multi-river acronym VRAEM, and the Huallaga region in the northeastern forest, where the remnants of the defunct Shining Path guerilla group remain. These areas grow *Erythroxylum coca* var. *coca,* Huánuco coca, whose broad and bitter leaves have always been linked to cocaine production.[36]

The two areas where *E. novogranatense* var. *truxillense* is grown are far removed from these cocaine-trafficking regions. Upper Marañon River Valley is the first area. This two-mile-deep river canyon forms a rain shadow, so the growing conditions down in the canyon are dry and similar to the area of Peru west of the Andes. I can attest to the flavor and quality of the coca grown here from the experience of chewing for many years in the Utcubamba region of northeastern Peru.

My most memorable chewing episode occurred while climbing up to Mount Shubet, the tallest peak in the relatively low-lying (at least for the Andes) department (state) of Amazonas, with the ethnohistorian and former mayor of the city of Chachapoyas Dr. Peter Lerche.[37] While we were ascending a windy and mist-shrouded trail, Peter and I observed a mule train appear out of the fog, guided by two campesinos, with bales of coca leaves as cargo. As we approached they appeared to panic. Two gringos coming out of the mist in this remote location was exceedingly rare. But after exchanging a few words with Peter, one of them looked at my mouth.

I had started to chew coca in the night because of the cold and had continued all through the morning trek, so my lips and teeth were stained green. Frankly, I had already chewed so much coca I was worried about my supply of leaves. Chewing and trekking in the Andes were at this point equivalent for me, and I had been doing both at a furious pace for hours. I was running out of coca, and this paucity would greatly add to the trip's difficulty. The two men told Peter they were bringing coca to the Utcubamba, probably to the famous market at Yerbabuena, from Cocabamba.[38] This was not exactly a legal enterprise, and that is the reason they were alarmed at seeing two gringos hiking alone in this remote place.

Coca is controlled in Peru like cigarettes are regulated in the States. For example, in the Chachapoyas market, the sanctioned coca stall is ignored because the leaves are dry and overpriced. But a few blocks from the Plaza de Armas, a knock on the door of a nondescript house, along with a request to purchase a *libra* (pound) bag of coca, will be quickly answered. In every region the semi-illicit coca vending varies, and avoiding taxes and regulation is the justification.[39] In any case, these entrepreneurs were suppling the vendors in the Utcubamba with some excellent coca. And to keep us happy, and somewhat complicit in their venture, they gracious filled our plastic bags with tasty *tupa coca* from the Upper Marañon for free.

The second locale associated with *E. novogranatense* var. *truxillense* is the Alto Chicama region approximately fifty miles northeast of the Peruvian coastal city of Trujillo (the namesake for this variety of coca), almost directly east of the pre-Columbian site of Huaca Prieta. According to the Peruvian government's 2008 study monitoring coca, this region specializes in growing *E. novogranatense* var. *truxillense*.[40] This area is also near the old-growth forest of Coto de Caza

Sunchubamba. This region I consider a possible pre-Columbian source for the difficult-to-transport *rocoto* hot pepper, which was found in a seven-thousand-year-old excavation at Huaca Prieta. Once again, I reference the enduring prevalence of certain flora and fauna in Peru over time and space. I am perplexed that Dillehay et al. found no plant remains of *E. novogranatense* var. *truxillense* at Huaca Prieta. From a geographical perspective, Huaca Prieta is certainly closer to the Alto Chicama than the very early coca center of Nanchoc Valley, uncovered by Dillehay's team in 2010.[41] But before leaving this discussion, I would like to point out that *E. novogranatense* var. *truxillense* is the flavoring agent for Coca-Cola, and the company to this day gets the *tupa coca* leaves from the Alto Chicama region.[42]

I need a moment here to clarify my position on the difference between coca and cocaine, and be assured, I have pondered this dichotomy for decades. I consider coca leaves to be food. Cocaine is a drug. Cocaine was first isolated from the leaf by Albert Niemann in 1860, and in my opinion, the powerful alkaloids from this substance have been a blight on the face of humanity since it was first concocted.[43] In contrast to cocaine's sordid 150-year flirtation with humanity, benign instances of coca chewing were recorded eight thousand years ago, and I am sure this date is conservative.[44] So, the ubiquitous Andean T-shirt that says *La hoja de coca ne es una droga* (the coca leaf is not a drug), in my opinion, speaks the truth.

Many years ago a good friend of mine, Jimmy Ward, who also happened to be a New York City narcotics cop, told me he wished all the fields of coca in the Andean nations were sprayed with chemicals and destroyed. From his perspective, witnessing firsthand the daily destruction of people's lives, I completely understood. He also retired from the force in the wake of the Violent Crime Control and Law Enforcement Act of 1994, because, if I can paraphrase his words, as an African American he was tired of putting young black males, booked for being in possession of small amounts of drugs, in prison for the rest of their lives. This law and the sentencing disparity were aimed at crack cocaine, which had become a scourge in urban African American communities. If, as I believe, coca is benign and cocaine is perverse, then crack is outright pornographic.

But several long Friday night discussions, while feasting on Chinese food after judo class, I convinced my friend that eliminating coca from the Andean world, likely a political and economic impossibility, would cause even more devastation to the indigenous and campesino populations. Coca is not only a social lubricant; it helps alleviate hunger and fatigue, and probably also altitude sickness. Unfortunately, there is curiously insufficient data supporting this last assumption. However, this is obvious to anyone who has hiked remote Andean trails and has witnessed many campesinos with green lips negotiating an impossible vertical path while carrying an even more incredible load. I believe an amendment should be made to the United Nations articles on the worldwide prohibition on coca (to be reviewed shortly) so as to allow for the worldwide production and consumption of the variety *E. novogranatense* var. *truxillense* (*tupa coca*). Again, this plant has been considered unique since the pre-Columbian era, and it is not at all suitable for illicit production of cocaine.[45] *Tupa coca* is grown on dry foothills, and it does not adapt to the clandestine jungle fields preferred by narcotraffickers. The production of *tupa coca* could be readily monitored by aerial reconnaissance.

In the nineteenth century the flavor component of the coca leaves was sought out by commercial interests seeking an additive for tonics: the most famous of which was Coca-Cola.[46] Full disclosure: I love Coca-Cola, particularly the Latin American Coca-Cola variant made with cane sugar and marketed in glass bottles. I was stunned and saddened when they introduced coca-less Coke in the mid-1980s. Thankfully that politically correct experiment was an abject failure.[47] Coca-Cola has firm Andean indigenous bona fides. Coca-Cola is the real Inca Kola, although Coca-Cola now owns both brands. However, a more apt name for Coca-Cola would be Moche-Cola, after the pre-Columbian people of northern Peru who thrived fifteen hundred years ago in the area where the modern city of Trujillo is located. The Alto Chicama was their territory. Several hundred years later the Chimú people dominated the same area, so Chimú-Cola would also be appropriate and perhaps has a better ring to it.

One would think the marketing geniuses at Coca-Cola would celebrate the beverage's links to the pre-Columbian Andean world, especially considering how indigenous identity is finally being celebrated, and rightly so, in the twenty-first century. Instead, the company runs away from this connection. Think how many times each day people all over the world see the word *coca* in Coca-Cola and make no association to the Andean bush. The word is hidden in plain sight, and I am sure that is intentional, because any positive reference to the *tupa coca* plant by this company was rendered impossible by the scandal that erupted at the beginning of the twentieth century over cocaine in the soft drink. Paul Gootenberg has extensively researched the almost cultlike relationship between the soft drink company and coca. Originally Coca-Cola did have small amounts of cocaine added to the drink mixture, and cocaine was removed in 1903, as people became aware of the drug's addictive qualities. However, the euphemistically named Merchandise No. 5 (extract of *E. novogranatense* var. *truxillense*) remains in the beverage to this day with only the dismal 1980s interlude as the exception.[48] The negative attention caused by initially adding cocaine would haunt the Coca-Cola company for decades, and the scandal has fostered a culture of denying any and all association with the plant.[49] In the 1980s, the height of the cocaine epidemic, a company spokesperson definitively stated that "ingredients from the coca leaf are used but there is no cocaine in it and it is all overseen by regulatory authorities."[50]

I want to take a minute to detail the strange process whereby Coca-Cola gets de-cocainized *tupa coca* into the soft drink. First, the company must acquire the coca leaves from where *E. novogranatense* var. *truxillense* is cultivated in northern Peru, the Alta Chicama region. Next, the company imports 175,000 kilos annually and ships them to the Stepan Chemical Company in Maywood, New Jersey, where the coca is de-cocainized.[51] The original company that initiated this process was Maywood Chemical Works, which after being family owned for decades was sold by family members to Chicago's Fortune 500 company Stepan Chemical Corporation in 1959.[52] The cocaine produced from this de-cocainizing process has always been a source of embarrassment to the Coca-Cola company, particularly when political interests focused on the dangers of uncontrolled narcotics in the early twentieth century. Maywood's and later Stepan's unprocessed cocaine was farmed out to companies that were expert in refining cocaine like Merck (yes, that Merck) and Mallinckrodt. The end product was then used for medical applications. Over time this whole system was overseen by Coca-Cola executives in collusion with the Federal Bureau of Narcotics (later the DEA) and was strictly regulated. And this special arrangement enabled Coca-Cola to stifle any coca-leaf competition.

In 1961, after years of political pressure from the United States, the UN Single Convention on Narcotic Drugs deemed coca cultivation a crime indistinguishable from the cultivation of the opium poppy.[53] But the intolerant tone of convention article 26 was immediately mitigated by article 27: "The Parties may permit the use of coca leaves for the preparation of a flavoring agent, which shall not contain any alkaloids, and, to the extent necessary for such use, may permit the production, import, export, trade in and possession of such leaves."[54] Article 27 specifically releases the Coca-Cola company from any wrongdoing in producing their internationally appreciated beverage. The article also gives the company an almost worldwide monopoly on coca-flavored products, because after 1961, no international startup would have the means or connections to create a system of de-cocainizing their product before marketing.

The real question here is Why should they have to de-cocainize their products? Remember cocaine remains mostly inactive in coca leaves without an alkali or a strong solvent such as ethanol. Without some catalyst the cocaine in Coca-Cola would pass unnoticed through your system (more on alcohol and coca in a minute). I suppose the absence of cocaine extraction would make a rum and Coke an even more pleasant experience, but for a normal cocaine "high," you would need to put down many of these cocktails, and it is likely you would become an alcoholic or get diabetes before any signs of cocaine addiction. Coca-Cola's original sin of using both cocaine and coca leaves forced the expensive and secretive de-cocainizing process.

A problem arises when we look at the specifics of producing Merchandise No. 5, the de-cocainized coca extract used to make Coca-Cola. Plowman has pointed out that extracting cocaine from *tupa coca* is an extremely difficult process, and therefore this variety of coca has always been poorly suited for cocaine production. "*E. coca,* Trujillo coca has long been valued for coca-flavored wines and tonics. In the last century [the nineteenth century], it was highly prized in the North American pharmaceutical industry for medical preparations. Because it is difficult to extract and crystallize cocaine from Trujillo coca leaves, this variety has rarely been exploited for commercial cocaine production."[55]

I presume the rare time cocaine is extracted from *tupa coca* is in the production of Coca-Cola's Merchandise No. 5. This unnecessary process, pointless because the alkaloids in the leaves are not activated, is very demanding, but I presume the early-twentieth-century chemists of Maywood Chemicals were up to the task. Gootenberg's research details the many elaborate steps Coca-Cola has used to rid themselves of cocaine, the annoying by-product this process produces.[56] If it was not for Gootenberg's detailed history of Coca-Cola's cocaine diaspora, I would speculate that the *E. novogranatense* var. *truxillense* used for flavoring still has alkaloids in the leaves, but this cocaine remains inactive in Coca-Cola. To daydream for a second, perhaps Huánuco coca is also processed at the facility as a ploy to hide the lack of *tupa coca* processing? I am also troubled by the chemicals that would be used to de-cocainize the *tupa coca.* Niemann's description of his synthesis of cocaine has a toxic medley of chemicals that include not only the previously discussed alcohol and CaO but also sulfuric acid, mercury nitrate, and sodium acetate.[57] Granted, twentieth-century chemists could have developed a cleaner cocaine-extracting process, but the illegal jungle cocaine-processing labs that plagued South America in the 1980s and 1990s were notorious for contaminating the forests. So, would you really want to use what is basically a by-product of cocaine production as a flavoring agent? This is pure speculation, and I certainly hope my musings do not cause Coca-Cola to repeat the disastrous coca-free abomination that was New Coke.

The inspiration for John Pemberton's seven-secret-ingredient concoction, which resulted in Coca-Cola, was Vin Mariani. Indeed, Pemberton's initial drink was Pemberton's French Wine Coca, which he claimed was superior to Vin Mariani. But as he was approaching the fin-de-siècle dawn of the temperance movement in the United States, Pemberton wisely moved on to a coca-infused soft drink.[58] Vin Mariani was the invention of an established Corsican chemist, Angelo Mariani, who named his wildly successful mixture of Bordeaux red wine and Bolivian coca leaves Vin Mariani à la Coca du Pérou.[59]

Mariani was working at the end of the nineteenth century, so his classification of coca lacked Plowman's years of botanical work. He refers to Bolivian coca, which he classifies as *Erythroxylum coca,* as being more delicate than Peruvian coca. He was oblivious to the fact that there were two separate species of cocaine-producing coca plants—*Erythroxylum coca* and *Erythroxylum novogranatense*—with two varieties in each species. It is then difficult to definitively state that Mariani used *E. novogranatense* var. *truxillense* in his Vin Mariani because of the deficiency in the nineteenth century's botanical information. However, the following quote reveals that Mariani was a coca aficionado and suggests it is quite possible he did have access to *tupa coca* for his Vin Mariani. He wrote: "The Coca leaf from Bolivia, smaller than the Peruvian leaf, is as much esteemed as the latter, although it contains less of the alkaloid. It possesses so exquisite and so soft an aroma, indeed, that the *coqueros* seek it in preference to any other."[60] This passage certainly seems to describe *E. novogranatense* var. *truxillense* precisely, even though the species and the variety were not identified at this time. Recent research on alkaloids in *E. novogranatense* var. *truxillense* used leaves from the Chapare and Yungas regions of Bolivia, so perhaps this variety has a history of cultivation in this country, and this region could have been the leaf source for Mariani's drinks and elixirs.[61]

Mariani was aware of the use of coca in the Inca state and in the colonial era, but he was as unaware of the term *tupa coca* as he was of the existence of *E. novogranatense* var. *truxillense*, even though he could have inadvertently stumbled on to the variety. Mariani was well informed about the use of *llypta* as an alkali in coca chewing, and he even provided several illustrations of paraphernalia in his book.[62] He mentioned that the first step Albert Niemann used to isolate cocaine in his 1860 experiment was to soak the leaves "in alcohol (at 55°), for several days."[63] This first step likely inspired the invention of Vin Mariani and the more potent Elixir Mariani. Vin Mariani involved soaking coca leaves in wine for a period of time. Mariani describes the method as follows:

> Vin Mariani contains the soluble parts of the Coca plant. The combination of Coca, with the tannin and the slight traces of iron which this wine naturally contains, is pronounced the most efficacious of tonics. The fresh Coca leaves that we employ, after careful selection, come from three different sources and are of incomparable quality. It is this that gives to our wine that special taste and agreeable aroma which renders it so acceptable to the sick. It is likewise to the combination and preparing of these three varieties of Coca leaf in our wine that we can attribute this important fact; during more than thirty years, no matter in how large doses taken, Vin Mariani has never produced cocainism, nor any other unpleasant effects.[64]

The amount of time the leaves are steeped in wine is omitted but, considering the great lengths Coca-Cola later used to guard their production secrets, perfectly reasonable.

Vin Mariani was wildly popular. In 1909 aviator Louis Blériot brought a small flask of Vin Mariani with him on his record-setting first flight across the English Channel. The coca wine was lauded by the inventor Thomas Edison and the writer Henrik Ibsen. The French sculptor Rodin was a fan as were the early science fiction writers Jules Verne and H. G. Wells. Mariani even mailed a case to Pope Leo XIII, which resulted in Mariani being awarded a papal gold medal.[65]

Elixir Mariani was made by mixing the coca leaves with a spirit. According to Mariani, the beverage was "three times as highly charged with the aromatic principles of the Coca leaf as the Vin Mariani."[66] It is important to point out that Mariani did not add cocaine to either beverage. But he did add "two milligrammes of Cocaine hydrochlorate [*sic*]" to his Pastilles Mariani. He was very candid about the use of either coca or cocaine or both in each of his concoctions.[67]

Gootenberg has noted that, although the Germans were fixated on cocaine (especially after Niemann's sythesis, the French and English were fascinated by the history and use of the coca leaf. The United States relished both coca and cocaine in the nineteenth century until the prohibitionist reaction of the early twentieth century, which ultimately threw the baby (coca leaves) out with the bathwater (cocaine).[68] To reiterate, I see coca leaves as a food or as, perhaps more accurately, a tonic. I believe the 1961 UN mandate prohibiting the worldwide use and import of coca leaves should be repealed, particularly in reference to *E. novogranatense* var. *truxillense*. Remember, it is very difficult to extract cocaine from *tupa coca*, and today the sophisticated Westerner has easy access to a plethora of pharmaceuticals that are just as powerful as or more powerful than cocaine.

Coca leaf use should be systematically and extensively studied as a remedy for altitude sickness, as a weight-loss supplement, and as a flavoring agent for myriad products. The Peruvian historian María Rostworowski considered coca leaves, specifically the fragrant leaves of *E. novogranatense* var. *truxillense*, as a herb as important as *ajíes* in pre-Columbian cooking.[69] Today, the master Peruvian chef Virgilio Martínez Véliz, the founder of Central Restaurant (one of the top fifty best restaurants in the world), routinely uses coca in his cerebral preparations, thematically focused on Peru's unique topography, flora, and fauna.[70] A few years ago, the first indigenous president of Bolivia pleaded in a *New York Times* opinion column to "let him chew his coca leaves."[71] We should listen to former President Evo Morales, a spokesman for many Andean people, who let his people chew their coca, saying roughly, "But give them only the best and let them chew *tupa coca*."

Finally, let us return to the acclaimed Peruvian *aguardiente de uva* (grape brandy), pisco, and specifically the famous cocktail made with this brandy, the pisco sour. Production of this quintessentially Peruvian spirit dates to the beginning of the seventeenth century. I will once more stress that this is an extraordinarily early date for distribution of a distilled beverage.[72] It is even more amazing when we consider the production and distribution of this spirit took place in colonial South America. The pisco sour consists of pisco (preferably a *puro* Quebranta) mixed with key-lime juice, sugar in the form of simple syrup, and egg white. The preferred method of blending the components is to shake the mix by hand, a technique perfected into a form of performance art at the Museo del Pisco. But more commonly, the cocktail elements are put in a high-speed mixer, then poured, and topped with a few drops of Angostura bitters.

Of interest here is a recent variant of this classic Peruvian drink, the coca sour, which is the modern-day return of Vin Mariani, or perhaps more specifically, the Elixir Mariani. The legendary Peruvian chef Don Cucho La Rosa is credited with creating the archetypical coca sour, but the cocktail also is linked with another founder of the Novoandina cuisine movement, a journalist, Bernardo Roca Rey.[73] The elements for the cocktail are identical to the pisco sour except that the pisco base—which consists of pisco, again preferably *puro* Quebranta or mixed *acholado*—is infused with coca leaves. Remember, I referred to the aromatic and nonaromatic grapes used in the production of Peruvian pisco, therefore a common nonaromatic Quebranta is an excellent base for a coca sour. The leaves should be

Garnishing a coca sour at Museo del Pisco. Photo by Robert Bradley.

steeped in the pisco until the spirit has a green tinge, and most of the bartenders I asked said this takes at least seven days. Because alcohol is a strong solvent, cocaine is released, and the beverage will have all the pleasant effects of Mariani's concoctions. There is a world of difference between a coca sour and a coca tea. They both contain cocaine, but because alcohol is a stronger solvent, more alkaloids are released in the coca sour than in the coca tea.[74] Keep in mind that drinking both will produce a positive urine analysis test within twenty hours of imbibing. But at least drinking coca sours will make it worth your trouble.

For the past six years I have frequented the Museo del Pisco restaurant/bar in Cuzco while leading my Peru study abroad trip. Of course, my beverage of choice there is their superb hand-shaken coca sour. This is not finished with an Angostura bitter splash but, instead, is garnished with coca leaves.

Cuzco is the epicenter of the coca sour phenomena for several reasons. Tourists go a bit coca crazy when they arrive at the Alejandro Velasco Astete International Airport in Cuzco. First, they are met at the airport by the coca hawkers, then they are presented with coca leaves and tea, ubiquitously served gratis, at every guesthouse, hostel, and hotel in the city. Coca is everywhere and for good reason. Most tourists are oblivious to the fact that Cuzco is only a few hours from the VRAEM, the largest narcotrafficking region in all of Peru. But the flow of coca leaves into Cuzco and the Sacred Valley of the Inca is the only place the two divergent worlds meet. From what I have seen, all the coca in the markets and hotels in Cuzco is, unfortunately, *Erythroxylum coca* var. *coca* (Huánuco coca). With the proximity of the VRAEM in mind, this makes perfect sense. So, the teas and coca sours of Cuzco are all flavored with a coarse and less tasty variety of coca that is more suited to cocaine production. The second-rate flavor makes me wonder what a coca sour would taste like if the pisco was infused with *E. novogranatense* var. *truxillense*? Unfortunately, the areas of production for *tupa coca* are far from the gringo trail, the heavily traveled tourist route from Lima to Cuzco to Machu Picchu and back.

To pisco connoisseurs, the coca sour and the pisco sour are gaudy creations that only diminish the excellent flavor of the hand-crafted Peruvian piscos. There is a great deal of value in this way of thinking. To find out how much, the next time you visit Peru, I urge you to locate a serious bar and ask for a shot of Biondi Pisco puro Albilla in a brandy snifter. However, pisco puro Quebranta is a less venerated spirit that serves as the most frequent base for pisco sours in Peru.[75] And since the National Institute of Culture of Peru declared the pisco sour a UNESCO Cultural Heritage in 2007, despite the pisco purists the cocktail is not fading into obscurity any time soon.[76] I would recommend a similar elevation for the coca sour, and I hope the Peruvian government will specify in the resolution that the coca sour must be made with *E. novogranatense* var. *truxillense*. This resolution would showcase some of the best things Peru has to offer:

their unique four-hundred-year-old brandy, an inventive handmade twentieth-century cocktail, and the finest coca, called "royal" by the Inca. Elevating this beverage could also start the move toward decriminalizing *E. novogranatense* var. *truxillense*. Obviously, the ineffectual war on drugs is coming to an end in the United States, so hopefully the ridiculous skirmish that resulted in prohibiting coca leaves will end with the acceptance of *E. novogranatense* var. *truxillense*.

Chapter 9
Foreign Influences

In this chapter I will dispense with the scientific names for non-indigenous South American flora and fauna because the origins and history of those plants and animals are beyond the scope of this book. Four exceptions are the tomato (*Solanum lycopersicum*), the collared peccary (*Dicotyles tajacu*), *culantro* (*Eryngium foetidum*), and *hierba lusia* (*Aloysia citrodora* Paláu). Even though the tomato was domesticated in Mexico, *S. lycopersicum*'s likely ancestors were wild Andean tomato species. Although the peccary was abundant throughout the neotropical Americas, there is very little evidence of this animal in the pre-Columbian record. The focus here will be on when they arrived and what influence these plants and animals had on Peruvian cuisine. Endemic *culantro* has an almost identical flavor to Old World cilantro, and endemic *hierba lusia* tastes like Asian lemongrass.

Christopher Columbus's legacy has not fared well with today's revisionist historians. Certainly, his voyages were more celebrated than scrutinized in the past, and perhaps reassessment was inevitable. However, the Columbian Exchange ushered in hundreds of years of ever-increasing globalization, which has only recently been framed as a possibly dubious phenomenon.[1] Looking back at the sixteenth century with twenty-first-century eyes is a pointless endeavor, because the first few decades of that early era were marked by a tumultuous trade of flora and fauna, both from the New World to the Old World and vice versa. And this frenzy was inevitable.

The Spanish arrived in the Americas as a bare-bones military force lacking the logistical support for the frontline forces. Initially, the conquistadors survived by eating and drinking indigenous foodstuffs. They equated unfamiliar foods—llamas, guinea pigs, potatoes, and quinoa, for instance—with familiar foods such as sheep, rabbits, truffles, and rice.[2] A prime example of this association is Pedro Cieza de León's first record of quinoa: "There is another very good food they call *quinoa,* which has a leaf like the Moorish chard; the plant grows almost to a man's height, and produces tiny seeds, some white, some red, of which they make drinks and which they also eat boiled, as we do rice."[3]

After the discord of the initial conquests gave way to colonial management, the growing Spanish population in the Americas longed for the animals and foods of their homeland.[4] This was compounded by the Spanish belief that Incan crops were inferior to, for example, wheat and barley.[5] Remember, according to the chronicler Cieza de León, wheat fields were already extensively planted throughout Peru by the time of the conquest era.[6] During the mid-sixteenth century, Old World beasts of burden and draft animals were particularly coveted. So much so that the widespread demand for these animals caused a price bubble that only burst at the end of the century, when the costs dropped more than 90 percent as these animals became abundant.[7]

The desire for draft animals and beasts of burden is not surprising considering the paucity of animal domestication in pre-Columbian South America. And the need for draft animals is obvious, considering Andean sowing technology of that time. The Andean foot plow (*chakitaqlla* or *taclla*) is a Stone Age instrument consisting of a wooden shaft called a *chanchaca,* measuring from five feet in height, and a footrest called a *taquilpo*. The farmer then places his weight on the *taquilpo* to break the earth and plant seeds. Each year at the village of Huilloc, my study abroad students have a chance to practice with a *taclla* during a *pachamanca,* a traditional barbeque of food cooked in the earth, with the Huilloc villagers. Every student who has used the *taclla* said the experience was exhausting. Therefore, when the Spanish introduced oxen and the *arado dental* ("scratch" plow) soon after the conquest, it was a technological breakthrough. So much so that, in 1580, Viceroy Toledo decreed that each Andean community purchase a plow with oxen to work the land.[8]

The llama and alpaca Andean domesticates are marginal beasts of burden compared to the donkey, the horse, and the mule. A male

Andean digging stick ceremony at Huilloc. Photo by Robert Bradley.

llama can only carry a sixty-five-pound load twelve miles a day before it needs to be rested after the third day.[9] A donkey can carry double that weight without rest, and horses and mules can carry at least six times that load or more, depending on the animal. And most important, you cannot ride a llama or alpaca unless you are a child or someone with a great sense of humor who can take a fall. Garcilaso noted that the Spanish lacked the agility of the native population when walking in the mountains. So, because of the roughness of the terrain, they naturally preferred riding horses.[10] I can say without doubt, after leading many study abroad treks and guiding tourists in the Andes, this tradition of outsiders relying on horses and mules to negotiate the rough Andean landscape is still alive and well today.

Obviously, these animals were essential, and too important to eat, but many of the animals brought in with the Spanish made it to the Peruvian table and have remained there to this day. The most important of these are chickens, cows, goats, pigs, and turkeys. There is an incredible number of chickens eaten in Peru, and any bus ride along the coastal Pan American Highway will confirm this assertion. For many years I looked at the enormous tent-like complexes lining the coastal desert and wondered if they were military training areas—only to find out they were chicken farms. These farms are prolific and efficient. Astonishingly enough, these farms deliver 80 percent of the broilers (chickens raised for meat production) to the wholesalers and retailers alive.[11] This freshness is perhaps another reason that *pollo a la braza,* or any other Peruvian chicken dish, is so good. Beef is mostly consumed in Peru as *lomo* (steak), the most famous dish being the famous Chinese-Peruvian stir-fry *lomo saltado.* Peru also has an excellent hamburger chain called Bembo's, which has grown to more than sixty stores since the first one was launched in the Lima barrio of Miraflores in 1988.

Cieza de León mentions goats several times in his conquest era chronicle. One passage is of particular interest because he states that the North Coast valley of Pacasmayo produced some of the best cattle and goats.[12] Garcilaso's record reveals a sixteenth-century "goat bubble" caused by the meager supply of goats in Cuzco, which then burst when the animals reproduced so prolifically they became commonplace.[13] Goats thrived in Peru shortly after their introduction, and Cieza de León's observation of the quality of goats on Peru's North Coast suggests that the dish *cabrito norteño* could have developed in this area very early in the colonial era. Finally, Peruvian food historian Sergio Zapata Acha recorded that, in 1858, a great quantity of special *cabrito* called *chivito de leche* were introduced to Lima from the North Coast, implying that the quality of goats from this region was already renowned.[14]

Puercos (pigs) are mentioned many times in the chronicles. Cieza de León recorded pigs thriving in the wild.[15] However, what he was referring to was the collared peccary (*Dicotyles tajacu*), a creature that in some ways resembles a pig but is not in the same animal family. There is scant faunal evidence of peccary in the pre-Columbian record, with a notable exception recorded at Nanchoc in northwestern Peru from ten thousand years ago.[16] But pigs were one of the first Old World animals taken to the Americas. Hernando Pizarro bought his own *puercos* with him from Panama during the first days of the conquest of Peru. In Peru the word *chancho* is typically used for pigs and pork. It is a humorous seventeenth-century nickname derived from the Spanish name *Sancho*.[17] Because of this, the term *chancho* is absent from the colonial record. I eat much more pork in the States than I do in Peru, with two notable exceptions. *Chicharrones* are not one of my exceptions, but they are the most common pork dish you are likely to encounter in Peru. These consist of pieces of pork and pork fat that are boiled until the water evaporates and then fried. *Chicharrones* are basically tastier and more elaborate versions of pork rinds. But even though *chicharrones* are ubiquitous throughout the country, Peru has one of the lowest per capita consumptions of pork in South America.[18]

My two favorite Peruvian pork dishes are sandwiches. The first is the *butiffara de jamón del país*, which consists of country ham on French bread with *sarza* (salsa criolla). This sandwich was my typical evening meal at Cuzco's Museo del Pisco bar, but the item has been removed from their abbreviated post-pandemic menu. The second is the *lechon a la leña* (suckling pig) sandwich on a Kaiser roll with the same *sarza*. The Peruvian sandwich chain La Lucha Sangucheria does an exceptional version of *lechon a la leña*. A final note on these sandwiches: several years ago when our family was staying in the coastal village of Pimentel, we frequented a sandwich shop that sold excellent *lechon a la leña* sandwiches. Unfortunately, the shop is now closed, but back then the owner told me they grilled the suckling pig in a device called La Caja China or La Caja Asadora. Although this grill is a relatively new import to Peru, the device has become very popular. A Caja China is basically a box on wheels with the interior lined with metal and a top tray placed over the interior chamber. The meat (chickens, suckling pig, etc.) is placed inside the chamber with spices and liquid marinade such as beer or wine. The top plate covers the meat, and coals are placed on top of the plate and ignited. After an hour, the plate is carefully lifted, and the meat is turned. Then the plate is placed back on the box, and the food is cooked for another hour. The grill was invented in Cuba and has been in use there for decades. According to the late anthropologist Sid Mintz, the China designation is a way of saying it is a clever and exotic invention and likely has nothing to do with Chinese immigrants to Cuba.[19] I expect the influence of this ingenious grill to be another interesting addition to the expanding Peruvian culinary tradition.

The last imported animal to mention is the oddly named turkey, which was brought to Peru from Mesoamerica by the Spanish. Both Juguería San Agustín in Trujillo and the La Lucha Sangucheria sandwich chain have excellent versions of the turkey sandwich served on a hard roll with *sarza*. In Peru, if you have a choice between a chicken or turkey sandwich, always take the turkey option, because you will never be served dry or bland turkey. Unlike in the States, turkey in Peru is almost never frozen, and the birds are always free-range. At Christmas the main course for many Peruvians is roast turkey.[20] These birds are not cheap. A few years ago, my family and I celebrated Christmas in my wife's village of Ferreñafe. At that time my father-in-law spent one hundred sols (about thirty dollars) for our holiday bird, and to make sure it was cooked to perfection he paid to have the local bakery cook the turkey. If he saw or ate one of our frozen turkeys that are free at Thanksgiving if you purchase one hundred dollars' worth of groceries, he would be aghast.

So, what were the most important edible plants in the Peruvian culinary tradition brought to Peru by the Spanish? The short list includes wheat, grapes, garlic, key limes, red onions, tomatoes, and cilantro. *Solanum lycopersicum* (tomato) is a strange global traveler like the potato. Tomatoes were domesticated in Mexico and not in South America; however, "the tomato derives from a genus of weedy Andean plants with red, orange, or green berries of currant to cherry size." Different wild species in South America include *L. peruvianum* and *L. pennellii*, which were widespread in Peru; *L. esculentum* var.

cerasiforme, which grows on the Andean eastern slopes; *L. chilense,* which is native to coastal deserts of northern Chile and southern Peru; *L. hirsutum,* which grows in high altitudes of Ecuador and Peru; and finally the curious *L. cheesmanii,* which is indigenous to the Galapagos Islands.[21] There is some evidence that wild tomatoes were eaten in pre-Columbian Peru, but there is no indication they were extensively domesticated.[22]

Tomatoes had made their way to Spain by 1523 but, more important, to Spanish-occupied Naples. The Italians embraced the tomato, to the point of making it their own. (A good comparison is the acceptance and then dominance of the peanut in sub-Saharan Africa after its introduction in the sixteenth century.) The Italians, using early "heirloom" gardening, changed the fruit of the tomato from a small marble-like yellow fruit to the larger red tomato we know today.[23] The domesticated tomato was probably reintroduced to Peru sometime during the colonial era. Jesuit missionary José de Acosta noted in his late sixteenth-century natural history that a sauce of hot peppers, tomatoes, and salt was universally found in the Caribbean, Mexico, and Peru.[24] Finally, some scholars have suggested that a wild cultivar was domesticated in Peru, but the distribution was not widespread.[25] Today, as in Mexico, the Roma tomato or plum tomato is the most widespread variety of tomato in Peru, which is curious because the biodiversity of wild tomato species in Peru obliges the need for heirloom cultivation. The results could be spectacular. For example, the twentieth-century experimentation with *L. peruvianum* in California lead to the development of the popular super-sweet species *L. chmielewskii.*[26]

The key lime, *limón sutil,* and the bitter orange came to the New World via the Spanish during the conquest era. Bitter orange was widely used in old Lima but now key lime has completely displaced bitter orange in Peruvian cooking, and in ceviche in particular.[27] The historian Juan Jose Vega has rightly noted that the technique of using *limón sutil* and bitter orange in cooking came to the Spanish from the Moors and is therefore ultimately a northern African influence.[28]

Grape vines were shipped to the colonies from the more proximately located Canary Islands almost from the beginning of the conquest era.[29] Grape production led to the development of the *aguardiente de uva* (grape brandy) called pisco, which is named after the port of Pisco on Peru's southern coast.[30] The first distillation of this brandy is tied to the Peruvian town of Ica in the early sixteenth century.[31] Finally, the sociologist Giovanni Bonfiglio has Moscatello Bianco di Alessandria (the grape for Pisco Italia) introduced into Peru by Italian enologists (scientists specializing in wine) at the beginning of the twentieth century, but this information contradicts early eighteenth-century Pisco Italia shipping manifests from Peru to California.[32]

The chronicler Acosta observed that garlic and onions were thriving in Peru in the sixteenth century. After this Sergio Zapata Acha noted that garlic flourished in the cold climates of Arequipa, Cajamarca, and the Lima highlands. The purple (red) or criolla onion is the primary onion used in Peruvian cuisine. It has a strong flavor and is cultivated mostly in the South Coast region of Peru.[33]

Cilantro (*Coriandrum sativum*) is a firmly established Old World herb found in Tutankhamen's tomb but originating in ancient Greece.[34] Cilantro was brought to the New World by the Spanish, but *culantro* (*Eryngium foetidum*, Mexican coriander, *sacha culantro, culantro de la selva*) is an endemic New World herb with an almost identical flavor profile to cilantro. In Peru today, *culantro* is almost exclusively used in the forested lowlands, but the nonnative cilantro is ever-present in the highland and coastal markets.[35]

The intellectual leader of Peru's early twentieth-century indigenous movement, José Carlos Mariátegui, believed that neither the Chinese nor the African contributed cultural values or creative energies to the formation of Peru.[36] It is true that the African and Chinese diasporas brought mostly workers—enslaved and semi-enslaved peoples—to Peru, so their primary goal upon arrival was survival and not to contribute to Peru's culture and creativity. But both groups made immense contributions to the Peruvian culinary tradition. In his tome on mid-nineteenth-century Lima, Manuel Atanasio Fuentes recorded that the celebrated Negro cooks of the time, the *Serapios,* fetched a high price for their services to elite Limeños.[37] Writing about the specifics of the African contributions to Peruvian cuisine is difficult because of the lack of research and documentation on the subject.[38] However, a clearly African contribution to Peruvian cuisine is *Lablab purpureus,* the *zarandaja* bean that serves as a side for ceviche in northern Peru. Beans were an integral part of the enslaved Afro-Peruvian diet, and ecogeographic surveys of *Lablab purpureus* have them as endemic to southeast Africa and Madagascar.[39] Piura and Lambayeque include communities of *Mangaches,* Afro-Peruvians with roots in Madagascar, who brought their own beans with them.[40] Therefore, the *zarandaja* beans wound up in ceviche, which is uniquely popular in these two places. Finding clear links after *zarandaja* beans remains problematic.

There are echoes of African influences in the Peruvian culinary tradition. For example, cooking stew in a pot was an African tradition brought to the Americas during the diaspora. And a classic Peruvian stew that has been associated with an African origin is *carapulcra,* which is made with a meat base combined with butter, onions, garlic, hot pepper, cumin or coriander, and toasted peanuts. *Carapulcra* is typically served with boiled yuca and rice or potatoes. But although it seems an Afro-Peruvian dish, the word *carapulcra* is listed in Holguín's 1608 Quechua dictionary as *ccalapurca, o pari rucru*. Holguín defines it as *el guisado cozido con piedra ardiendo* (a stew cooked on heated rocks).[41] Fuentes states that *carapulcra* was "the daily food of the poorer inhabitants of Peru," in the same section where he mentions that the *Serapios* were Negro cooks and very famous in their day.[42] The links here that suggest *carapulcra* came from an African culinary tradition are obvious, but why is the term defined in a Quechua dictionary?

It is true that enslaved Africans had already been in Peru for decades before Holguín completed his work, but *carapulcra* likely is a fusion or criollo recipe, which comes from an indigenous/African mix. In the early nineteenth century Adán Felipe Mejía defined *carapulcra* as *zambicholo*.[43] In Mejía's day, using a word like *zambicholo* would not raise an eyebrow, but today the term is considered derogatory. *Zambi* comes from Zambo or Sambo, a negative term used for blacks in the Americas, which has thankfully disappeared. The term *cholo* was brought to Peru from a Cariban dialect. *Cholo* was defined by Garcilaso as word for a mongrel dog and was used by the Spanish to demean the indigenous population.[44] Despite his most problematic expression, Mejía's intent was to link *carapulcra* to both the African and the native Peruvian traditions. The peanuts for *carapulcra* are also telling. Peanuts are used in some Peruvian dishes, but peanuts are very common in African-influenced recipes. Remember, peanuts spread so quickly throughout Africa after the conquest that early botanists believed they were endemic to the continent.[45]

Anthony Bourdain's beloved organ meat, offal, could also be another echo of African influence on Peruvian cooking. *Anticuchos* (grilled beef heart), *rachi* (grilled cow stomach), *choncholí* (grilled beef intestine), *cau cau* (beef or chicken tripe stew), *chanfainita* (stew with beef lungs) are all made with offal—and all from animals (cows and chickens, for example) that, like the enslaved Africans, came to Peru with the Spanish. There are examples of Inca eating raw llama heart, but this consumption was ceremonial and not a widespread practice.[46] The habit of eating offal began in the colonial era. Of the five dishes mentioned, notice two are stews.

The most famous and most common dish of this type is *anticuchos* (grilled beef hearts). In Peru it seems as if *anticucho* street vendors pop up on every other town corner in the early evening. The street cooks grill their *antichuchos* over an *algarrobo* fire and then serve the beef hearts with potatoes, *choclo* (corn on the cob), and a fiery *ají* sauce. The *algarrobo* wood used by these cooks could be another echo of an African past. Sociologist José Carlos Luciano noted that in the colonial era Africans gravitated toward the *leña* trade, supplying indispensable firewood (*algarrobo*) to the cities and the countryside. Therefore, this enterprise could be an African link to *anticuchos*, because they controlled the fuel that supplied the street vendors.[47]

Luciano also has enslaved Africans providing the labor for sugar, wine, and olive production.[48] This makes sense because these three agricultural crops are imports that were unknown to the indigenous population. The history of *guarapo* certainly resonates with Luciano's observation. Additionally, the historian Rachel Sarah O'Toole has pointed out that sugarcane syrup traded by enslaved Africans was "used to make an alcohol drink or to strengthen *chicha*."[49] Africans working vineyards during the seventeenth century would have been eyewitnesses to the growth of the distilled spirit pisco. Remember, Fuentes had the beverage of choice for the *bozales* as *achichadito*, which was very strong and made from the cane trash after the syrup had been extracted.[50] So, *achichadito* is likely a distilled spirit made from the by-products of fermentation, like Italian grappa, Greek rakija, Spanish *orujo*, and Serbian *komovica*.[51] It seems that the fermenting of *guarapo* and the distillation *aguardiente de caña* are clear African contributions to Peru and Latin America.

African slaves were freed in Peru in 1854. This emancipation, although a godsend to the enslaved, was a disaster for Peruvian businessmen who were experiencing the guano boom and a market demanding increased sugar exports to Europe. These hacienda owners needed workers. So they pushed the passage of the *Ley china* law, which allowed the introduction of an indentured workforce from China to replace the slave trade. Between 1849 and 1874, one hundred thousand coolies, almost all male, were brought to Peru.[52]

Peru's *Tusán* or *Tusheng* Chinese immigrants came almost exclusively from Canton province and worked for an eight-year contract under slavelike conditions. The center for the coolie trade was the Portuguese colony of Macao largely because of the lack of protection in this place for the Chinese workers exploited in the trade.[53] From the beginning, the Chinese were apart from Peruvian culture. The workers lived in their own facilities and cooked and ate their own food, of which rice was the main ingredient. As the first few decades of the semi-slave coolie years waned in 1874, some enterprising *Tusheng* workers imported food items and Chinese goods and formed storerooms, which became the centers of the workers' lives. Here they ate, smoked opium, drank alcohol, and gossiped. Soon the area of central Lima near the main market became the center of the immigrant Chinese community in the city. The *Tusheng* flourished in other coastal cities as well, notably in Chiclayo, Trujillo, and Huacho, but Lima was the epicenter. Capon Street became Chinatown, which expanded as Chinese import companies prospered. Every enterprise had a kitchen in the back to feed the growing Chinese population of the city, and the propensity for them to eat traditional meals soon created the taverns and then the first Chinese restaurants. Chinese taverns that maintained "a certain kind [of] oriental flavor" were frequented by Chinese and poor Peruvians, but taverns located in the center of Chinatown were frequented mainly by Chinese.[54]

Like the Africans, good Chinese cooks were sought after by Lima's upper classes. Fuentes mentions their skill in the kitchen and how many of them became cooks in Lima's elite households.[55] This trend continued into the early twentieth century when it became increasingly fashionable for the privileged to have an adept Chinese cook in their kitchen who not only prepared excellent Chinese food but also the superb criollo dishes these cooks had acquired.[56]

In 1909, 1912, and 1919 angry protests took place in Lima as a result of price increases and the lack of jobs. The Limeño workers were also incensed by the spectacular rise of the *Tusheng,* who had not only escaped lives of indentured servitude but who now prospered. During this time Chinese people were openly attacked by enraged mobs, and their thriving tavern businesses were often condemned by racist publications, even though the poor Limeño workers were the ones who benefited the most from these affordable food venues.[57] Perhaps then José Carlos Mariátegui's racist criticism of the Chinese, published during this era, is not surprising.

The early twentieth century was also a time for *Tusheng* advancement, because this era ushered in the rise of the *chifa*. But first, a note on the word *chifa,* which is used only in Peru. Many etymologies have *chifa* coming from the Mandarin word *chifan* (to eat rice), but as we know, the *Tusheng* were from Canton province where Cantonese is spoken. The Cantonese term for eating rice is *sek fan,* and when pronounced by a Cantonese speaker, it sounds very similar to *chifan.* This word for a Chinese tavern, and now restaurant, first appeared in *El Comercio,* Peru's *New York Times,* in an article dated March 14, 1920, about the opening of an elegant Chinese restaurant in Lima.[58]

In an interesting contrast to Mariátegui's intellectual contempt for the Chinese, beginning around 1915 Lima's intellectuals and bohemians were the first to frequent the Chinese establishments in order to enjoy the exotic food and surroundings and the opium, and soon many non-avant-garde elites followed. By the 1930s thousands of upper- and lower-class Limeños frequented Chinatown's Capon Street daily for lunch and dinner. Upscale locales like Kuong Tong and San Joy Lao became venues where elite parties and events were celebrated.[59] And in the later part of the twentieth century, *chifas* proliferated throughout Peru, even in the remote Andean towns.

What foods did the Chinese bring to Peru? First, lots of vegetables, which are now all grown in Peru. A sampling includes *cebolla china* (spring onion), *calabaza china* (wax gourd), *col china* (napa cabbage), *pac choi* (bok choy and baby bok choy), *colantao* (snow peas), and *gau choy* (Chinese chives). Imported condiments include Chinese cinnamon, *kión* (ginger), and *tau si* (fermented and salted black soybeans). *Sillau* (soy sauce), wantons, noodles, crystal noodles, rice, tamarind, soybean paste, tofu, pickled turnip, and sesame oil were imported; now they are made in Peru. As an example, the first Peruvian manufactured soy sauce was made in 1920.[60]

My experience with *chifas* has been limited because if I am in a coastal Peruvian city I typically eat seafood, especially ceviche, for the main afternoon meal. Also, although *chifas* are as omnipresent in Peru as *pollo a la braza* restaurants, most of these locales have simple

The dining room of Mococho. Photo by Robert Bradley.

uninteresting menus focused on *arroz chaufa* (fried rice) and *tallarines chinos* (lo mein). And more than twenty years ago I became very affected in my views of Cantonese cuisine. During this time I lived in Lower Manhattan, and every Friday I played judo at Oishi's on Leonard Street. After practice my dojo friends and I would walk a few blocks to the famous restaurant Sun Lok Kee in Chinatown. The restaurant closed in 2002 after a fire, much to the chagrin of all of us. We were not sad because of the ambiance—physically, the restaurant was awful, with annoying lighting, tables and chairs that must have been lifted from a firehouse, and surly waiters. The closing made us sad because the food was spectacular. Our group's favorite appetizers were sauteed Chinese chives, razor clams, and geoduck, the last two being mollusks brought to the city from the West Coast. And we finished each meal with whole cooked fish served "family style." My wife loves *arroz chaufa* and *tallarines chinos*—so much so that she will not eat Chinese food without fried rice. I am ambivalent about both, but I love whole fish. Mococho Restaurant in Huanchaco serves Cantonese-style whole fish, which is better than any offering I ever had at Sun Lok Kee. The reason it is so good is because the owner Ricardo Sulem Wong uses both Chinese and Peruvian herbs and spices to flavor the fish.[61]

Earlier I mentioned the Chinese Peruvian stir-fry *lomo saltado* as a matter of fact, which was disingenuous because the origin of the dish is far from settled. I make *lomo saltado* often, and when I do I use a wok and soy sauce, so it feels like an Asian stir-fry to me. But the Peruvian food historian Sergio Zapata Acha has *lomo saltado* originating in the criollo tradition with pork as the main ingredient. He also imagines the dish as European and not Chinese influenced.[62] Even the Peruvian journalist Mariella Balbi, a specialist in Chinese Peruvian culinary history, cedes that sautéed beef with onions and tomatoes is a common recipe in southern Europe, but she notes that the way in which the ingredients are chopped and prepared and the fact that no other Peruvian dish is sautéed could be an indication of *Tusheng* origin. Balbi does go on to point out that soy sauce was added to the dish in the 1930s by Japanese-owned taverns that served Peruvian food.[63] I think it is best to call *lomo saltado* an indigenous-, European-, Chinese-, and Japanese-inspired Peruvian classic—a super-criollo recipe ubiquitous in all manner of Peruvian restaurants. And the dish works well with several different main ingredients: chicken, pork, shrimp, and so on (my take on this classic is below).

The nineteenth century saw a slight surge of Italian immigrants to Peru, attracted by the economic impact of the guano boom. I say slight because the number of Italian immigrants was in the low thousands, about one-tenth of the number of Chinese coming in during the coolie trade. About 80 percent of the Italian émigrés came from Italy's northwestern Liguria region, with the port city of Genoa being the capital.[64] I have eaten pasta in Peru, but since I grew up in a place where they made fresh raviolis and mozzarella around the corner, I was not impressed. However, the Italian food I do seek out in Peru is pizza, which comes to the country, like the rest of the world (except Chicago), from Naples. Pizzerias took off in Peru during the 1960s, and today there are many establishments in the coastal cities and on the gringo trail tourist centers in and around Cuzco.[65]

A real Italian import that has become a Peruvian staple is my wife's beloved *panetón* (in Italian, *panettone*). *Panetón* is a fruitcake infinitely better than what gets traded in the States during the Christmas season. *Panetón* is also mostly consumed in Peru during the Christmas holidays and *Fiestas Patrias de Perú* (Peruvian national holidays), which is celebrated on and around July 28. Here in south Texas, *panetón* is in stock right before Thanksgiving, but the supply normally runs out before Navidad. *Panetón* is in the Milan style, spongy with raisins and fruit embedded in the cake.[66] During the season there are a great many varieties of *panetón* available in the markets and bodegas of Peru, including many Italian imports, but big Peruvian brands like D'Onofrio dominate the market. Like pizza, *panetón* is a relatively new addition to the Peruvian culinary tradition, having only been introduced to the country after World War II.[67]

Nikkei is the term for Peruvians of Japanese descent who came to Peru from Okinawa and mainland Japan. Although both are part of the larger Japanese community, the division between the Japanese and the Okinawans is very pronounced in Peru.[68] About thirty thousand Japanese sojourners arrived in Peru during the years 1899 and 1923 to work in the sugarcane industry, but they quickly became disillusioned with the harsh conditions of the plantations and turned to the cotton trade as demand for Peruvian cotton increased during World War I.[69] With their intense work ethic, the Japanese also established businesses (notably restaurants and taverns) in a relatively noncompetitive commercial environment.[70] These restaurants originally served traditional criollo food, but over time the Japanese influence on these Peruvian classics started to coalesce. La Buena Muerte (The Good Death), a whimsically named Japanese restaurant founded in 1959 by Minoru Kunigami, was one of the first innovators in the emerging style that would become Nikkei cuisine.[71] Basically,

Kunigami's dishes used less *ají*, incorporated traditional Japanese condiments like miso, soy sauce, and wasabi, and finally stressed seafood dishes.[72] Nikkei cooks did not have the vast supply of products from their homeland like the Chinese cooks, so they learned to be innovative. For example, they made *dashi* (the base for miso soup) by drying tuna at home, and they made soba noodles and *mochi* (sweet rice cakes) out of *yuca*.[73] But Nikkei cuisine started on the road to international fame in 1973 when a young master sushi chef named Nobu Matsuhisa opened his restaurant Matsuei in Lima.[74] Nobu would go on to build a restaurant empire that spanned the globe and introduced the world to Japanese Peruvian fusion cuisine.[75]

Nobu has also been credited with the invention of *tiradito* ceviche, which is made from thinly sliced raw fish accented by a touch of lime and *ají*, influenced in this case by the precise cuts of fish from the Japanese sashimi tradition. The master chef Mitsuharu Tsumura and the writer Josefina Barrón have Nobu using yuzu fruit, the bitter fruit that flavors *ponzu* sauce, in his *tiraditos* instead of key lime. They go on to favorably compare yuzu fruit to bitter orange.[76] This is a fascinating comparison, because Fuentes has nineteenth-century ceviche made with bitter orange, and according to Valderrama, the bitter orange is almost nonexistent in Peru today, except for in the city of Huacho.[77] But Valderrama takes issue with *tiradito* being invented by Nobu and cites the tradition of northern Peruvian and Callao fisherman slicing off thin strips of fish to make their ceviche meal. Additionally, he states that the famous Peruvian chef Don Cucho, Luis La Rosa, credited Peruvian Carlos Araujo for the thin slicing because the chef had a famously sharp Japanese knife.[78]

Going even further into the deep influence of the Japanese on the Peruvian seafood tradition, Chef Tsumura has suggested that the practice of appreciating fresh fish quickly marinated with lime juice comes from twentieth-century Japanese immigrants.[79] Until the 1980s, Valderrama has Limeños marinating the fish for hours in key lime juice as does Fuentes (in bitter orange juice) in his record of nineteenth-century cooking. However, I am sure that Valderrama and Fuentes are discussing the practices of elite city dwellers, who were mostly descendants of European ancestry. Certainly, the Nikkei influence changed the cooking time to a quick rinse of *limón sutil*. But outside of Lima, particularly on the North Coast, there is little Japanese influence on cuisine.[80] Tsumura and Barrón continue with the narrative of Japanese transformation of Peruvian culinary practices by anecdotally noting the Peruvian disdain for eel and octopus in the late twentieth century. They tell of fishermen near Lima throwing away octopi and of a merchant in Lima's central market being flabbergasted when Chef Nobu wanted to buy some eels, because usually nobody wanted them.[81]

I have two problems with these stories. First, I have bought fish from Peruvian fishermen and I have interviewed a very famous one for an article of mine, and I know they are loath to throw any catch away.[82] Second, vendors in the markets in Peru are not in the practice of stocking things people don't want. And as far as eels go, the archaeological record at the North Coast Moche site of Huaca de la Luna, dated roughly fifteen hundred years ago, has remains of snake eels.[83] Also, even though faunal remains of boneless octopi would be almost an impossibility, images of the creatures are a common theme in Moche art.[84] Finally, if Dillehay's work at Huaca Prieta is indicative of anything, it is that pre-Columbian Peruvians were familiar with and made use of all maritime resources, including seaweed, snails, bivalves, sharks, boney fish, and so on.[85] This is not to say that Nikkei cuisine did not have a significant impact on Peruvian cuisine, particularly seafood. It did. Nikkei cuisine is an internationally known style of cooking, and this cuisine brought distinction and fame to the Peruvian culinary tradition. Certainly, Chef Mitsuharu Tsumura's restaurant Maido, one of the best restaurants in the world, serves as a fine example of the sublime heights that can be reached by Nikkei cuisine.

I want now to briefly discuss one of my favorite restaurants, which unfortunately closed more than a decade ago. Siam de los Andes, located in the mountain town of Huaraz, was a wonderful

Thai restaurant, a rarity in Peru. The late owner and chef Naresuan Buttham made spectacular Thai food and had the distinction of not only having some of the best Thai food in South America but also being one of the most expensive restaurants in Peru. One night, many years ago, I ordered a delicious bowl of Tom Yum Goong soup. As I was appreciating the flavor of the lemongrass in the soup I wondered where Naresuan got this plant, because no species are native to the Americas and lemongrass is not used in Chinese or Japanese cooking. When Naresuan came to the bar where I was eating, he told me the lemongrass is called *hierba lusia* in Peru and it is sold in every market. During my research for this book, I found out that *hierba lusia* is not in the genus *Cymbopogon*, so it is not actually lemongrass, and it is dissimilar to all the lemongrass species from Southeast Asia, Africa, and Australia. Instead *hierba lusia* is in the genus *Aloysia*. Lemon verbena (*Aloysia citrodora* Paláu) is endemic to the Americas, and the likely origin for this plant is Salta and Jujuy provinces in northwestern Argentina.[86] Lemon verbena's flavor profile is like lemongrass but stronger. Lemon verbena was the main flavoring for Inca Kola—created by José Lindley, the son of the Scottish immigrant José Robinson Lindley, in 1935, the year marking Lima's four-hundredth anniversary. Inca Kola is cherished in Peru and sought out by Peruvian émigrés in other countries worldwide.[87] One more note on lemon verbena: when I am in Peru and have a kitchen available, I sometimes make a fish stew using soy, *ají amarillo*, spring onions, *hierba lusia*, wine, and *tollo* (again, the generic name for any predatory cartilaginous fish), and the stew is wildly popular with my wife and her family.

Bob's *Lomo Saltado*

- 1½ lbs. sirloin steak
- 4 *ají amarillos* or Anaheim peppers deveined and deseeded
- 3 cloves garlic
- 2 tbsp. vegetable oil
- 4 Roma tomatoes
- 1 red onion
- ¼ cup soy sauce
- 2 oz. pisco or 4 oz. of white wine
- 2 tbsp. chopped cilantro

I grill the steak very rare, preferably with mesquite charcoal, and then cut the meat into thin strips. I chop a medium-sized red onion into eight sections and separate the pieces. Next, I cut up four Roma tomatoes into four quarters and deseed the quarters (two heirloom tomatoes work well here too). If I am in Peru, I would then deseed the *ají amarillos* and cut them into 3-inch strips, but this pepper is almost impossible to get fresh in the United States. The paste in a jar works to a point, but the flavoring is not the same. Lacking fresh *ají amarillo,* I use fresh Anaheim peppers, which again are not *ají amarillo,* but they will suffice. The last prep is to cut up a handful of cilantro leaves and crush and chop some garlic cloves. I have all the ingredients laid out so I can reach them fast because the stir-fry needs to advance quickly. First, fry the garlic in a few tablespoons of vegetable oil until it browns slightly. Then add the onions and cook until they soften, followed by the *ají amarillo* and tomatoes. Stir quickly and add the strips of steak, then the soy sauce, and/or the pisco/white wine. Cover the ingredients and let them simmer briefly. Finally, add cilantro and stir. I serve the *lomo saltado* with hand-cut double-fried french fries and rice. To bring fire to the dish, blend a deseeded and deveined *rocoto* with a key lime and salt.

Bob's *Tusán Nikkei Sudado*

2 lbs. *tollo*
4 *ají amarillos* (Anaheim peppers are a fair substitute)
2 bunches of spring onions
1 cup dry white wine
½ cup soy sauce
1 tbsp. cilantro
1 tbsp. *hierba luisa* or lemongrass
2 cloves of garlic
2 tbsp. vegetable oil

In a large pot fry the garlic in oil, then the *ají* and the chopped spring onion, then braise the *tollo,* which should be cut into portion-sized chunks. Add the wine and soy and simmer over medium to low heat for half an hour. With five minutes left of the cooking cycle, add the chopped cilantro and *hierba luisa* or prepped lemongrass.

Conclusion

As I am writing this last chapter, the SARS-CoV-2 (COVID 19) pandemic has taken over people's lives and ruined many plans for going on two years. My family and I have been lucky during this pandemic; we had mild symptoms and the only disruption was the dreaded online-only 2020–21 academic year. My wife's family in Peru was less lucky, however. They experienced a spike of deaths and cases not only in summer 2020 but also in early winter 2021 when the Lambda corona virus variant took hold, even though Peru had the world's most stringent lockdown protocols. In the end Peru would have by far the highest per capita death rate in the world, with two hundred thousand COVID deaths in a population of less than thirty-three million. Adding insult to injury, Peruvians suffered through one week of three different presidents in November 2020, a symptom of the chaos caused indirectly by the effects of the pandemic.

For now, the storm has passed in Peru. According to the US State Department's travel advisory, Peru is a category 2 risk, meaning "travel with caution." This rating implies that travel is back to normal—in the more than twenty years that I have been going to Peru, the country has always been a category 2. Crime and terrorism (both easily avoided) keep Peru from the highest rating of category 1. While writing this text, I watched in horror as the virus spread not only in the United States but like wildfire in Peru. I tried not to have selfish thoughts, but I kept thinking "I need to go there and finish my research." All this became moot when the University of Texas system cancelled all foreign travel until summer 2022.

I returned to Peru in July 2022 for my study abroad course focused on the grueling Vilcabamba trek. Before leaving the States, I was concerned with the effect of the pandemic on air travel, lodging, and restaurants. After all, I was writing a guide and a history of Peru's ascendance to the No. 1 culinary destination in the world, and airline disruptions, lockdowns, and severe quarantines are in direct conflict with my project. But I was happy to note that not one of the restaurants or hotels I discussed had either permanently or temporarily closed. Most of what I saw in Peru were restaurants with abbreviated menus and streets with an eerie paucity of tourists. I am confident this will change as the world moves on from COVID.

My chapter on ceviche would have been much longer with the research I expected to accomplish after my summer programs in 2020 and 2021. I planned to visit the *chifas* of Lima's San Bartolo barrio and explore the *cevicherías* of the port of Callao and the Chorrillos District in Lima. I also intended to visit the five pisco-producing regions in the south and spend time sampling *rocoto* dishes in Arequipa, but the virus infringed on my plans. Again, with all the suffering the pandemic has caused the world, I feel guilty lamenting the disruption that COVID brought to my work, but I would be a hypocrite not to say so. My future study will focus on southern Peru and in particular the pisco region.

Going forward, I hope all the projects outlined above will at some point be accomplished, and these, along with a much-needed trip to the Amazon River city of Iquitos, will be the highlights of my future research. COVID seems to be waning, or should I say going from a pandemic to an endemic malady, which we will all have to endure like the common cold. I believe at some point the pent-up human desire to travel, eat, and explore will explode—even though, in my opinion, the pandemic clearly revealed that our leaders had too little faith in us and we had too much faith in them. But moving on, the Spanish flu was followed by a decade deemed the Roaring Twenties, a time period of economic and cultural advancement. Let us hope that we move into a similar dynamic in the very near future.

The city of Chachapoyas and the surrounding towns and villages in northeastern Peru are the areas in which I traveled the most in my early career. This region was all part of the pre-Columbian Chachapoya culture until it was conquered by the Inca in the late fifteenth century. Discussion of my travel in this region is minimal in this book, especially considering the time I have spent there. The main reason for this omission is that I haven't been to the Chachapoya region in more than a decade. Why? Basically, I could never get funding for the numerous projects I submitted to myriad granting agencies. I could be a terrible grant writer, but I do not think this is the case. I believe the reason lies in the fact that the field of Andean studies has turned away from adventure archaeology in the past few decades, maybe for the best and maybe not. From the beginning, Chachapoya studies have always been marked by cloud forest expeditions in search of remote ruins, with the adventures of Gene Savoy being the most famous.[1]

This lack of funding is how my study abroad trips became the focus of my research. For more than a decade I have led students from Texas's Rio Grande Valley to Peru, and I am compensated for teaching this class, just as any professor is compensated for teaching a summer course. However, my expenses and my meals, airfare, and hotels are also paid by my university. This funding enabled me to travel to Peru each summer and to conduct research before, during, and after each trip. For my first trip, I tried to take students to the Chachapoya region, but the trip failed because of a lack of student interest. I recovered by taking students to Peru's North Coast the next two seasons, always in June, but even these exceptional tours of Peru's magnificent Moche culture and the gastronomic center of the country were extremely difficult to "make" (getting enough students to sign on in order to make the travel economically viable). Then I made the turn to Cuzco and Machu Picchu, and my problems were solved.

If you want to travel to Peru and learn the absolute least about the country and its people, by all means stay on the "gringo trail"—that is, Lima (Miraflores) to Cuzco to Machu Picchu and back. This is the itinerary for most foreign travelers to Peru. And although I understand the focus on these locales, I still find the myopic concentration on the Machu Picchu journey frustrating. I spent almost a decade going to

Peru without visiting Machu Picchu, and most of my travel then was to remote cloud forest areas, like the environs of Machu Picchu but lacking the crowds. On my last post-pandemic trip to the town below Machu Picchu, I did not even walk up to the famous ruin.

But ever since the Peruvian photographer Martín Chambi Jiménez snapped his iconic photograph of Machu Picchu, which every visitor is obliged to imitate, the Inca emperor Pachacuti Inca Yupanqui's royal estate started on the path of being loved to death.[2] Well then, if I am so critical of this circuit, why did I include numerous destinations in Miraflores, the Sacred Valley of the Inca, and Aguas Calientes (Machu Picchu)? The simple answer is because I had to. A great many readers of this book will travel this route first. But I hope some of my recommendations resonate with you (after you explore the "gringo trail") and persuade you to embark on some of the less-traveled circuits outlined in this book.

The former Peruvian president Alberto Fujimori once cited three unrivaled pre-Columbian locations in Peru: Machu Picchu, Chavín de Huántar, and Kuelap. Today, mining companies have strewn the road from Huaraz to Chavín de Huántar with contaminated soil, making the four-hour bus ride a grim outing (at least it was like that on my last visit in 2013). Of the three, Kuelap is by far the most neglected by the modern gaze, even though it has been known to the West since the mid-nineteenth century. In contrast, Hiram Bingham's lost (and misinformed) expedition introduced Machu Picchu to the Western world in the early twentieth century. Despite this late entry, Machu Picchu has somehow attracted the lavish attention of one million foreign visitors annually. Kuelap, even with the new cable car access to the top of the mountain, attracts a fraction of this number.

Going forward, I do not see how Machu Picchu can sustain this multitude of tourists. When I first went to Machu Picchu in 2008, I took my time walking around the site and even enjoyed an extended coca chew in a rocky alcove looking off to the east. Doing this today would be impossible because each year more crowd-control restrictions are put in place. In 2017 our study abroad group had to hire a guide even though I was an Andean specialist with almost two decades of experience. To my horror, the guide informed my students that Machu Picchu was an Inca university (a conceptionally and historically ludicrous suggestion). In 2018 we were shocked to be told to walk in the same direction with all the other tourists, making us feel like we were trapped in one of Disney World's endless line dividers. In 2019, after hiking up to Machu Picchu from Aguas Calientes (always my favorite part of the trip), I chewed some coca at the head of the trail before the bus parking lot, and after hearing the noise of the buses and the crowds I turned away and started down the mountain without entering the site. Finally, on this last trip, I did not even bother to walk up.

Perhaps I am a spoiled Andeanist, and I want this beautiful locale all to myself? Fair enough, but I hope this book will in a clear and concise manner attract you to join me in enjoying the other wonderful places in Peru, beyond the crowds. And in these places, you will visit ancient ruins while dining in some of the most important centers of Peru's culinary boom. In the introduction, I outlined the tension between the North American and European scholars' criticism of Peru's gastronomic miracle and the Peruvian school's celebration of the boom, led by the scholars of the Universidad de San Martín de Porres Press. But recently I was delighted to read the food and cultural studies scholar Raúl Matta's interview with a Peruvian journalist and cultural critic, Mirko Lauer, who is the author of a book entitled *The Peruvian Gastronomic Revolution*, by the same Universidad de San Martín de Porres Press.[3] The article is published online with free access, so I encourage you to seek it out in the journal the *Anthropology of Food*.

Notably, Lauer does not see the Peruvian gastronomic boom continuing, because the movement's ability to move forward has been lost—or more precisely, it has become leaderless. For example, Gastón Acurio's cooking, while always at the high end of the restaurant market, is firmly rooted in the Peruvian culinary tradition. So, whether you are having posh *chicharrones* at his restaurant Chicha in Cuzco, or *ceviche de maracuyá* at La Mar in Lima, you know you are firmly grounded in Peru. Earlier I said *chicharrones* (pork rinds) were a common dish throughout the country. There is nothing common about Aucrio's *chicharrones* at Chicha, certainly not the price, but again the connection to the country is apparent. *Ceviche de maracuyá* as a dish is not common, but recall that earlier *maracuyá* is suggested as a substitute for key lime in pre-Columbian ceviche. In any case the Peruvian bona fides of the recipe are secure. Lauer then is correct by calling Gastón Acurio inclusive. However, Lauer sees Virgilio Martínez, the new face of the culinary boom, as "*desinclusión*," which I will translate as exclusive or restricted.[4]

Lauer uses a music analogy to explain his comments, but here I want instead to use culinary tradition to explain why I think he is correct. As I hinted before, Martínez is an eccentric but brilliant chef. His theoretical approach to food can be favorably compared to the molecular gastronomic approach of, for example, Wylie Dufresne. Chef Dufrense's cuisine was grounded in the science of chemistry and physics. But the basis for Chef Martínez's is not cooking; instead, his foundation is the science of biology and the social science of anthropology. The cerebral concepts outlined on his sister's Mater Iniciativa website speak to the links (or at least the similarity) of his approach to the molecular gastronomic one. Virgilio Martínez's is then firmly placed in an intellectual Western culinary tradition.

Additionally, Chef Martínez shares a twenty-first-century Western foraging gastronomic tradition exemplified by Chef René Redzepi of Noma in Copenhagen, Denmark. To an elite global audience, a restaurateur foraging for food for the menu of his or her internationally renowned venue seems at once eccentric, brilliant, and a bit dangerous. It goes back to our earliest origins as hunter-gatherers, yet this method feels remarkably modern because of its sustainability and deep environmental understanding. But Peruvians have been continuously foraging for food for at least ten thousand years. On any given day, you can sit on the *malecón* at Huanchaco and watch people harvest *mococho*, the edible seaweed. Highlanders forage for *yuyo* and *tarwi* growing around or in between crops. And highlanders sift through high-mountain ponds in search of the nutritious blue-green algae *cushuro*. Also, remember the 1986 study of an Aymara village, where individuals distinguished between different species of wild potato by tasting bitter and nonbitter varieties. All this was done even though these semi-wild potatoes had extremely high glycoalkaloid (poison) levels. These villagers were doing this in the hope of domesticating a new species of wild potato. This is extreme foraging. So, whereas Chef Redzepi's hunt for wild Nordic ingredients to rediscover "ancestral motivations that they didn't even know they had," Chef Martínez's project is quite different.[5] Most of the exotic items Martínez is foraging are readily available in local markets. He is not then rediscovering ancestral motivations because these motivations never disappeared in the Andean world. What he is really doing is discovering foods such as *tarwi* and *cushuro* for the elite neoliberal world. With this in mind, Lauer's critique is clear. Martínez is then *des-inclusión* (exclusive), because although he is an incredibly creative and inspiring chef his project is one designed for the global elite. Peruvian foodstuffs are this artist's palette, not his raison d'être.

Lauer ends his interview with Matta noting that, according to the World Bank, the poverty rate in Peru has fallen 30 percent over the past few decades, which was also the era of the Peru's gastronomic boom. Lauer sees, as I do, that the kitchen elevated many of these Peruvian's lives. The boom then is not just the growth of world-class restaurants in Lima, although Lauer notes that the Peruvian gastronomic revolution has not avoided becoming a Lima gastronomic revolution. He sees some spillover into the colonial city of Arequipa but very little to the North Coast city of Chiclayo.[6] Perhaps this is the way forward? Often in this text I have highlighted Chiclayo's famous gastronomic customs. I specifically singled out the towns of Lambayeque, Ferreñafe, and Monsefú as places with ancient culinary traditions. I even expanded out from Chiclayo to discuss the city of Trujillo, three hours south of Chiclayo, and the city of Huacho, a few hours to the north of Lima. These places should be promoted as the next fulcrum of Peru's gastronomic revolution.

The Commission for the Promotion of Peruvian Exports and Tourism (PROMPERÚ) could and should start a campaign to promote these regions. Travel to Huacho would link the city's best *cevicherías* and *chifas* with tourism to the oldest city in the Americas, Caral. The *cevicherías* of Trujillo and the fishing village of Huanchaco can be coupled with travel to the Moche Huaca de la Luna and the magnificent El Brujo complex and museum. And speaking of Trujillo, recall the discussion of the most flavorful variety of coca, *Erythroxylum novogranatense* var. *truxillense,* which is named after the city. The coca fields that supply Coca-Cola with *tupa* coca leaves are about an hour outside the city. And I say this in all seriousness, these fields should be tourist destinations. In the Western world even the hardest of drugs are on their way to legalization, with the only outlier being the deadly narcotic fentanyl. With this growing tolerance in mind, keeping in place the UN Single Convention on Narcotic Drug restriction on coca cultivation is farcical. Growing coca should be legal in the West with cultivation prosecuted only if the grower initiates the chemical process of turning the leaves into cocaine. And coca, specifically *Erythroxylum novogranatense* var. *truxillense,* could be marketed as a remedy for altitude sickness, as a weight-loss supplement, as a soothing tea, and as a flavoring agent for gum and candy. And Coca-Cola leading this campaign would be of great benefit to the company's image, transitioning the corporation from a diabetes delivery system to disadvantaged youth into a company that has and is promoting one of the greatest flavoring agents of the indigenous Americas! If tour buses start to visit coca plantations in the Alto Chicama, I am sure booths would soon spring up selling all manner of things coca. Additionally, Peru should move to honor the coca sour just like the pisco sour, which was made UNESCO Cultural Heritage in 2007, and the historic trinity of pisco punch, pisco sour, and coca sour should be part of a countrywide marketing campaign, with the epicenter being Peru's North Coast.

Finally, Chiclayo would be the crown jewel of these gastronomic and archaeological excursions with visits to the Museo Tumbas Reales de Sipán in Lambayeque complemented by lunch at a venue such as El Cántaro. A visit to the market of Monsefú and Terminal Santa Rosa could be highlighted by an afternoon meal of *panquitas de lifes* at Los Delfines. A lodge such as Los Horcones de Túcume could be encouraged to provide guests with time and transportation to pick out their own fish at Terminal Santa Rosa for a luncheon later in the day at the lodge. Indeed, it is perhaps auspicious that this area was mostly left out of Peru's gastronomic revolution because it can become the focus of Peru's gastronomic boom 2.0. Would I relish returning to Terminal Santa Rosa only to see a multitude of tourists bent on outbidding me for that day's catch? No, I would not. But I would have a sense of inner satisfaction to see such progress. And yes, these outings could all include a three-day junket to Machu Picchu at the excursion's end—if only to satisfy the bucket list.

Notes

Introduction

1. Bird, Hyslop, and Dimitrijevic Skinner 1985, 241.

2. Cabello Balboa 1951, p. 327.

3. McDonell 2019; Matta 2014; Hall 2020; López-Canales 2019; and García 2021 are but a few examples from the second school.

4. León Canales 2013, p. 357.

5. Uceda, Mujica, and Morales 1997, p. 131.

6. Garcilaso de la Vega 1989, p. 504.

7. Valderrama and Ugás 2009, p. 36.

8. León Canales 2013, pp. 199–201.

9. Fuentes 1866, p. 130.

10. Kipling quoted from Asbury 1933, p. 227.

11. Because many highlanders have left the Andes for the opportunities of the coast, the male tradition of coastal *chicha* brewers has waned.

12. Cabello Balboa 1951, p. 327.

13. Ranere et al. 2009.

14. Staller, Tykot, and Benz 2006.

15. Reader 2009, pp. 27.

16. McDonell 2015, pp. 70–85.

17. Personal communication with campesinos in Huaraz, Peru, and National Research Council 1989, pp. 181–82.

18. Dillehay and Piperno 2014.

19. Andres, Ugás, and Bustamante 2006, pp. 333–40.

20. Rostworowski cited from Villavicencio 2007, p. 128.

21. Plowman 1984, pp. 125–63.

22. Streatfeild 2002, pp. 59–61, 81–82.

23. Mariátegui, Urquidi, and Basadre 1971, p. 279.

24. Fuentes 1866, p. 125.

25. Fuentes 1866, p. 122.

26. Balbi 1999, pp. 10–12.

27. Balbi provides a nice explanation of the origin of the word in the Cantonese language, which means either "to cook rice" or "to eat rice." Balbi 1999, p. 124.

28. Balbi 1999, pp. 128–38.

29. Masterson and Funada-Classen 2004.

30. Matsuhisa and Shih 2018.

31. For example, Chef Mitsuharu Tsumura's book *Nikkei es Perú* suggests Limeño ignorance of the edibility and deliciousness of many of the creatures in their abundant maritime environment. But, again, one look at the shell and bone remains at Huaca Prieta clearly reveals that Peruvians have been eating all

kinds of things from the sea for thousands of years. Tsumura and Barrón 2013, p. 29; for Bird's analysis, see Bird 1985, pp. 241–43.

32. Tegel 2016, p. 24.

Chapter 1

1. DeMasi and Weiner 2011.

2. Miroff 2014.

3. Personal communication with Ricardo Sulem Wong, December 21, 2021.

4. According to Wikipedia, "The World's Best 50 Restaurants" is a list produced by UK media company William Reed, which originally appeared in 2002. The Lima restaurants have moved up in 2022. https://www.theworlds50best.com/list/1-50.

5. Obama, Konner, Davis et al. 2021.

6. Lazar 2018.

7. González Holguín 1608, p. 261.

8. Twain 1951, pp. 361–62.

9. "Lagniappe" 2019.

10. The Sacred Valley of the Inca runs about thirty miles, as the condor flies, from Pisac to Ollantaytambo, where travelers take the train into Aguas Calientes and Machu Picchu. The valley's allure is that it is lower in altitude and much warmer than Cuzco. In many places there are also stunning views of the mountains.

11. Alva and Donnan 1993, pp. 19–25.

12. Shady, De Haro, and Delgado 2007.

13. Mujica and Maio 2007, pp. 49, 36, 37, 240.

14. Briones Vela 2013, pp. 18–19.

15. Remains of these scallops were found at Huaca Prieta dating back to more than eleven thousand years ago. Dillehay 2017, pp. 211, 215.

16. Heyerdahl, Sandweiss, and Narváez 1995, pp. 6–7.

Chapter 2

1. Dillehay 2011, p. 77.

2. Diversity is the theme of the Monte Verde study in coastal Chile (Dillehay 1989, p. 815), and in Peru (Dillehay 2011, p. 5).

3. Moseley 1974, pp. 7–11.

4. Moseley 1992, p. 87.

5. Dillehay 2011, pp. 187–88.

6. Paterson 2008, pp. 54–56.

7. Childe 1951.

8. Blanton 1981, p. 107.

9. Silverman 2004, pp. 35–36.

10. Moseley 1974, pp. 43–48.

11. Shady, De Haro, and Delgado 2007, p. 24.

12. Dillehay 2017, pp. 203–5.

13. Donnan and McClelland 1999, p. 67.
14. Donnan 1976, pp. 92–93.
15. Cobo and Hamilton 1990, p. 237.
16. Chardon 1980, pp. 294–302.
17. Dillehay 2017, p. 420.
18. Dillehay 2017, p. 418. For the making of the paddle and images in Moche art, see Donnan 1976, p. 92. Cobo also refers to them in Cobo and Hamilton 1990, p. 237. The cane paddle is shown in Donnan 1976, p. 93.
19. Cobo and Hamilton 1990, p. 238.
20. The record of Naymlap and his retinue was recorded in the sixteenth-century chronicle of Father Miguel Cabello Balboa. See Cabello Balboa 1951, p. 327. For the landing near Chotuna, see Wester La Torre 2010, p. 181. Alana Cordy-Collins has suggested Naylamp's invasion could be instead a record of a rich *Spondylus princeps* merchant's return. The shell of *S. princeps* (the spiny Pacific oyster) was more valuable than gold in the pre-Columbian Andean world. Moseley and Cordy-Collins 1990, p. 412.
21. See Geoffrey Conrad in Moseley and Cordy-Collins 1990, p. 237. The story of Taycanamo was recorded in the 1614 manuscript by the Anonymous Trujillano. See Kosok 1965, p. 89.
22. Sarmiento, Bauer, and Smith-Oka 2007, bk 46.
23. Mann 2011, pp. 139–56.
24. Julien 1985.
25. Cushman 2013.
26. Sater 2007.
27. Smil 2001.
28. Leon and Kraul 2014.
29. Philipe Béarez personal communication 2020.
30. Dillehay 2017, pp. 205–6, gives the most organized listing; León Canales 2013 records the earlier archaeological record.
31. Cerrón-Palomino, Pontificia Universidad Católica del Perú 2000, pp. 151–62; Valderrama 2010, pp. 166–70.
32. Valderrama 2010, pp. 48–52.
33. Cobo and Mateos 1964, pp. 289–90.
34. Uceda, Mujica, and Morales 1997, p. 136.
35. Uceda, Mujica, and Morales 1997, p. 131.
36. Valderrama 2010, p. 167.
37. Valderrama 2010, p. 169.
38. Tsumura and Barrón 2013, p. 29.
39. Valderrama 2010, pp. 11–12.
40. Fuentes 1866, pp. 121–27.
41. Jurafsky 2014, pp. 41–45.
42. Alcalde Mongrut (Compadre Guisao) 2005, pp. 21–22.
43. Alcalde Mongrut (Compadre Guisao) 2005, p. 21.
44. Valderrama 2010, p. 169.
45. Alcalde Mongrut (Compadre Guisao) 2005, pp. 22–24. The use, type, and history of ajíes in Peruvian cuisine is a fascinating and complex topic.

46. Lynch 1980, p. 116.

47. Blanchard 1992, p. 77; Maass et al. 2010.

48. Saavedra 2016.

49. This etymology is from Galen Brokaw, professor and head of the Modern Languages and Literatures Department at Montana State University.

50. León Canales 2013, p. 262.

51. Dillehay 2017, p. 426; Noriega Cardó 2016, p. 6. For the reconciliation of the scientific names, see Agardh and Agardh 1842.

52. Aaronson 2000, p. 232.

53. Valderrama 2010, p. 106.

54. Dillehay 2017, pp. 205–6, 216, 228, 242.

55. Bradley 2012.

56. León Canales 2013, p. 12.

57. Resolución Ministerial 2015.

58. Bird, Hyslop, and Dimitrijevic Skinner 1985, p. 39.

59. Valderrama 2010, p. 77.

60. Dillehay 2017, pp. 318, 320.

61. Bonavia 1985, p. 90.

62. Replicas of this mural confront visitors arriving at Lima's Jorge Chávez on their way through customs.

63. Gálvez and Runcio 2009, pp. 55–87.

64. Tschudi 1844, pp. 22, 25.

65. Eigenmann 1922, p. 57.

66. Uceda, Mujica, and Morales 1997, p. 171.

67. These culinary notes are from my visit to the restaurant Los Delfines and the central market of Monsefú in December 2013.

68. Middendorf 1959, pp. 152–53.

Chapter 3

1. Andrews and Eshbaugh 1984, pp. 2–4.

2. Andrews 1999, p. 52.

3. Dillehay 2017, p. 645.

4. Andrews and Eshbaugh 1984, pp. 87–114.

5. Dillehay 2017, p. 645.

6. Andrews 1999, p. 52.

7. Garcilaso de la Vega and Craesbeeck 1609, p. 421 (Spanish); Garcilaso de la Vega 1989, p. 504 (translation).

8. Keegan and Hofman 2017.

9. Garcilaso de la Vega and Craesbeeck 1609, p. 505.

10. González Holguín 1608, p. 210.

11. RMC/JOT 2009.

12. Ugás and Mendoza 2012, pp. 15, 16.

13. Alvarez Novoa, Arquíñigo Vidal, and Cayllahua Muñoz 2017.

14. Fuentes 1866, pp. 134–35.

15. Mann 2011, pp. 123–63.
16. Rice 2011, pp. 179–80.
17. Mann 2011, p. 146.
18. Cabieses, Vargas, Viacava, and Wust 2006, p. 66.
19. PromPerú 2016, p. 22.
20. For the identification of wakatay (huacatay), see León Canales 2013, p. 474; for the recipes, see Zapata Acha 2009, p. 648.
21. Garcilaso de la Vega and Craesbeeck 1609, p. 474.
22. Balta Campbell 2009.
23. Andrews and Eshbaugh 1984, p. 119.
24. Alcalá and Brown 2014, p. 333.
25. Dillehay 2017, pp. 651, 655.
26. León Canales 2013, p. 204.
27. Wood 2002.
28. Rowe 1946, pp. 231–32.
29. Dillehay 2017, p. 654.
30. Cabieses, Vargas, Viacava, and Wust 2006, p. 59.
31. Dillehay 2017, pp. 645, 651.
32. Cabieses, Vargas, Viacava, and Wust 2006, p. 59; Dillehay 2017, p. 645.
33. Cabieses, Vargas, Viacava, and Wust 2006, p. 59; Valderrama and Ugás 2009, p. 39.
34. PromPerú 2016, pp. 31, 32.
35. Andrews 1999, pp. 4–17.
36. Garcilaso de la Vega and Craesbeeck 1609, p. 422.
37. Andrews 1999, p. 121.
38. León Canales 2013, p. 205; Cabieses, Vargas, Viacava, and Wust 2006, pp. 60, 61.
39. Valderrama and Ugás 2009, p. 39.
40. Dillehay 2017, p. 646; Bird, Hyslop, and Dimitrijevic Skinner 1985, p. 236.
41. Cabieses, Vargas, Viacava, and Wust 2006, p. 60.
42. Valderrama and Ugás 2009, p. 39; PromPerú 2016, p. 35.
43. Andrews and Eshbaugh 1984, pp. 115–17.
44. Andrews and Eshbaugh 1984, p. 119.
45. Cabieses, Vargas, Viacava, and Wust 2006, p. 60.
46. Valderrama and Ugás 2009, p. 43.
47. Dillehay 2017, p. 655.
48. Twain 1866. http://www.twainquotes.com/18661025u.html.
49. Morton and Dowling 1987.
50. Vanhove and Van Damme 2013.
51. Staff, National Research Council 1988, p. v; Peña, Sharp, and Wysoki 2002, p. 200.
52. Morton and Dowling 1987.
53. Castañeda-Vildózola et al. 2010.
54. González Holguín 1608, pp. 329, 174. Many thanks go to my colleagues Gladys Jiménez and Jim Sykes for their assistance in this identification.

55. Vanhove and Van Damme 2013.
56. Dillehay 2017, p. 369.
57. León Canales 2013, p. 201.
58. Vanhove and Van Damme 2013.
59. Staff, National Research Council 1988, p. 229.

Chapter 4

1. Fuentes 1866, p. 130.
2. "Alcohol through the Ages," p. 26.
3. Gutiérrez Sarmiento and Pulla Aguirre 2017.
4. Gutiérrez Sarmiento and Pulla Aguirre 2017, p. 3.
5. Bradley 2013.
6. Galloway 1989.
7. Monzote 2008, p. 25.
8. Philologist Gerald Taylor has *guarapo* (*warapu*) entering with the Spanish and has the word listed as common in his linguistic study of the northeastern Chachapoyas region of Peru. Taylor 2000, pp. 91, 105.
9. Hildebrandt 1969, p. 131; Zapata Acha 2009, p. 375.
10. See Zapata Acha 2009, p. 375, for the seventeenth-century statistics; Rice 2011, pp. 224–25, for the capacity of botijas.
11. Zapata Acha 2009, p. 375.
12. O'Toole 2012, pp. 112, 208.
13. Adorno and Guamán Poma de Ayala 2001.
14. Guamán Poma de Ayala 1613.
15. Guamán Poma de Ayala 1613, pp. 704 (718) is only one example. The term *bozales* first is used for muzzled slaves, but in the later colonial and early republican eras it is a generic term for young enslaved African males.
16. Espinoza Soriano 1967, p. 318.
17. Bowser states that during the early conquest period and the Inca rebellion, a strong distrust developed between the Blacks and the indigenous peoples, which benefited both the Spanish and the enslaved Blacks. Bowser 1977, p. 26.
18. Fuentes 1866, p. 127.
19. I believe this analogy works even though the list of spirits is all grape-based. Bordiga 2018, p. 63.
20. Rice has noted by the eighteenth century, 89–90 percent of the wine produced in southern Peru was being distilled into brandy. Therefore, Peru had one of the largest productions of distilled spirits in the early modern world. Rice 2011, p. 181.
21. Vasconcelos and Jaén 1997.
22. Commager 1966, p. 244.
23. Andrews 2004, pp. xi. Aguirre shows a more drastic decline from 1792 to 1845. Aguirre 1995, p. 47.
24. Andrews 2004, p. 167.
25. Bradley 2019, p. 3.
26. Cobo and Hamilton 1990, p. 198.

27. Staller, Tykot, and Benz 2006, pp. 449–50. For the etymology of *chicha* see Hildebrandt 1969, p. 131.

28. Aikhenvald and Dixon 2006.

29. Alvarez Novoa, Vidal, and Cayllahua Muñoz 2017, vol. 2, pp. 265–66.

30. Moore 1989, p. 686.

31. According to Hayashida, the Piura *chicha* makers boil twice, whereas the Lambayeque brewers only boil once. Hayashida 2008, pp. 163–67. But this boiling likely varies from *chichería* to *chichería,* because Cayllahua Muñoz has his brewer boiling the beer twice in Lambayeque. Alvarez Novoa, Vidal, and Cayllahua Muñoz 2017, vol. 2, pp. 265–66.

32. Bird 2010. I must state that I am appalled by the adaptation of this flash pasteurization, especially for vin de garde (wines that improve with age), because the process can destroy some of the subtle flavors of fine wines.

33. Cobo and Hamilton 1990, pp. 172–74. Hayashida, after Morris, has the chosen women brewers relocated from Cuzco to provincial centers as a display of hospitality. Hayashida 2008, p. 162.

34. Hayashida 2008, p. 165.

35. Moore 1989, p. 686.

36. Acosta 2008, p. 148.

37. Goode and Harrop 2011.

38. Hayashida 2008, pp. 165–66; Alvarez Novoa, Vidal, and Cayllahua Muñoz 2017, vol. 1, p. 163, and vol. 2, pp. 265–66.

39. Jennings and Bowser 2009, pp. 10–11.

40. Cabello Balboa 1951, p. 327.

41. Many thanks for this exact translation to my colleague and friend Ignacio López-Calvo, PhD, the UC Merced Presidential Chair in the Humanities and Professor of Latin American Literature and Culture in the Department of Literatures, Languages and Cultures.

42. Moseley and Cordy-Collins 1990.

43. Alvarez Novoa, Vidal, and Cayllahua Muñoz 2017, vol. 2, p. 265.

44. Hayshida has pointed this out clearly in Jennings and Bowser 2009, p. 234.

45. Arriaga and Keating 1968, p. 34.

46. In his 1977 Master's thesis, James Szabo observed that the preponderance of Moche ceramic sherds he studied were vitrified, making them nonporous, so they would not leak during any long fermentation process. Szabo 1977, p. 51.

47. Hayashida 2008, p. 172.

48. Hardwick 1995, pp. 56–57. Lambic is a type of beer brewed in the Pajottenland region of Belgium southwest of Brussels and in Brussels itself since the thirteenth century (Wikipedia).

49. Hayashida 2008, p. 172.

50. Donnan and McClelland 1999, p. 20.

51. My colleague Mark Andersen, a UTRGV biologist, believes that most contaminants would collect at the "T" juncture at the top of the ceramic.

52. Donnan and McClelland 1999, pp. 20–21.

53. There is a beautiful drawing of a cántaro covered with a cotton cloth here in Alvarez Novoa, Vidal, and Cayllahua Muñoz 2017, vol. 2, p. 248.

54. Forbes 1970, pp. 20–21, 33, 57.

55. Serra Puche and Lazcano Arce 2016, p.53.

56. Schuler 2005, pp. 83–109.

57. Rice 2011, p. 158; Huertas Vallejos 2004, pp. 53–54, 59.

58. Rice records the staggering amounts of alcohol consumed by the Spaniards and natives at Potosí, and she notes that by the late eighteenth century, 80–90 percent of the wine produced in southern Peru was distilled into brandy. Rice 2011, pp. 180–81. For the restrictions on the colonial wine trade, see Rice 2011, pp. 138–53.

59. Rice 2011, pp. 137–38.

60. Rice and Huertas Vallejos both refer to Cieza de León's early colonial record, where he comments on the enormous extent of Peruvian viniculture even in his time. Rice 2011, pp. 144–45; Huertas Vallejos 2004, p. 50; Cieza de León and Pease 2005.

61. Rice 2011, pp. 149–53.

62. Mann 2011, p. 155.

63. Rice 2011, pp. 180–81.

64. Mann 2011, p. 223.

65. Toro Lira 2010, p. 9.

66. Toro Lira 2010, p. 20.

67. Toro Lira 2010, p. 26.

68. Schuler 2005, pp. 26–29.

69. Emen 2015.

70. Rice 2011, p. 155.

71. Schuler 2005, p. 20. The Peruvians insist that this separates their pisco from Chile's spirit, because the Chileans can distill past proof and then add water later. See Kulp 2015.

72. Schuler 2005, pp. 40–42.

73. Brown uses the proportion of botijas for this ratio. Brown 1986, p. 44.

74. Schuler 2005, p.29.

75. Emen 2015.

76. Emen 2015.

77. Toro Lira 2010, pp. 37–65. Asbury has Nicol creating the pisco punch recipe, but this is likely an overstatement. Asbury 1933, p. 226.

78. Duggan and Abiol 2015, p. 65.

79. McDonnell and Abiol 2015, pp. 64–65.

80. Toro Lira 2010, p. 10.

81. Schiaffino 2006, pp. 5–6.

82. Schiaffino 2006, pp. 6–7.

83. A suggestion from my sour-loving colleague Mark Andersen.

84. Bronson 1973, p. 236.

85. Bronson 1973, p. 240.

Chapter 5

1. Mint Museum Online Database 2008.

2. Cobo and Hamilton 1990, pp. 48–50.

3. Matsuoka et al. 2002.

4. Motley, Zerega, and Cross 2006, pp. 67–68.

5. Piperno and Flannery 2001.

6. León Canales 2013, p. 138.

7. Food and Drug Administration 2020.

8. Motley, Zerega, and Cross 2006, pp. 70–80. In their chapter on maize, Buckler and Stevens explore both locations as epicenters for domestication of corn even though the two regions are five hundred miles apart.

9. Piperno and Flannery 2001.

10. Ranere et al. 2009.

11. Dillehay 2017, p. 663.

12. Kistler et al. 2018. The odd term race is applied to the many varieties of maize that are genetically diverse and locally adapted. Villa et al. 2005.

13. Staller and Carrasco 2010, pp, 358–59.

14. Katz, Hediger, and Valleroy 1974, p. 767.

15. Karttunen 1983, p. 171.

16. Katz, Hediger, and Valleroy 1974.

17. Katz, Hediger, and Valleroy 1974, p. 771. Juniper ash is used in Native American cooking to create an alkali solution. Sherman and Dooley 2017.

18. Staller, Tykot, and Benz 2006, pp. 451–54; Jennings and Bowser 2009.

19. Although flour tortillas are now considered authentic Mexican fare, they were first made in the colonial era when the Spanish brought wheat to the New World.

20. Moseley 1974.

21. Burger and Van der Merwe 1990.

22. León Canales 2013, p. 510. Both Betanzos and Cobo mention tortillas in their chronicles. The Betanzos chronicle is particularly important because it was written during the early conquest era before the Spanish colonized the Inca world. Betanzos, Hamilton, and Buchanan 1996, p. 254; Cobo and Hamilton 1990, p. 198.

23. Coe 1994, pp. 113–14.

24. Cieza de León and Pease 2005, p. 100.

25. Cobo and Hamilton 1990, p. 198.

26. González Holguín 1608, p. 94.

27. Cobo and Hamilton 1990, p. 198; González Holguín 1608, p. 146.

28. Although his book is dedicated to Peruvian tamales (which came to Peru with the Spanish), Rodríguez Pastor does a fine job recording all the regional recipes throughout the country. And all of these preparations require butter or lard. Rodríguez Pastor 2007, pp. 511–66.

29. Coe 1994, pp. 117–18.

30. Kerr and Coe 1989, p. 963.

31. Zapata Acha 2009, pp. 397–99.
32. González Holguín 1608, p. 355.
33. Montaguth 2020.
34. González Holguín 1608, p. 175.
35. Zapata Acha 2009, p. 499.
36. González Holguín 1608, p. 153.
37. González Holguín 1608, p. 175; Cobo and Hamilton 1990 p. 198.
38. Rodríguez Pastor 2007, p. 22.
39. González Holguín 1608, pp. 115, 61.
40. Zapata Acha 2009, p. 163.
41. Grobman Tversqui et al. 1961, p. 175.
42. For images, see Guardia 2008, pp. 14, 22; for details, see Reader 2009, p. 52.
43. González Holguín 1608, p. 376.
44. Reader 2009, pp. 21–23.
45. Reader 2009, p. 23.
46. Motley, Zerega, and Cross 2006, p. 285.
47. Johns and Keen 1986, p. 437.
48. Johns 1986, p. 63.
49. Cieza de León, De Onís, and Von Hagen 1959, p. 271.
50. León Canales 2013, p. 11.
51. Cieza de León, De Onís, and Von Hagen 1959, p. 164.
52. Reader 2009, p. 27.
53. Motley, Zerega, and Cross 2006, p. 285.
54. Reader 2009, pp. 26–27; Guardia 2008, p. 36.
55. Because several of Cieza de León's written works languished in obscurity for hundreds of years, the Spanish historian Francisco López de Gómara's *Historia general de las Indias* (1552) is the first published record of potatoes. Hawkes and Francisco-Ortega 1993, p. 1.
56. Cieza de León, De Onís, and Von Hagen 1959, p. 44.
57. Mann 2011, p. 198.
58. Hawkes and Francisco-Ortega 1993, pp. 1–7.
59. Guardia 2008, p. 76.
60. Mann 2011, p. 200.
61. For Drake and Raleigh, see Reader 2009, pp. 86–87; for the sweet potato in English theater, see Reader 2009, pp. 77–79.
62. Reader 2009, pp. 94–98; Mann 2011, p. 198.
63. Mann 2011, p. 198.
64. Reader 2009, pp. 111–13.
65. Reader 2009, pp. 119–22.
66. Mann 2011, pp. 198, 210–11, 227.
67. Reader 2009, p. 163.
68. *P. infestans* destroys all nightshades, not just potatoes. Mann 2011, pp. 220–22.
69. Mann 2011, p. 199.
70. Mann 2011, p. 226.
71. Mann 2011, 231–37.

72. *The Botany of Desire* 2009.

73. León Canales 2013, p. 116; Lang et al. 2021, pp. 1, 10. The Lang et al. paper is a fascinating study from eleven Chinese researchers, which is quite apropos, because today China is by far the leading world producer of potatoes.

74. Peru has many fresh cheeses, but queso fresco from any Latin American market is a good substitute.

75. Reader 2009, p. 145.

Chapter 6

1. Cieza de León, De Onís, and Von Hagen 1959, p. 44.
2. National Research Council (U.S.) 1989, p. 11.
3. McDonell 2015, p. 76.
4. León Canales 2013, pp. 128, 125.
5. McDonell 2021, p. 390.
6. León Canales 2013, p. 128.
7. McDonell 2021, pp. 390, 385.
8. McDonell 2015, p. 80.
9. Gonzalez-Lamas 2018.
10. McDonell 2021, p. 391.
11. McDonell 2021, p. 400.
12. National Research Council (U.S.) 1989, p. 139.
13. León Canales 2013, p. 124.
14. National Research Council (U.S.) 1989, p. 139.
15. Zapata Acha 2009, p. 416.
16. National Research Council (U.S.) 1989, pp. 139, 143; León Canales 2013, p. 124.
17. León Canales 2013, pp. 124–25.
18. National Research Council (U.S.) 1989, pp. 125, 139.
19. Cruz et al. 2014, p. 2.
20. Nafici 2017.
21. Giusti-Lanham and Dodi 1978, p. 277.
22. Montagné and Harvey Lang 1988, p. 495.
23. León Canales 2013, p. 181.
24. National Research Council (U.S.) 1989, p. 181.
25. León Canales 2013, p. 183; National Research Council (U.S.) 1989, p. 188.
26. Garcilaso de la Vega and Craesbeeck 1609, p. 418.
27. González Holguín 1608, p. 222.
28. National Research Council (U.S.) 1989, p. 187.
29. León Canales 2013, p. 181.
30. Thanks to longtime Huaracinos Gladys Jiménez and Jim Sykes for this information.
31. National Research Council (U.S.) 1989, p. 188.
32. León Canales 2013, p. 182.
33. Thanks again to Huaracinos Gladys Jiménez and Jim Sykes.
34. Aaronson 2000, p. 232.

35. For the synonym name, see Zapata Acha 2009, p. 251; for the Spanish Quechua, see González Holguín 1608, p. 375. Holguín's entry is interesting. Specifically, it reads *Ouas redonditas* (Spanish) to *Llullucha* (Quechua). *Ouas* is Ovas, possibly related to huevas or eggs. Thanks to Ignacio López-Calvo, professor of Latin American literature and culture at UC Merced, for this analysis. However, Galen Brokaw, head of the Modern Languages and Literatures Department at Montana State University states: "I don't think that ova is related to hueva. Hueva comes from the Latin ova, but ova referring to algae comes from the Latin ulva, which I think originally referred to marsh grass rather than algae. In any case, these two nouns belong to different declension classes in Latin." Karttunen links it to the Nahuatl (Aztec) term *apachtli*, which is insect larvae, or a plant that grows in water, marsh hay: ovas que se crían dentro del agua (M), planta que crece detro del río, heno. Karttunen 1992, p. 11.

36. Aaronson 2000, p. 231.

37. Ponce 2014, p. 117.

38. McDonell 2019.

39. Chef's Table 2017. For the neurotoxic aspects of Andean *Nostoc*, see Ponce 2014, p. 116.

40. Seminario "Arte, Cultura e Identidad sobre la Mesa" and Weston 1993, pp. 39–40.

41. Milon et al. 2020, pp. 4, 43.

42. Martínez-Véliz 2008.

43. León Canales 2013, pp. 440, 474.

44. Zapata Acha 2009, p. 390.

45. León Canales 2013, p. 492.

46. León Canales 2013, pp. 249–50.

47. Garcilaso de la Vega and Craesbeeck 1609, p. 419.

48. Karttunen 1992, p. 273.

49. Dillehay 2017, p. 383.

50. Smith 2015, p. 156.

51. Alva and Donnan 1993, pp. 93–94.

52. León Canales 2013, p. 159.

53. Smith 2002, p. 7.

54. Stalker and Wilson 2016. The first chapter has an excellent record of early colonial sources recording the peanut.

55. Smith 2002, pp. 7–9.

56. León Canales 2013, p. 26. For the African production, see Scott 2016.

57. Smith 2015 p. 157.

58. Smith 2002, pp.12–14.

59. Krampner 2013, pp. 24–28.

60. Carver 1983.

61. Smith 2015 p. 155.

62. Christakis 2008.

63. Smith 2015 pp. 176–78.

64. Krampner 2013, p. 4.

65. Christakis 2008.

Chapter 7

1. Silverman and Isbell 2008, pp. 121–29.
2. Sandweiss and Wing 1997, pp. 47, 49 (quote).
3. González Holguín 1608, p. 78.
4. Cieza de León and Pease 2005, p. 366.
5. Arriaga and Keating 1968, p. 47.
6. Garcilaso de la Vega and Craesbeeck 1609, p. 278.
7. Pigière et al. 2012, pp. 1020–23.
8. There are many different variations of this sauce, but the essential ingredients are *hucatay* and *ají*.
9. Pearson 1948, p. 346.
10. León Canales 2013, pp. 289–90.
11. Cieza de León and Pease 2005, p. 279.
12. Garcilaso de la Vega and Craesbeeck 1609, pp. 432, 277.
13. Lemons, Victor, and Schaffer 2003, pp. 345–54. For the origin of the chacu, see Garcilaso de la Vega and Craesbeeck 1609, p. 272.
14. Jiménez 1996, pp. 1–6; Nilsson 2005, p. 21.
15. McKirdy 2016.
16. Phipps and Solazzo 2020.
17. D'Altroy 2002, pp. 12–13, 320–21.
18. Ferreguetti, Pereira, and Bergallo 2018.
19. Hosken et al. 2021, pp. 366–67.
20. Hemming 1970, pp. 330, 435.
21. Luján 2017, pp. 9, 18.
22. Bradley 2017.
23. Thanks for this information from my former student Erich Keller who is building his house in the forest near the southern Peruvian town of Salvación.
24. Sanz 2016, p. 201.
25. According to Huanchaco restaurant owner Ricardo Sulem Wong, the medium loche is grown in the Chao and Virú Valleys near Trujillo, but the smaller true loche (uno pequeño, el verdadero) comes from Lambayeque and costs three times the price.
26. Personal communication with Ricardo Sulem Wong, December 19, 2021. For the Moche reference, see León Canales 2013, p. 465.
27. Caritas of Peru 2012.
28. Andres, Ugás, and Bustamante 2006, p. 333.
29. Metropolitan Museum of Art 2008.
30. Garcilaso spent time noting that a pre-Columbian ethnic group relished eating the flesh of dogs. Garcilaso de la Vega 1989, p. 335.
31. Gepts 1998, p. 1124.
32. Sanz 2016, p. 204.
33. Uceda, Mujica, and Morales 1997, p. 135.
34. Mejía 1969, p. 73.
35. Holderread 2001, p. 79.
36. Goldhammer 2014.

37. Silverman and Isbell 2008, pp. 121–22.
38. Stahl, Muse, and Delgado Espinoza 2006, pp. 657–58.
39. Silverman and Isbell 2008, p. 122.
40. Stahl, Muse, and Delgado Espinoza 2006, p. 661.
41. Donkin 1989, pp. 16–18.
42. Stahl, Muse, and Delgado Espinoza 2006, p. 657.
43. Donnan 1976, p. 13.
44. Garcilaso de la Vega and Craesbeeck 1609, p. 435; González Holguín 1608, p. 379.
45. Stahl 2005, p. 916.
46. Peruvian writer Adán "El Corregidor" Mejía recommended grinding your own *ají mirasol* from the dried peppers. This can work nicely if the dried peppers were purchased in a Peruvian market where they haven't been in a bag for months. It is also interesting to note that the famous author was a Limeño (a person from Lima), which indicates why he left loche out of his recipe. It also speaks to the regionality of this squash's use. Curiously, Mejía cites the quality of the flor rice from the village of Ferreñafe, which is a center for loche production. Mejía 1969, pp. 72–77.
47. Solís 2012.
48. Kauffman 2012; Gonzales-Lara 2020, pp. 1–2.
49. Gonzales-Lara 2020, pp. 2–3.
50. León Canales 2013, pp. 6–7; Palacios et al. 2011, p. 166.
51. León Canales 2013, pp. 189, 191.
52. Dillehay 2017, p. 368.
53. Pasiecznik et al. 2001, p. 10; Depenthal and Meitzner Yoder 2018.
54. Salazar Zarzosa et al. 2021.
55. Gonzales-Lara 2020, p. 4.
56. Gonzales-Lara 2020, p. 3.
57. For the Mexico origin, see León Canales 2013, p. 227; for Huaca Prieta, see Dillehay 2017, p. 379.
58. Karttunen 1992, p. 7.
59. Cieza de León and Pease 2005, pp. 59, 80, 185.
60. González Holguín 1608, p. 187.
61. Giusti-Lanham and Dodi 1978, p. 185.
62. You can substitute either ½ dried *ají mirasol* or 2 tbsp. *ají amarillo* paste, if necessary.

Chapter 8

1. Gagliano 1994, p. 7; Gootenberg 2008, p. 16.
2. This process is described in Hesse 2002, p. 350. Hesse also defines alkaloids, a term first proposed by Meisser in 1819, as nitrogen-containing substances of natural origin, mostly from plants but also from animals, with a greater or lesser degree of basic character, many of which are physiologically active. Hesse 2002, pp. 4–5.

3. Katz, Hediger, and Valleroy 1974, pp. 768–69; Misra, Ragland, and Baker 1993, p. 111.

4. Siegel et al. 1986, p. 40; Jenkins et al. 1996, p. 6.

5. In a summer 2003 trip to La Paz, I had my first experience with the small Bolivian bags of coca and llypta.

6. Julien 1998.

7. The gourd is called a *calero* in Spanish, but the Quechua term *puro* is likely more ancient and therefore more precise.

8. Pacini and Franquemont 1986, p. 35.

9. The story of the coca club in Chachapoyas came up in a personal conversation with the former mayor of Chachapoyas, Dr. Peter Lerche.

10. Donnan 1978, p. 35; Mujica and Maio 2007, p. 215.

11. Plowman 1979; Dillehay et al. 2010.

12. Dillehay et al. 2010, pp. 950, 948.

13. Engel 1957; Shady Solis and Leyva 2003.

14. Dillehay et al. 2010, p. 949.

15. Moseley 1974; Wust 2006.

16. Plowman 1984, pp. 130–37; Rostworowski 1988, p. 65.

17. González Holguín 1608, p. 159.

18. Plowman 1979; Plowman 1984.

19. Plowman 1979, p. 52; Dillehay et al. 2010, p. 940.

20. Acock et al. 1996, pp. 49–53.

21. Rostworowski 1988.

22. Villavicencio 2007, p. 128.

23. Bradley 2019.

24. Karttunen 1983, p. 171.

25. Wingate 1985, pp. 9–22.

26. Engel 1957, p. 68.

27. Josephson and Carroll 1974.

28. Donnan 1978, pp. 116–19; Plowman 1984, p. 142; Villavicencio 2007, p. 207.

29. Matienzo 1967; Murra cited in Julien 1998, p. 129; Pacini and Franquemont 1986, pp. 49–52.

30. Dobyns 1963.

31. Julien 1998, p. 129.

32. Burger 1992; Morris and Thompson 1985.

33. Dillehay et. al. 2010, p. 940.

34. Plowman 1984, p. 138; Dillehay 2010, p. 940.

35. The Valle de los Ríos Apurímac, Ene y Mantaro (VRAEM, the Valley of the Apurímac, Ene and Mantaro Rivers) is a geopolitical area in Peru. It is one of the major areas of coca production in Peru. The area is extremely poor (paraphrased from Wikipedia).

36. See Gobierno de Perú 2008, p. 13, for the data; see Plowman and Rivier 1983, p. 642, for the description of different coca varieties.

37. To avoid confusion, especially for the pre-Columbian aficionados, Chachapoyas is (1) the name for a pre-Columbian polity conquered by the Inca

around 1470, (2) a term for their pre-Hispanic territory, and (3) a modern city in northeastern Peru, which is the capital of the department of Amazonas.

38. You can easily find the town of Cocabamba on Google Earth and note that it is at about thirteen difficult mountain miles from Yerbabuena as the condor flies.

39. After working for years in the Utcubamba Valley, I am most familiar with the coca shops there, but the street on the southwest corner of Cuzco's San Pedro market has several stores selling coca and llypta. Finally, during a visit to the town of Huamachuco, twenty years ago, I was surprised to see an entire street dedicated to coca sales, likely to service the wildcat miners in the region.

40. Gobierno de Perú 2008.

41. Dillehay et al. 2010, p. 940.

42. Streatfeild 2002, p. 190. Gootenberg has the Department of La Libertad, Peru, as the source for Coca-Cola's coca, and the Alto Chicama is in the department of La Libertad. Gootenberg 2008, pp. 82–83. Gootenberg has also noted that Otuzco Province, in La Libertad, is the only coca-producing region in Peru on the western side of the Andes, and according to a 1940 document related to the sourcing of Coca-Cola's coca, the leaves came from twenty-five *chacras* (farms) in this area. Gootenberg 2004, pp. 244–45.

43. Gootenberg 2008, p. 22.

44. Dillehay 2010, p. 948.

45. Dillehay 2010, p. 948.

46. Plowman 1984, p. 138.

47. Streatfeild 2002, p. 190.

48. Gootenberg 2008, p. 62. Merchandise No. 5 is the fifth of seven secret ingredients that are closely guarded from public knowledge by the Coca-Cola company.

49. Pendergrast 1993, pp. 90–91.

50. May 1988, p. D1.

51. Streatfeild 2002, p. 190.

52. Gootenberg 2008, p. 199.

53. Gootenberg 2008, p. 207.

54. UN Conference for the Adoption of a Single Convention on Narcotic Drugs 1961, article 27.

55. Plowman 1984, p. 138.

56. Gootenberg 2004.

57. Niemann 1860, pp. 146–47.

58. Gootenberg 2008, pp. 28–29.

59. Gootenberg 2008, p. 25.

60. Mariani 1896, p. 10.

61. Moore et al. 1994, p. 359.

62. Mariani 1896, p. 26.

63. Mariani 1896, p. 36.

64. Mariani 1896, p. 52.

65. Streatfeild 2002, pp. 60–61.

66. Mariani 1896, p. 60.

67. Mariani 1896, p. 62.
68. Gootenberg 2008, pp. 26–27.
69. Villavicencio 2007, p. 128.
70. Dua 2019.
71. Morales Ayma 2009.
72. Rice 2011, p. 145.
73. See Acurio 2006, bk. 9, for the link to Don Cucho.
74. Hesse specifically mentions aqueous methanol (MeOH) as an agent used to isolate alkaloids from plants, and although consuming this chemical can cause blindness and death, this alcohol is structurally like ethanol (EtOH). Therefore, ethanol is a good agent to extract cocaine from coca leaves, again proved by Mariani's concoctions. Hesse 2002, p. 116. And although water is the universal solvent, it is a very weak isolator of alkaloids from coca. Finally, Siegel et al. specifically mention that in the 1980s, individuals experimented with infusing coca tea with alcohol instead of water to enhance the effects of the cocaine in the tea leaves. Siegel et al. 1986, p. 40.
75. For example, making a pisco sour with Biondi Pisco Italia would be like making a whisky sour with Delamain Cognac Pale & Dry XO.
76. Resolución Directoral National 2007.

Chapter 9

1. Mann 2011, p. xvi.
2. Covey 2021, p. 312.
3. Cieza de León, De Onís, and Von Hagen 1959, p. 44.
4. Covey 2021, p. 317.
5. National Research Council (U.S.) 1989, p. 11.
6. Cieza de León and Pease 2005, p. 100.
7. Covey 2021, p. 317.
8. Gade and Rios n.d.
9. D'Altroy 2002, pp. 34–35.
10. Garcilaso de la Vega and Craesbeeck 1609, p. 482.
11. Shimizu 2011, p. 16.
12. Cieza de León and Pease 2005, p. 189.
13. Garcilaso de la Vega and Craesbeeck 1609, p. 486.
14. Zapata Acha 2009, p. 136.
15. Cieza de León and Pease 2005, p. 35.
16. León Canales 2013, p. 282; Dillehay 2011, pp. 194, 201.
17. Zapata Acha 2009, p. 264.
18. Nolte 2017.
19. Sifton 2004.
20. León Canales notes the oddity of having the turkey, a foreign import, as the centerpiece of the Peruvian Christmas table. León Canales 2013, p. 25.
21. National Research Council (U.S.) 1989, pp. 191.
22. León Canales 2013, p. 248. For the archaeological evidence, see Cook and Parrish 2005, pp. 139, 147, 155.

23. National Research Council (U.S.) 1989, pp. 191–93.
24. Acosta 2008, p. 155.
25. León Canales 2013, p. 249.
26. National Research Council (U.S.) 1989, pp. 192–93.
27. Cerrón-Palomino, Pontificia Universidad Católica del Perú 2000, pp. 151–62.
28. Seminario "Arte, Cultura e Identidad sobre la Mesa," and Weston 1993, pp. 158–60.
29. Rice 2011, pp. 137–38.
30. Schuler 2005, pp. 83–109.
31. Rice 2011, p. 158; Huertas Vallejos 2004, pp. 53–54, 59.
32. Seminario "Arte, Cultura e Identidad sobre la Mesa," and Weston 1993, p. 246.
33. Acosta 2008, p. 171; Zapata Acha 2009, pp. 52, 199.
34. Dalby 2000, p. 126.
35. Thanks to longtime Huaracinos Gladys Jiménez and Jim Sykes for this information.
36. Mariátegui, Urquidi, and Basadre 1971, p. 279.
37. Fuentes 1866, p. 125.
38. Seminario "Arte, Cultura e Identidad sobre la Mesa," and Weston 1993, p. 171.
39. Blanchard 1992, p. 77; Maass et al. 2010.
40. Saavedra 2016.
41. González Holguín 1608, p. 68.
42. Fuentes 1866, pp. 122, 125.
43. Mejía 1969, pp. 68–69.
44. Garcilaso de la Vega and Craesbeeck 1609, p. 505.
45. Smith 2002, pp. 7–9.
46. Arriaga and Keating 1968, p. 42.
47. Luciano cited in Seminario "Arte, Cultura e Identidad sobre la Mesa," and Weston 1993, p. 172.
48. Luciano cited in Seminario "Arte, Cultura e Identidad sobre la Mesa," and Weston 1993, p. 171.
49. O'Toole 2012, pp. 112, 208n178.
50. Fuentes 1866, p. 127.
51. Bordiga 2018, p. 63.
52. Look Lai and Tan 2010, p. 143.
53. Stewart 1951, pp. 30–31, 42.
54. Balbi 1999, pp. 28, 52–54, 62.
55. Fuentes 1866, p. 88.
56. Balbi 1999, p. 48.
57. Balbi 1999, p. 92.
58. Balbi 1999, p. 124.
59. Balbi 1999, pp. 138–40.
60. Seminario "Arte, Cultura e Identidad sobre la Mesa," and Weston 1993, p. 226; Balbi 1999, p. 34.
61. Bradley 2012, p. 72.

62. Zapata Acha 2009, pp. 438–39.
63. Balbi 1999, p. 102.
64. Seminario "Arte, Cultura e Identidad sobre la Mesa," and Weston 1993, pp. 239–40.
65. Seminario "Arte, Cultura e Identidad sobre la Mesa," and Weston 1993, pp. 250–51.
66. Zapata Acha 2009, p. 542.
67. Seminario "Arte, Cultura e Identidad sobre la Mesa," and Weston 1993, p. 244.
68. Masterson and Funada-Classen 2004, p. 64.
69. Seminario "Arte, Cultura e Identidad sobre la Mesa," and Weston 1993, p. 259; Masterson and Funada-Classen 2004, p. 64.
70. Masterson and Funada-Classen 2004, p. 66.
71. Long 2001, p. 271.
72. Takenaka 2019, pp. 3, 66; Seminario "Arte, Cultura e Identidad sobre la Mesa," and Weston 1993, p. 262.
73. Takenaka 2019, p. 4.
74. Tsumura and Barrón 2013, p. 134.
75. Takenaka 2019, p. 5.
76. Tsumura and Barrón 2013, p. 134.
77. Fuentes 1866, pp. 121–27; Valderrama 2010, p. 106.
78. Valderrama 2010, p. 22.
79. Tsumura and Barrón 2013, p. 29.
80. Valderrama 2010, pp. 11–12; Fuentes 1866, p. 126.
81. Tsumura and Barrón 2013, pp. 28, 62, 134.
82. Bradley 2012, p. 73n3.
83. León Canales 2013, pp. 356–57.
84. Donnan 1976, p. 34.
85. Dillehay 2017, pp. 203–5.
86. Di Leo Lira et al. 2013, p. 252.
87. Alcalde 2009, p. 34.

Conclusion

1. Savoy 1970. For my own modern take on this survey archaeology, see Bradley 2017.
2. Chambi 1993, p. 33; Burger and Salazar 2004.
3. Matta 2019.
4. Matta 2019.
5. Tesauro 2017.
6. Matta 2019.

Bibliography

Aaronson, Sheldon. 2000. "Algae." In *The Cambridge World History of Food*, edited by Kenneth F. Kiple and Kriemhild Coneè Ornelas, 231–49. Cambridge: Cambridge University Press.

Acock, M., J. Lydon, E. Johnson, and R. Collins. 1996. "Effects of temperature and light levels on leaf yield and cocaine content in two *Erythroxylon* species." *Annals of Botany* 78:49–53.

Acosta, Josef. 2008 [1590]. *Historia natural y moral de las indias*. Investigaciones Sociales. Lima: Universidad Nacional Mayor de San Marcos.

Acurio, Gastón. 2006. *Las cocinas del Perú*. Lima: El Comercio.

Adorno, Rolena, Felipe Guamán Poma de Ayala, and Kongelige Bibliotek (Denmark). 2001. *Guaman Poma and his illustrated chronicle from colonial Peru: From a century of scholarship to a new era of reading = Guaman Poma y su crónica ilustrada del Perú colonial: un siglo de investigaciones hacia una nueva era de lectura*. Copenhagen: Museum Tusculanum Press, University of Copenhagen & the Royal Library.

Agardh, C., and J. Agardh. 1842. "*Gigartina chamissoi*." In *Algae maris mediterranei et adriatici*, observationes in diagnosin specierum et dispositionem generum. pp. [i]–x, 1–164. Paris: Apud Fortin, Masson et Cie.

Aguirre, Carlos. 1995. *Agentes de su propia libertad: los esclavos de Lima y la desintegración de la esclavitud, 1821–1854*. Lima: Fondo Editorial, Pontificia Universidad Católica del Perú.

Aikhenvald, Alexandra Y., and Robert M. W. Dixon. 2006. *Grammars in contact: A cross-linguistic typology*. Oxford: Oxford University Press.

Al-Ahmed, N., S. Alsowaidi, and P. Vadas. 2008. "Peanut allergy: An overview." *Allergy, Asthma and Clinical Immunology* 4:139. https://doi.org/10.1186/1710-1492-4-4-139.

Alcalá, Luisa Elena, and Jonathan Brown. 2014. *Painting in Latin America, 1550–1820: From conquest to independence*. New Haven: Yale University Press.

Alcalde, Cristina. 2009. "Between Incas and Indians: Inca Kola and the construction of a Peruvian-global modernity." *Journal of Consumer Culture* 9:31–54. https://doi.org/10.1177/1469540508099700.

Alcalde Mongrut, Ricardo (Compadre Guisao). 2005. *De la mar y la mesa: jocundas historias con viejas recetas*. Lima: Escuela Profesional de Turismo y Hotelería, Universidad de San Martín de Porres.

"Alcohol through the Ages." 2020. *Archaeology Magazine* (November/December): 26–33. https://www.archaeology.org/issues/398-2011.

Allchin, Frank Raymond. 1979. "India: The ancient home of distillation?" *Man* 14:55–63.

Alva, Walter, and Christopher B. Donnan. 1993. *Royal tombs of Sipán*. Los Angeles: Fowler Museum of Cultural History, University of California.

Alvarez Novoa, Isabel, Ronald Arquíñigo Vidal, George Yuri Cayllahua Muñoz, and Universidad de "San Martín de Porres." 2017. *Picanterías y chicherías del Perú: patrimonio cultural de la nación.* Lima: Fondo Editorial USMP: Facultad de Ciencias de la Comunicación Turismo y Psicología.

Andres, T. C., R. Ugás, and F. Bustamante. 2006. "Loche: A unique pre-Columbian squash locally grown in north coastal Peru." In *Proceedings of Cucurbitaceae 2006*, edited by G. J. Holmes, 333–40. Raleigh, NC: Universal Press.

Andrews, George Reid. 2004. *Afro-Latin America, 1800–2000*. Oxford: Oxford University Press.

Andrews, Jean. 1999. *The pepper trail: History and recipes from around the world.* Denton: University of North Texas Press.

Andrews, Jean, and W. Hardy Eshbaugh. 1984. *Peppers: The domesticated Capsicums*. Austin: University of Texas Press.

Arriaga, Pablo José de, and L. Clark Keating. 1968 [1621]. *The extirpation of idolatry in Peru.* Lexington: University of Kentucky Press.

Asbury, Herbert. 1933. *The Barbary coast: An informal history of the San Francisco underworld.* New York: A. A. Knopf.

Balbi, Mariella. 1999. *Los chifas en el Perú: historia y recetas = Chinese restaurants, "chifas," in Peru: History and recipes.* Lima: Escuela Profesional de Turismo y Hotelería, Universidad de San Martín de Porres.

Balta Campbell, Aida. 2009. "The syncretism in the painting of the School Cuzqueña." In *Cultura,* vol. 23, 101–13. Lima: Universidad de San Martín de Porres.

Betanzos, Juan de, Roland Hamilton, and Dana Buchanan. 1996. *Narrative of the Incas*. Austin: University of Texas Press.

Bird, David. 2010. *Understanding wine technology: A book for the non-scientist that explains the science of winemaking*. Newark, UK: DBQA Publishing.

Bird, Junius Bouton, John Hyslop, and Milica Dimitrijevic Skinner. 1985. "The preceramic excavations at the Hucaca Prieta, Chicama Valley, Peru." *Anthropological Papers of the Museum of Natural History* 62, no. 1: 1–295.

Blanchard, Peter. 1992. *Slavery and abolition in early republican Peru*. Wilmington, DE: SR Books.

Blanton, Richard E. 1981. *Ancient Mesoamerica: A comparison of change in three regions*. New York: Cambridge University Press.

Bonavia, Duccio. 1985. *Mural painting in ancient Peru*. Bloomington: Indiana University Press.

Bordiga Matteo. 2018. *Post-fermentation and -distillation technology: Stabilization, aging, and spoilage*. Boca Raton: CRC Press.

The Botany of Desire. 2009. Anonymous Public Broadcasting Service. https://video.alexanderstreet.com/watch/the-botany-of-desire.

Bowser, Frederick P. 1977. *El esclavo africano en el Perú colonial, 1524–1650*. Mexico: Siglo Veintiuno.

Bradley, Robert. 2012. "Sudado de Raya, an ancient Peruvian dish." *Gastronomica* 12, no. 4 (Winter 2012): 68–73.

Bradley, Robert. 2013. "A Western mirage on the Altiplano." In *Buen gusto and classicism in the visual cultures of Latin America, 1780–1910*, edited by Paul B.

Niell and Stacie G. Widdifield, 157–75. Albuquerque: University of New Mexico Press.
Bradley, Robert. 2017. "Architectural anomalies in the Northeastern Forest of Peru." In *Visual culture of the ancient Americas: Contemporary perspectives.* Online addenda. http://www.columbia.edu/cu/arthistory/faculty/Pasztory/Festschrift.html.
Bradley, Robert. 2019. "Innovative ingesting of alkaloids in ancient South America." *Anthropology of Food.* October. https://journals.openedition.org/aof/10377.
Briones Vela, Hilderbrando. 2013. *Pimentel, historia, tradición, identidad.* Chiclayo, Peru: Emdecosege S.A.
Bronson, William. 1973. "Secrets of pisco punch revealed." *California Historical Quarterly* 52, no. 3 (Fall): 229–40.
Brown, Kendall W. 1986. *Bourbons and brandy: Imperial reform in eighteenth-century Arequipa.* Albuquerque: University of New Mexico Press.
Burger, Richard L. 1992. *Chavin and the origins of Andean civilization.* New York: Thames and Hudson.
Burger, Richard L., and Lucy C. Salazar. 2004. *Machu Picchu: Unveiling the mystery of the Incas.* New Haven: Yale University Press.
Burger, Richard L., and Nikolaas J. Van der Merwe. 1990. "Maize and the origin of highland Chavín civilization: An isotopic perspective." *American Anthropologist* 92:85–95.
Cabello Balboa, Miguel. 1951. *Miscelánea antártica: una historia del Perú antiguo.* Lima: Facultad de Letras Instituto de Etnología, Universidad Nacional Mayor de San Marcos.
Cabieses, Fernando, Raúl Vargas, Juan Viacava, and Walter H. Wust. 2006. *Ajíes del Perú = Aji peppers of Peru.* Lima: Fundación Backus.
Cánepa Koch, Gisela. 2011. *Cocina e identidad: la culinaria peruana como patrimonio cultural inmaterial.* Lima: Ministerio de Cultura.
Caritas of Peru. 2012. *Loche de Lambayeque: Cultivation manual.* Lima: Caritas of Peru.
Carver, George Washington. 1983. *How to grow the peanut and 105 ways of preparing it for human consumption.* Tuskegee, AL: Eastern National Park and Monument Association for Tuskegee Institute.
Castaneda-Vildózola, A., C. Nava-Díaz, J. Váldez-Carrasco, C. Ruiz-Montiel, L. Vidal-Hernández, and S. Barrios-Matias. 2010. "Distribution and host range of Bephratelloides cubensis Ashmead (Hymenoptera: Eurytomidae) in Mexico." In *Neotropical Entomology* 39, no. 6: 1053–55.
Cerrón-Palomino, Rodolfo, Pontificia Universidad Católica del Perú. 2000. "Nota etimológica: el topónimo Lima." *Lexis* 24, no. 1: 151–62.
Chambi, Martín. 1993. *Martín Chambi: Photographs, 1920–1950.* London: Smithsonian Institution Press.
Chardon, Roland. 1980. "The elusive Spanish League: A problem of measurement in sixteenth-century New Spain." *Hispanic American Historical Review* 60, no. 2 (May): 294–302.
Chef's Table. 2017. *Chef's Table.* Season 3. Netflix.
Childe, V. Gordon. 1951. *Man makes himself.* New York: New American Library.

Christakis, Nicholas. 2008. "This allergies hysteria is just nuts." *British Medical Journal* 337:a2880.

Cieza de León, Pedro de, Harriet De Onís, and Victor Wolfgang Von Hagen. 1959. *The Incas*. Norman: University of Oklahoma Press.

Cieza de León, Pedro de, and Franklin Pease G. Y. 2005. *Crónica del Perú: el señorío de los Incas*. Caracas: Fundación Biblioteca Ayacucho.

Cobo, Bernabé, and Roland Hamilton. 1990. *Inca religion and customs*. Austin: University of Texas Press.

Cobo, Bernabé, and Francisco Mateos. 1964. *Obras del P[adre] Bernabé Cobo*. Madrid: M. Rivadeneyra.

Coe, Sophie D. 1994. *America's first cuisines*. Austin: University of Texas Press.

Commager, Henry Steele. 1966. *Freedom and order: A commentary on the American political scene*. New York: G. Braziller.

Cook, Anita Gwynn, and Nancy A. Parrish. 2005. "Gardens in the desert: Archaeobotanical analysis from the lower Ica Valley, Peru." *Andean Past* 7:135–56.

Covey, Alan. 2021. "Foodways under Spanish Colonial Rule." In *Andean foodways: Pre-Columbian, colonial, and contemporary food and culture*, edited by John Staller, 311–35. Springer NatureEBook.

Cruz, Mercedes, Severo Malpartida, Hamilton Beltrán, Valérie Jullian, and Geneviève Bourdy. 2014. "Hot and cold: Medicinal plant uses in Quechua speaking communities in the high Andes (Callejon de Huaylas, Ancash, Peru)." *Journal of Ethnopharmacology* 155. https://doi.org/10.1016/j.jep.2014.06.042.

Cushman, Gregory T. 2013. *Guano and the opening of the Pacific world: A global ecological history*. Cambridge: Cambridge University Press. https://doi.org/10.1017/CBO9781139047470.

Dalby, Andrew. 2000. *Dangerous tastes: The story of spices*. Berkeley: University of California Press.

D'Altroy, Terence N. 2002. *The Incas*. Malden, MA: Blackwell.

DeMasi, Deborah, and Kenneth B. Weiner. 2011. *International project financing*. 4th ed. Huntington, NY: Juris Publishing.

Depenthal, Johanna, and Laura S. Meitzner Yoder. 2018. "Uso y conocimiento comunitario del algarrobo (Prosopis pallida) e implicaciones para la conservacion del bosque seco peruano." *Ciencias ambientales* 52, no. 1: 49–70.

Di Leo Lira, P., C. M. van Baren, S. López, A. Molina, C. Heit, C. Viturro, M. P. de Lampasona, et al. 2013. "Northwestern Argentina: A center of genetic diversity of lemon verbena (*Aloysia citriodora* Paláu, Verbenaceae)." *Chemistry and Biodiversity* 10:251–61.

Dillehay, T., and D. Piperno. 2014. "Agricultural origins and social implications in South America." In *The Cambridge world prehistory*, edited by Colin Renfrew and Paul G. Bahn, 970–85. New York: Cambridge University Press.

Dillehay, Tom D. 1989. *Monte Verde: A late Pleistocene settlement in Chile*. Washington, DC: Smithsonian Institution Press.

Dillehay, Tom D. 2011. *From foraging to farming in the Andes: New perspectives on food production and social organization*. New York: Cambridge University Press.

Dillehay, Tom D. 2017. *Where the land meets the sea: Fourteen millennia of human history at Huaca Prieta, Peru*. 1st ed. Austin: University of Texas Press.

Dillehay, Tom D., Jack Rossen, Donald Urent, Anathasios Karathanasis, Victor Vasquez, and Patricia Netherly. 2010. "Early Holocene coca chewing in northern Peru." *Antiquity* 84, no. 326: 939–53.

Dobyns, Henry F. 1963. "An outline of Andean epidemic history to 1720." *Bulletin of the History of Medicine* 37, no. 6: 493–515.

Donkin, R. A. 1989. *The Muscovy duck, Cairina moschata domestica: Origins, dispersal, and associated aspects of the geography of domestication*. Rotterdam: A. A. Balkema.

Donnan, Christopher B. 1976. *Moche art and iconography*. Los Angeles: Latin American Center, UCLA.

Donnan, Christopher B. 1978. *Moche art of Peru: Pre-Columbian symbolic communication*. Los Angeles: Museum of Cultural History, University of California.

Donnan, Christopher B., and Donna McClelland. 1999. *Moche Fineline painting: Its evolution and its artists*. Los Angeles: Fowler Museum of Cultural History, UCLA.

Dua, Tanya. 2019. "Here's what a 12-course meal at Lima's Central—one of the best restaurants in the world—looks and tastes like." *Business Insider*. https://www.businessinsider.com/wildest-dishes-central-no-6-restaurant-in-world-photos-lima-2019-6.

Eigenmann, Carl H. 1922. *The fishes of western South America: Part I. The freshwater fishes of northwestern South America, including Colombia, Panama, and the Pacific slopes of Ecuador and Peru, together with an appendix upon the fishes of the Rio Meta in Colombia*. Pittsburgh: Published by the authority of the Board of Trustees of the Carnegie Institute.

El Bizri, Hani R., John E. Fa, Mark Bowler, Joao Valsecchi, Richard Bodmer, and Pedro Mayor. 2018. "Breeding seasonality in the lowland paca (*Cuniculus paca*) in Amazonia: interactions with rainfall, fruiting, and sustainable hunting." *Journal of Mammalogy* 99, no. 5: 1101–11.

Emen, Jake. 2015. "Pisco: A complete guide to the brandy from South America." *Eater*. October 6. https://www.eater.com/drinks/2015/10/6/9385867/the-complete-guide-to-pisco.

Engel, F. 1957. "Early sites on the Peruvian coast." *South-Western Journal of Anthropology* 13, no. 1 (Spring): 54–68.

Espinoza Soriano, Waldemar. 1967. *Los señoríos étnicos de Chachapoyas y la Alianza Hispano-Chacha: siglos XV–XVI*. Lima: Academia Nacional de la Historia.

Ferreguetti, Atilla C., Bruno C. Pereira, and Helena G. Bergallo. 2018. *Zoologia* (Curitiba, Brazil) 35:1–5.

Food and Drug Administration. 2020. "GMO crops, animal food, and beyond." *Agricultural Biotechnology*. September 28. https://www.fda.gov/food/agricultural-biotechnology/gmo-crops-animal-food-and-beyond#:~:text=Corn%20is%20the%20most%20commonly,%2C%20livestock%2C%20or%20other%20animals.

Forbes, R. J. 1970. *A short history of the art of distillation: From the beginnings up to the death of Cellier Blumenthal*. Leiden: E. J. Brill.

Fuentes, Manuel Atanasio. 1866. *Lima; or sketches of the capital of Peru, historical, statistical, administrative, commercial and moral*. London: Trübner.

Gade, Daniel Wayne, and Roberto Rodríguez Rios. 1972. "Chaquitaclla, the native footplough and its persistence in Central Andean agriculture." *Tools & Tillage* 2 (1972/1975): 3–15.

Gagliano, Joseph A. 1994. *Coca prohibition in Peru: The historical debates*. Tucson: University of Arizona Press.

Galloway, J. H. 1989. *The sugar cane industry: An historical geography from its origins to 1914*. Cambridge: Cambridge University Press.

Gálvez Mora, César A., and María Andrea Runcio. 2009. "El Life (*Trichomycterus* sp.) y su importancia en la iconografía mochica." *Archaeobios* 1, no. 3: 55–87.

García, María Elena. 2021. *Gastropolitics and the specter of race: Stories of capital, culture, and coloniality in Peru*. Berkeley: University of California Press.

Garcilaso de la Vega. 1989. *Royal commentaries of the Incas and general history of Peru*. Translated by Harold Livermore. Austin: University of Texas Press.

Garcilaso de la Vega and Pedro Craesbeeck. 1609. *Primera parte de los commentarios reales: que tratan del origen de los Yncas, reyes que fueron del Peru, de su idolatria, leyes, y gouierno en paz y en guerra: de sus vidas y conquistas, y de todo lo que fue aquel imperio y su republica, antes que los españoles passaran a el*. Lisbon: En la officina de Pedro Crasbeeck.

Gepts, Paul. 1998. "Origin and evolution of common bean: Past events and recent trends." *HortScience HortSci* 33, no. 7: 1124–30.

Gill, Nicholas. 2018. *The chifas of San Borja*. newworlder.com. October 18. https://www.newworlder.com/article/19569/the-chifas-of-san-borja?fbclid=IwAR0XGbaifM_k-lcm-8hKA7eRvCb1USu8aKEQJF6U011y2rnRx2XnOQZ3Pqo.

Giusti-Lanham, Hedy, and Andrea Dodi. 1978. *The cuisine of Venice and surrounding northern regions*. Woodbury, NY: Barron's.

Gobierno de Perú. Naciones Unidas. 2008. *Monitoreo de cultivos de coca*. Comisión Nacional para el Desarrollo y Vida sin Drogas (DEVIDA).

Goldhammer, Zach. 2014. "Why Americans call turkey 'turkey.'" *The Atlantic*. November 26. https://www.theatlantic.com/international/archive/2014/11/why-americans-call-turkey-turkey/383225.

González Holguín, Diego. 1608. *Vocabvlario dela lengva general de todo el Perv llamada lengua Qquichua, o del Inca. Corregido y renovado conforme ala propriedad cortesana del Cuzco. Diuidido en dos libros, que son dos Vocabularios enteros en que salen a luz de nueuo las cosas q̃ faltauan al Vocabulario. Y la suma de las cosas que se aumentan se vea enla hoja siguiente*. Lima (Impresso en la Ciudad de los Reyes): Por Francisco del Canto.

Gonzalez-Lamas, Rosa. 2018. *Olive Oil Times*. https://www.oliveoiltimes.com/world/peru-rediscovers-its-own-olive-oils/64165.

Gonzales-Lara, Jorge Yeshayahu. 2020. *La historia del pollo a las brasas peruano: patrimonio cultural e identidad gastronómica*. La Diaspora Digital Magazine: Actualidad-Analisis e Informacion Digital.

Goode, Jamie, and Sam Harrop. 2011. *Authentic wine: Toward natural and sustainable winemaking*. Berkeley: University of California Press.

Gootenberg, Paul. 2004. "Secret ingredients: The politics of coca in US-Peruvian relations, 1915–65." *Journal of Latin American Studies* (May): 233–65.

Gootenberg, Paul. 2008. *Andean cocaine: The making of a global drug*. Chapel Hill: University of North Carolina Press.
Grobman Tversqui, Alexander, Wilfredo Sergio Salhuana, Ricardo Sevilla Panizo, and Paul C. Mangelsdorf. 1961. *Races of maize in Peru, their origins, evolution and classification*. Washington, DC: National Academy of Sciences–National Research Council.
Guamán Poma de Ayala, Felipe. 1613. *Guaman poma: el primer nueva corónica y buen gobierno*. Copenhagen: Museum Tusculanum Press, University of Copenhagen, 2002. http://www5.kb.dk/permalink/2006/poma/info/en/frontpage.htm.
Guardia, Sara Beatriz. 2008. *Peruvian potato: History and recipes*. Lima: Fondo Editorial, Universidad de San Martín de Porres.
Gutiérrez Sarmiento, Paola Adriana, and Tatiana Fabiola Pulla Aguirre. 2017. "Aplicación de técnicas de cocción en la elaboracion de recetas de sal y dulce utilizando guarapo." Proyecto de intervención previa a la obtención del título de: "Licenciada en Gastronomía y Servicio de Alimentos y Bebidas." Thesis. Universidad de Cuenca, Ecuador.
Hall, Amy Cox. 2020. "Cooking up heritage: Culinary adventures of Peru's past." *Bulletin of Spanish Studies*, 97, no. 4: 593–613.
Hamblin, James. 2013. "Why we took cocaine out of soda." *The Atlantic*. January 31. https://www.theatlantic.com/health/archive/2013/01/why-we-took-cocaine-out-of-soda/272694.
Hardwick, William A. 1995. *Handbook of brewing: Food science and technology*. New York: CRC Press.
Hawkes, J. G., and Javier Francisco-Ortega. 1993. *The early history of the potato in Europe*. Wageningen, The Netherlands: Kluwer Academic Publishers.
Hayashida, Frances. 2008. "Ancient beer and modern brewers: Ethnoarchaeological observations of chicha production in two regions of the North Coast of Peru." *Journal of Anthropological Archaeology* 27:161–74.
Hemming, John. 1970. *The conquest of the Incas*. New York: Harcourt, Brace, Jovanovich.
Hesse, Manfred. 2002. *Verlag Helvetica Chimica Acta*. Zürich: Wiley-VCH.
Heyerdahl, Thor, Daniel H. Sandweiss, and Alfredo Narváez. 1995. *Pyramids of Túcume: The quest for Peru's forgotten city*. New York: Thames and Hudson.
Hildebrandt, Martha. 1969. *Peruanismos*. Lima: Moncloa-Campodónico.
Holderread, Dave. 2001. *Storey's guide to raising ducks*. Pownal, VT: Storey Books.
Hosken, Fábio Morais, Matheus Henrique Vargas de Oliveira, Jessica Moraes Malheiros, Eduardo Henrique Martins, Felipe Norberto Alves Ferreira, Walter Motta Ferreira, et al. 2021. "Experimental ethology of intensively reared lowland pacas (Cuniculus Paca)." *Tropical Animal Health and Production* 53, no. 3: 367.
Huertas Vallejos, Lorenzo. 2004. *Historia de la producción de vinos y piscos en el Perú*. Talca, Chile: Instituto de Estudios Humanísticos, Universidad de Talca.
Jenkins, Amanda, Teobaldo Llosa, Ivan Montoya, and Edward J. Cone. 1996. "Identification and quantitation of alkaloids in coca tea." *Forensic Science International* 77, no. 3: 179–89.

Jennings, Justin, and Brenda J. Bowser. 2009. *Drink, power, and society in the Andes*. Gainesville: University Press of Florida.

Jiménez, Jamie. 1996. "The extirpation and current status of wild chinchillas *Chinchilla lanigera* and *C. brevicaudata*." *Biological Conservation* 77, no. 1: 1–6.

Johns, T. 1986. "The detoxification function of geophagy and the domestication of the potato." *Journal of Chemical Ecology* 12:635–46.

Johns, Timothy, and Susan L. Keen. 1986. "Taste evaluation of potato glycoalkaloids by the Aymara: A case study in human chemical ecology." *Human Ecology* 14, no. 4: 437–52.

Josephson, Eric, and Eleanor E. Carroll. 1974. *Drug use: Epidemiological and sociological approaches*. New York: Halstad Press.

Julien, Catherine. 1985. "Guano and resource control in sixteenth-century Arequipa." In *Andean ecology and civilization,* edited by S. Masuda, I. Shimada, and C. Morris, 185–231. Tokyo: University of Tokyo Press.

Julien, Catherine. 1998. "Coca production on the Inca frontier: The Yungas of Chuquioma." *Andean Past* 5:129–60.

Jurafsky, Dan. 2014. *The language of food: A linguist reads the menu*. New York: W. W. Norton.

Karttunen, Frances E. 1983. *An analytical dictionary of Nahuatl*. Austin: University of Texas Press.

Karttunen, Frances E. 1992. *An analytical dictionary of Nahuatl*. Norman: University of Oklahoma Press.

Katz, Solomon H., M. L. Hediger, and L. A. Valleroy. 1974. *Traditional maize processing techniques in the New World*. Vol. 184. Lancaster, PA: American Association for the Advancement of Science.

Kauffman, Jonathan. 2012. "The bird is the word: Surveying the Bay Area's Peruvian rotisseries." Dining. *San Francisco Weekly*. 04/18/2012 4:00 am. https://www.sfweekly.com/dining/the-bird-is-the-word-surveying-the-bay-areas-peruvian-rotisseries.

Keegan, William F., and Corinne L. Hofman. 2017. *The Caribbean before Columbus*. New York: Oxford University Press.

Kerr, Justin, and Michael D. Coe. 1989. *The Maya vase book: A corpus of rollout photographs of Maya vases*. New York: Kerr Associates.

Kistler, L., Maezumi S. Y., J. Gregorio de Souza, N. A. S. Przelomska, F. Malaquias Costa, O. Smith, H. Loiselle, et al. 2018. "Multiproxy evidence highlights a complex evolutionary legacy of maize in South America." *Science* 362, no. 6420 (December 14): 1309–13.

Kosok, Paul. 1965. *Life, land, and water in ancient Peru; an account of the discovery, exploration, and mapping of ancient pyramids, canals, roads, towns, walls, and fortresses of coastal Peru with observations of various aspects of Peruvian life, both ancient and modern*. New York: Long Island University Press.

Krampner, Jon. 2013. *Creamy and crunchy: An informal history of peanut butter, the all-American food*. New York: Columbia University Press.

Kulp, Kayleigh. 2015. "Peru vs. Chile: South America's great pisco war." *The Daily Beast*. October 18. https://www.thedailybeast.com/peru-vs-chile-south-americas-great-pisco-war.

"Lagniappe." 2019. Merriam-Webster.com. https://www.merriam-webster.com/dictionary/lagniappe.

Lauer, Mirko, and Vera Lauer. 2006. *La revolución gastronómica peruana*. Lima: Escuela Profesional de Turismo y Hotelería, Universidad de San Martín de Porres.

Lazar, Allie. 2018. "How Malena Martínez is changing the future of Peruvian cuisine." *Eater*. June 29. https://www.eater.com/2018/6/29/17509624/malena-martinez-mater-iniciativa-central-restaurant-peru-virgilio-martinez-interview.

Lemons, John, Reginald Victor, and Daniel Schaffer. 2003. *Conserving biodiversity in arid regions: Best practices in developing nations*. Boston, MA: Kluwer Academic.

Leon, Adriana, and Chris Kraul. 2014. "Peru wins maritime border dispute with Chile over key fishing grounds." *Los Angeles Times*. https://www.latimes.com/world/la-xpm-2014-jan-27-la-fg-wn-peru-territorial-dispute-chile-20140127-story.html.

León Canales, Elmo. 2013. *14000 años de alimentación en el Perú*. Lima: Escuela Profesional de Turismo y Hotelería, Universidad de San Martín de Porres.

Long, Susan Orpett. 2001. "Negotiating the 'good death': Japanese ambivalence about new ways to die." *Ethnology* 40, no. 4: 271–89.

Look Lai, Walton, and Chee-Beng Tan. 2010. *The Chinese in Latin America and the Caribbean*. Leiden: Brill.

López-Canales, Jorge. 2019. "Peru on a plate: Coloniality and modernity in Peru's high-end cuisine." *Anthropology of Food*. https://doi.org/10.4000/aof.10138.

Luján, Marta. 2017. *Spanish in the Americas: A dialogic approach to language contact*. https://doi.org/10.1075/slcs.185.181uj.

Lynch, Thomas F. 1980. *Guitarrero Cave: Early man in the Andes*. New York: Academic Press.

Maass, Brigitte L., Maggie R. Knox, S. C. Venkatesha, Tefera Tolera Angessa, Stefan Ramme, and Bruce C. Pengelly. 2010. "Lablab purpureus—A crop lost for Africa?" *Tropical Plant Biology* 3:123–35.

Mann, Charles C. 2011. *1493: Uncovering the new world Columbus created*. New York: Knopf.

Mariani, A. 1896. *Coca and its therapeutic application*. New York: J. N. Jaros.

Mariátegui, José Carlos, Marjory Urquidi, and Jorge Basadre. 1971. *Seven interpretive essays on Peruvian reality*. Austin: University of Texas Press.

Martínez-Véliz, Virgilio. 2008. "The taste of extreme altitude." *Alpine Modern Café*. Boulder, Colorado. https://www.alpinemodern.com/inspirations/the-taste-of-extreme-altitude-central-restaurant-virgilio-martinez.

Masterson, Daniel M., and Sayaka Funada-Classen. 2004. *The Japanese in Latin America*. Urbana: University of Illinois Press.

Matienzo, Juan de. 1967. *Gobierno del Peru*. Edited by G. Lohmann Vellena. Paris: Travaux de l'Institut Français d'Etudes Andines 11 (Français).

Matsuhisa, Nobuyuki, and David Shih. 2018. *Nobu: A memoir*. Old Saybrook, CT: Tantor Media.

Matsuoka, Y., Y. Vigouroux, M. M. Goodman, G. J. Sanchez, E. Buckler, and J. Doebley. 2002. "A single domestication for maize shown by multilocus microsatellite genotyping." *Proceedings of the National Academy of Sciences of the United States of America* 99, no. 9: 6080–84.

Matta, Raúl. 2014. "Dismantling the boom of Peruvian cuisine." *Revista: Harvard Review of Latin America* (Fall). https://archive.revista.drclas.harvard.edu/book/dismantling-boom-peruvian-cuisine.

Matta, Raúl. 2019. "La revolución gastronómica peruana: una celebración de 'lo nacional' entrevista a Mirko Lauer." *Anthropology of Food* [Online] 14. http://journals.openedition.org/aof/9982. https://doi.org/10.4000/aof.9982.

May G. 1988. "How Coca-Cola obtains its coca." *New York Times*. July 1, Business Day, D1.

McDonell, Emma. 2015. "Miracle foods: Quinoa, curative metaphors, and the depoliticization of global hunger politics." *Gastronomica: The Journal of Critical Food Studies* 15, no. 4: 70–85.

McDonell, Emma. 2019. "Creating the culinary frontier: A critical examination of Peruvian chefs' narratives of lost/discovered foods." *Anthropology of Food*. https://journals.openedition.org/aof/10183.

McDonell, Emma. 2021. "Commercializing the 'lost crop of the Inca': Quinoa and the politics of agrobiodiversity in 'traditional' crop commercialization." In *Andean foodways: Pre-Columbian, colonial, and contemporary food and culture*, edited by John Staller. Springer NatureEBook. https://search.ebscohost.com/login.aspx?direct=true&scope=site&db=nlebk&db=nlabk&AN=2696319.

McDonnell, Duggan, and Luke Abiol. 2015. *Drinking the devil's acre: A love letter to San Francisco and her cocktails.*

McKirdy, Tim. 2016. "This ugly chinchilla is an Argentinian delicacy." *Munchies: Food by Vice*. https://www.vice.com/en/article/z4g33a/this-ugly-chinchilla-is-an-argentinian-delicacy.

Means, Philip Ainsworth. 1931. *Ancient civilizations of the Andes*. New York: Charles Scribner's Sons.

Mejía, Adán Felipe. 1969. *De cocina peruana: exhortaciones*. Lima: Talleres Gráf. P.L. Villaneuva.

Metropolitan Museum of Art. 2008. Squash Bottle. Moche. 2nd–4th century. Gift of Judith Riklis. Accession Number 1983.546.7. https://www.metmuseum.org/art/collection/search/314682.

Middendorf, Ernst W. 1959. *Las lenguas aborígenes del Perú: proemios e introducciones al quechua, al aimará y al mochica*. Lima: Facultad de Letras, Universidad Nacional Mayor de San Marcos.

Milon, Pohl, Roberto Hugo Alcántara Estela, Carlos Fernando Jiménez Guerrero, and Diego Bernardi Espinoza. 2020. *Tipificación y determinación de los cambios en la composición de la microbiota presente en los distintos procesos de elaboración del tocosh de papa (Solanum tuberosum)*. Lima: Universidad Peruana de Ciencias Aplicadas (UPC).

Mint Museum Online Database. 2008. Maize Cob Effigy. Inka (Southern Highlands, Peru). 1438–534 CE. http://www.mintmuseums.org/resources/collection-database/item/2008.81.7/maize-cob-effigy.

Miroff, Nick. 2014. "Gastón Acurio, South America's super chef." *Washington Post*. World. July 23. https://www.washingtonpost.com/world/gaston-acurio-south-americas-super-chef/2014/07/23/2f7f05bd-a50b-4142-a5c3-b3206f216eac_story.html.

Misra, Mahendra K., Kenneth W. Ragland, and Andrew J. Baker. 1993. "Wood ash composition as a function of furnace temperature." *Biomass and Bioenergy* 4, no. 2: 103–16.

Montagné, Prosper, and Jenifer Harvey Lang. 1988. *Larousse gastronomique: The new American edition of the world's greatest culinary encyclopedia*. New York: Crown.

Montaguth, Sherly. 2020. "Battle over 15-year GMO ban extension rages in Peru as farmers breed and cultivate illegal biotech seed." *Genetic Literacy Project*, December 1. https://geneticliteracyproject.org/2020/12/01/battle-over-15-year-gmo-ban-rages-in-peru-as-farmers-breed-and-cultivate-illegal-biotech-seed/#:~:text=GM%20Crops%20are%20not%20a,such%20as%20corn%20and%20soy.

Monzote, Reinaldo Funes. 2008. *From rainforest to cane field in Cuba: An environmental history since 1492*. Chapel Hill: University of North Carolina Press.

Moore, J. M., P. A. Hays, D. A. Cooper, J. F. Casale, and J. Lydon. 1994. "1-Hydroxytropacocaine: An abundant alkaloid of *Erythroxylum novogranatense* var. *Novogranatense* and var. *Truxillense*." *Phytochemistry* 36, no. 2: 357–60.

Moore, Jerry D. 1989. "Pre-Hispanic beer in coastal Peru: Technology and social context of prehistoric production." *American Anthropologist* 91:682–95.

Morales Ayma, Evo. 2009. "Let me chew my coca leaves." *New York Times*, March 13. https://www.nytimes.com/2009/03/14/opinion/14morales.html.

Morris, Craig, and Donald E. Thompson. 1985. *Huánuco Pampa: An Inca city and its hinterland*. London: Thames and Hudson.

Morton, Julia F., and Curtis F. Dowling. 1987. *Fruits of warm climates*. Miami: J. F. Morton.

Moseley, Michael Edward. 1974. *The maritime foundations of Andean civilization*. Menlo Park, CA: Cummings.

Moseley, Michael Edward. 1992. *The Incas and their ancestors: The archaeology of Peru*. New York: Thames and Hudson.

Moseley, Michael Edward, and Alana Cordy-Collins. 1990. *The northern dynasties: Kingship and statecraft in Chimor: A symposium at Dumbarton Oaks, 12th and 13th October 1985*. Washington, DC: Dumbarton Oaks Research Library and Collection.

Motley, Timothy J., Nyree Zerega, and Hugh Cross. 2006. *Darwin's harvest: New approaches to the origins, evolution, and conservation of crops*. http://www.degruyter.com/doi/book/10.7312/mot113316.

Mujica B., Elias, and Eduardo Hirose Maio. 2007. *El Brujo: Huaca Cao, centro ceremonial moche en el valle de Chicama*. Lima: Fundación Wiese.

Nafici, Saara. 2017. "Weed of the month: Pigweed." *Urban Gardening and Ecology. Brooklyn Botanical Garden*. August 12. https://www.bbg.org/news/weed_of_the_month_pigweed.

National Research Council (U.S.). 1989. *Lost crops of the Incas: Little-known plants of the Andes with promise for worldwide cultivation*. Washington, DC: National Academy Press.

Niemann, Albert. 1860. *Ueber eine neue organische Base in den Cocablättern*. https://doi.org/10.1002/ardp.18601530202.

Nilsson, G. 2005. *Endangered species handbook*. http://www.endangeredspecieshandbook.org.

Nolte, Gaspar E. 2017. "Pork consumption in Peru—Lots of room to grow." *USDA Foreign Agricultural Service Gain Report*. May 9. http://agriexchange.apeda.gov.in/marketreport/Reports/Peruvian_Pork_Market_Lima_Peru_3-28-2017.pdf.

Noriega Cardó, Cristóbal. 2016. *Algas marinas para la alimentación de los peruanos*. Lima: Universidad de San Martín de Porres.

Obama, Michelle, Jeremy Konner, Tonia Davis, Priya Swaminathan, Alex Braverman, and Barack Obama. 2021. *Waffles+Mochi*. Higher Ground Productions. Episode 3. March 16, 2021. Netflix.

Odell, Kate. 2016. "Ask a Somm: What are oxidative wines?" *Eater*. June 24. https://www.eater.com/2016/6/24/12019360/oxidative-wine-oloroso-sherry-rioja.

O'Toole, Rachel Sarah. 2012. *Bound lives: Africans, Indians, and the making of race in colonial Peru*. Pittsburgh: University of Pittsburgh Press.

Pacini, Deborah, and Christine Franquemont, eds. 1986. *Coca and Cocaine: Effects on People and Policy in Latin America*. Proceedings of the Conference "The Coca Leaf and Its Derivatives—Biology, Society, and Policy," April 25–26, 1985, sponsored by the Latin American Studies Program (LASP), Cornell University, Ithaca, New York. Cambridge, MA: Cultural Survival.

Palacios, R. A., A. D. Burghardt, J. T. Frías-Hernández, V. Olalde-Portugal, N. Grados, L. Alban, and O. Martínez-de la Vega. 2011. "Comparative study (AFLP and morphology) of three species of Prosopis of the Section Algarobia: P. juliflora, P. pallida, and P. limensis. Evidence for resolution of the 'P. pallida-P. juliflora complex.'" *Österreichisches Botanisches Wochenblatt*. https://doi.org/10.1007/s00606-011-0535-y.

Pasiecznik, Nick, Peter Felker, P. Harris, L. N. Harsh, Gaston Cruz, J. Tewari, K. Cadoret, and L. J. Maldonado. 2001. *The Prosopis juliflora–Prosopis pallida complex: A monograph*. https://doi.org/10.1016/S0378-1127(02)00559-5.

Paterson, Andrew H. 2008. *Genetics and genomics of cotton*. New York: Springer.

Pearson, Oliver P. 1948. "Life history of mountain viscachas in Peru." *Journal of Mammalogy* 29, no. 4: 345–74.

Peña, Jorge E., Jennifer L. Sharp, and M. Wysoki. 2002. *Tropical fruit pests and pollinators: Biology, economic importance, natural enemies, and control*. Wallingford, UK: CABI.

Pendergrast M. 1993. *For God, country and Coca-Cola: The unauthorized history of the great American soft drink and the company that makes it*. New York: Charles Scribner's Sons.

Phipps, Elena, and Caroline Solazzo. 2020. "Viscacha: Luxury, fate and identification in pre-Columbian textiles." *Hidden Stories/Human Lives: Proceedings of the Textile Society of America 17th Biennial Symposium*. October 15–17. https://digitalcommons.unl.edu/tsaconf.

Pigière Fabienne, Wim Van Neer, Cécile Ansieau, and Marceline Denis. 2012. "New archaeozoological evidence for the introduction of the guinea pig to Europe." *Journal of Archaeological Science* 39:1020–24.

Piperno, D. R., and K. V. Flannery. 2001. "The earliest archaeological maize (Zea mays L.) from highland Mexico: New accelerator mass spectrometry dates and their implications." *Proceedings of the National Academy of Sciences of the United States of America* 98, no. 4: 2101–3.

Plowman, T. 1979. *The identity of Amazonian and Trujillo coca*. Boston, MA: Botanical Museum, Harvard University.

Plowman, T. 1984. "The origin, evolution and diffusion of coca, Erythroxylon spp., in South and Central America." In *Pre-Columbian plant migration*, edited by Doris Stone, 25–163. Boston, MA: Peabody Museum of Archaeology and Ethnology, Harvard University.

Plowman, T., and L. Rivier. 1983. "Cocaine and cinnamoylcocaine content of erythroxylum species." *Annals of Botany* 51, no. 5: 641–59.

Ponce, Ernesto. 2014. *Nostoc: un alimento diferente y su presencia en la precordillera de Arica*. Arica, Chile: Facultad de Ciencias Agronómicas, Universidad de Tarapacá.

PromPerú. 2016. "Pimientos, rocotos y ajíes." *Capsicum del Perú*. https://issuu.com/promperu/docs/capsicum.

Quispe, Gloria. 2018. "Picante de yuyo o espinaca." *Entérate*. https://enteratesemanal.wixsite.com/enterate/copia-de-4-deporte-1-3.

Ranere A., D. Piperno, I. Holst, R. Dickau, and J. Iriarte. 2009. *The cultural and chronological context of early Holocene maize and squash domestication in the Central Balsas River Valley, Mexico*. National Academy of Sciences. http://www.pubmedcentral.nih.gov/articlerender.fcgi?artid=2664064.

Reader, John. 2009. *Potato: A history of the propitious esculent*. New Haven, CT: Yale University Press.

Resolución Directorial Nacional. 2007. No. 1180. September 7. Lima. https://andina.pe/ingles/noticia-peru-celebrates-national-pisco-sour-day-597696.aspx.

Resolución Ministerial. 2015. El Peruano. No. 441-2015-PRODUCE. https://busquedas.elperuano.pe/normaslegales/prohiben-extraccion-de-la-especie-mantarraya-gigante-con-cua-resolucion-ministerial-n-441-2015-produce-1329586-2.

Rice, Prudence M. 2011. *Vintage Moquegua: History, wine, and archaeology on a colonial Peruvian periphery*. Austin: University of Texas Press.

RMC/JOT. 2009. "INIA Arequipa investigó 200 variedades de rocoto para promover su cultivo." *Andina: Agencia Peruana de Noticias*. https://andina.pe/agencia/noticia-inia-arequipa-investigo-200-variedades-rocoto-para-promover-su-cultivo-255349.aspx.

Rodríguez Pastor, Humberto. 2007. *La vida en el entorno del tamal peruano*. Lima: Escuela Profesional de Turismo y Hotelería, Universidad de San Martín de Porres.

Rostworowski de Diez Canseco, María. 1988. *Conflicts over coca fields in sixteenth-century Perú*. Ann Arbor: Museum of Anthropology, University of Michigan.
Rowe, John Howland. 1946. "Inca culture at the time of the Spanish conquest." *Handbook of South American Indians* Vol. 2. Washington, DC: Government Printing Office.
Saavedra, S. 2016. *Programa de animación sociocultural para el fortalecimiento de la identidad y desarrollo comunitario: ven y disfruta en la Mangachería* (tesis en historia y gestión cultural). Programa Académico de Historia y Gestión Cultural, Facultad de Humanidades, Universidad de Piura, Perú.
Salas, José Antonio. 2002. *Diccionario mochica-castellano, castellano-mochica*. Lima: Escuela Profesional de Turismo y Hotelería, Universidad de San Martín de Porres.
Salazar Zarzosa, Pablo, Glenda Mendieta-Leiva, Rafael M. Navarro-Cerrillo, Gastón Cruz, Nora Grados, and Rafael Villar. 2021. "An ecological overview of Prosopis pallida, one of the most adapted dryland species to extreme climate events." *Journal of Arid Environments* 193. https://doi.org/10.1016/j.jaridenv.2021.104576.
Sandweiss, Daniel, and Elizabeth Wing. 1997. "Ritual rodents: The guinea pigs of Chincha, Peru." *Journal of Field Archaeology* 24, no. 1: 47–58.
Sanz, Nuria. 2016. *The origins of food production = Los orígenes de la producción de alimentos*. Mexico City: UNESCO, Oficina en México.
Sarmiento de Gamboa, Pedro, Brian S. Bauer, and Vania Smith-Oka. 2007. *The history of the Incas*. Austin: University of Texas Press.
Sater, William F. 2007. *Andean tragedy: Fighting the war of the Pacific, 1879–1884*. Lincoln: University of Nebraska Press.
Savoy, Gene. 1970. *Antisuyo: The search for the lost cities of the Amazon*. New York: Simon and Schuster.
Schiaffino, José Antonio. 2006. *El origen del pisco sour: el Morris Bar, el Hotel Maury y el Gran Hotel Bolívar*. Tacna, Peru: Don César.
Schuler, Johnny. 2005. *Pasión por el pisco*. Lima: QW Editores S.A.C.
Scott, Michon. 2016. "Climate and chocolate." Climate.gov. February 10. https://www.climate.gov/news-features/climate-and/climate-chocolate.
Seminario "Arte, Cultura e Identidad sobre la Mesa," and Rosario Olivas Weston. 1993. *Cultura identidad y cocina en el Perú*. Lima: Escuela Profesional de Turismo y Hotelería, Universidad San Martín de Porres.
Serra Puche, Mari Carmen, and Jesús Carlos Lazcano Arce. 2016. *El mezcal, una bebida prehispánica*. Mexico City: Estudios Etnoarqueológicos.
Shady, Ruth, Patricia Courtney De Haro, and Erick Delgado. 2007. *The social and cultural values of Caral-Supe, the oldest civilization of Peru and the Americas, and their role in integrated sustainable development*. Lima: Proyecto Especial Arqueológico Caral-Supe, Instituto Nacional de Cultura.
Shady Solis, Ruth, and Carlos Leyva. 2003. *La ciudad sagrada de Caral-Supe: los orígenes de la civilizatión andina y la formación del estado prístino en el antiguo Perú*. Lima: Proyecto Especial Arqueológico Caral-Supe, Instituto Nacional de Cultura.

Sherman, Sean, and Beth Dooley. 2017. *The Sioux chef's indigenous kitchen*. Minneapolis: University of Minnesota Press.
Shimizu, Tatsuya. 2011. "Development of broiler integration in Peru." *Chiba: Inst. of Developing Economies, Japan External Trade Organization*. http://hdl.handle.net/2344/1085.
Siegel, Ronald K., Mahmoud A. Elsohly, Timothy Plowman et al. 1986. "Cocaine in herbal tea." *JAMA* 255, no. 1: 40.
Sifton, Sam. 2004. "Roasting a pig inside an enigma." *New York Times*. Food Section. January 7.
Silverman, Helaine. 2004. *Andean archaeology*. Malden, MA: Blackwell.
Silverman, Helaine, and William Harris Isbell. 2008. *Handbook of South American archaeology*. New York: Springer.
Smil, Vaclav. 2001. *Enriching the earth: Fritz Haber, Carl Bosch, and the transformation of world food production*. Cambridge, MA: MIT Press.
Smith, Andrew F. 2002. *Peanuts: The illustrious history of the goober pea*. Urbana: University of Illinois Press.
Smith, Matthew. 2015. *Another person's poison: A history of food allergy*. https://openlibrary.org/books/OL27186562M.
Smith, Michael Ernest. 1996. *The Aztecs*. Malden, MA: Blackwell.
Solís, Héctor. 2012. "Nueva receta de Héctor Solís: Arroz con pato a la chiclayana." Lamula.pe. June 14. https://gastronomia.lamula.pe/2012/06/14/nueva-receta-de-hector-solis-arroz-con-pato-a-la-chiclayana/admin.
Staff, National Research Council. 1988. *Lost crops of the Incas: Little-known plants of the Andes with promise for worldwide cultivation*. Washington, DC: National Academies Press.
Stahl, Peter W. 2005. "An exploratory osteological study of the Muscovy duck (*Cairina moschata*) (Aves: Anatidae) with implications for neotropical archaeology." *Journal of Archaeological Science* 32, no. 6: 915–29.
Stahl, Peter W., Michael C. Muse, and Florencio Delgado Espinoza. 2006. "New evidence for pre-Columbian Muscovy Duck *Cairina moschata* from Ecuador." *Ibis* 148, no. 4 (October): 657–63.
Stalker, H. T., and Richard F. Wilson. 2016. *Peanuts: Genetics, processing, and utilization*. http://search.ebscohost.com/login.aspx?direct=true&scope=site&db=nlebk&db=nlabk&AN=1134278.
Staller, John E., and Michael D. Carrasco. 2010. *Pre-Columbian foodways: Interdisciplinary approaches to food, culture, and markets in ancient Mesoamerica*. New York: Springer.
Staller, John E., Robert H. Tykot, and Bruce F. Benz. 2006. *Histories of maize: Multidisciplinary approaches to the prehistory, linguistics, biogeography, domestication, and evolution of maize*. Amsterdam: Elsevier Academic Press.
Stewart, Watt. 1951. *Chinese bondage in Peru*. Durham: Duke University Press.
Stolberg, Victor. 2011. "The use of coca: Prehistory, history, and ethnography." *Journal of Ethnicity in Substance Abuse* 10, no. 2: 126–46.
Streatfeild, Dominic. 2002. *Cocaine: An unauthorized biography*. New York: Thomas Dunne Books.

Szabo, James Robert. 1977. *Ceramic firing technology in the Moche Valley, Peru*. PhD dissertation, California State University Northridge.

Takenaka, Ayumi. 2019. "'Nikkei food' for whom? Gastro-politics and culinary representation in Peru." *Anthropology of Food* [Online]. 14. http://journals.openedition.org/aof/10065. https://doi.org/10.4000/aof.10065.

Taylor, Gérald. 2000. *Estudios lingüísticos sobre Chachapoyas*. Lima: Fondo Editorial UNMSM.

Tegel, Simeon. 2016. "Why Peru's gastronomy is a bigger draw for tourists than the Incas." *The Independent*. https://www.independent.co.uk/news/world/americas/why-peru-s-gastronomy-bigger-draw-tourists-incas-a6805026.html.

Tesauro, Jason. 2017. "One of the world's most famous chefs wants to help you forage for your food." *Washington Post*. Food Section. June 29. https://www.washingtonpost.com/lifestyle/food/one-of-the-worlds-most-famous-chefs-wants-to-help-you-forage-for-your-food/2017/06/29/b59a1d34-5ceb-11e7-9fc6-c7ef4bc58d13_story.html.

Toro Lira, Guillermo. 2010. *History of pisco in San Francisco: A scrapbook of first hand accounts*. Lima: LibrosGTL.

Tschudi, Johann Jakob von. 1844. *Untersuchungen über die Fauna peruana*. St. Gallen: Scheitlin und Zollikofer.

Tsumura, Mitsuharu, and Josefina Barrón. 2013. *Nikkei es Perú*. Lima: Telefonica. http://site.ebrary.com/id/11021861.

Twain, Mark. 1866. "Kau and Waiohinu." *Sacramento Daily Union*. October 25. http://www.twainquotes.com/18661025u.html.

Twain, Mark. 1951. *Life on the Mississippi*. New York: Harper.

Uceda, Santiago, Elias Mujica B., and Ricardo Morales. 1997. *Investigaciones en la Huaca de la Luna, 1995*. Trujillo: Facultad de Ciencias Sociales, Universidad Nacional de La Libertad.

Ugás, Roberto, and Víctor Mendoza. 2012. *El punto de ají: investigaciones en capsicum nativos*. Nos. 1–2. Programa de Hortalizas. UNALM.

UN Conference for the Adoption of a Single Convention on Narcotic Drugs. 1963. *Single convention on narcotic drugs, 1961: Including schedules, final act, and resolutions, as agreed by the United Nations Conference for the Adoption of a Single Convention on Narcotic Drugs*. New York: United Nations.

Valderrama, Mariano. 2010. *Cebiche: The taste of Peru*. 1st ed. Lima: Facultad de Ciencias de la Comunicación Turismo y Psicología, Universidad de San Martín de Porres.

Valderrama León, Mariano, and Roberto Ugás. 2009. *Ajíes peruanos: sazón para el mundo*. Lima: Sociedad Peruana de Gatronomía.

Vanhove, W., and P. Van Damme. 2013. "Value chains of cherimoya (Annona cherimola Mill.) in a centre of diversity and its on-farm conservation implications." *Tropical Conservation Science* 6, no. 2: 158–80.

Vasconcelos, José, and Didier Tisdel Jaén. 1997. *The cosmic race: A bilingual edition*. Baltimore, MD: Johns Hopkins University Press.

Velasco-Chong, Jonas Roberto et al. 2020. "Tocosh flour (*Solanum tuberosum* L.): A toxicological assessment of traditional Peruvian fermented potatoes." *Foods* (Basel, Switzerland) 9, no. 6 (June 2): 719.

Villa, Tania Carolina Camacho, Nigel Maxted, Maria Scholten, and Brian Ford-Lloyd. 2005. "Defining and identifying crop landraces." *Plant Genetic Resources* 3, no. 3: 373–84.

Villavicencio, Maritza, ed. 2007. *Seminario historia de la cocina peruana*. Lima: Universidad de San Martín de Porres.

Wester La Torre, Carlos. 2010. *Chotuna-Chornancap: "templos, rituales y ancestros Lambayeque."* https://www.academia.edu/29886677/Chotuna_-_Chornancap_Templos_rituales_y_ancestros_Lambayeque.

Wingate, Michael. 1985. *Small-scale lime-burning: A practical introduction*. London: Intermediate Technology Publications.

Wood, Frances. 2002. *The Silk Road: Two thousand years in the heart of Asia*. Berkeley: University of California Press.

Wust, Walter H. 2006. *La pesca en el Antiguo Perú*. Lima: Wust Ediciones.

Yan, L., Y. Zhang, G. Cai, Y. Qing, J. Song, H. Wang, X. Tan et al. 2021. *Genome assembly of primitive cultivated potato Solanum stenotomum provides insights into potato evolution*. September 27. *G3* (Bethesda) 11 (10): jkab262. https://doi.org/10.1093/g3journal/jkab262.

Zapata Acha, Sergio. 2009. *Diccionario de gastronomía peruana tradicional*. Lima: Fondo Editorial, Facultad de Ciencias de la Comunicación, Turismo y Psicología, Universidad de San Martín de Porres.

Index

Page numbers in italic type indicate images or image captions.

Milton Keynes UK
Ingram Content Group UK Ltd.
UKHW040629230823
427276UK00001B/34